JERUSALEM 3000

OR HADASH

LET A NEW LIGHT SHINE

A NEW CURRICULUM WRITTEN BY:
DR. BETSY DOLGIN KATZ, RJE

Produced by
The Association of Reform Zionists
of America (ARZA)

In cooperation with the
Union of American Hebrew Congregations
Department of Education

ARZA President: Marcia L. Cayne ז״ל
ARZA Acting President: Philip Meltzer
ARZA Executive Director: Rabbi Ammiel Hirsch
ARZA Jerusalem 3000 Chairman: Alan D. Bennett
Research Assistant: Ari Kelman
Editor: Alan D. Bennett
Department of Education Director: Seymour Rossel

UAHC PRESS   1995

This book is printed on acid-free paper
Copyright © 1995 by the UAHC Press
Manufactured in the United States of America
1 2 3 4 5 6 7 8 9 10

June 11, 1995
י"ג בסיון התשנ"ה

Dear Friends,

It is with great pleasure that I extend my greetings to the participants attending the adult education study program, who will be among us as we celebrate the 3000th anniversary of Jerusalem.

The Association of Reform Zionists of America, whose efforts and programs ensure the continuation and strengthening of the Jewish people both in Israel and in the Diaspora, are to be praised for its efforts and attachment to the State of Israel.

Your dedicated efforts in helping to create a society which reflects Jewish values and the Zionist vision are truly appreciated.

We are happy to learn of the planned visit to our country by a contingent of participants next summer, and extend to you a warm welcome.

To those of you who will be visiting Israel for the first time, I wish a special B'ruchim Ha'bayim - welcome - with the hope that it will be only the beginning of many more such visits.

With warm wishes from Jerusalem,

Sincerely yours,

Yitzhak Rabin

Rabbi Ammiel Hirsch
Executive Director
Association of Reform
Zionists of America
838 Fifth Avenue
New York, New York 10021-7064
U.S.A.

Jerusalem, Israel

עיריית ירושלים
Municipality of Jerusalem
بلدية اورشليم-القدس

ראש העיר
Mayor of Jerusalem
رئيس البلدية

Jerusalem, May 31, 1995
2 Sivan 5755

The Association of Reform Zionists of America
838 Fifth Avenue
New York, New York 10021

Dear Friends,

I was delighted to learn that ARZA's Jerusalem 3000 study program will be concluded in the City of Jerusalem in the summer of 1996.

As the participants will have a unique opportunity of sharing in our year-long Trimillennium celebrations, I cannot think of a more ideal setting to complete the in-depth adult education program, than the eternal capital city.

During this historic time, when we will be reconfirming and strengthening our commitment of solidarity with the world Jewish community, ARZA will be an important force in reinforcing these bonds.

Furthermore, education is the backbone of our heritage and a vital tool to ensure a positive and strong Jewish identity. Because I firmly believe in the importance of education for the continuation of the Jewish people, I have taken on the Jerusalem's education portfolio as my personal responsibility; therefore, I am particularly pleased that ARZA is bringing their innovative adult education program to Israel.

Please accept my best wishes for much success with the program, and I look forward to welcoming you to Jerusalem in the summer of 5756\1996.

Yours sincerely,

Ehud Olmert

J10\007

כיכר ספרא 1, ת.ד. 775, ירושלים, 91007, טלפון 02-297997, פקס' 02-296014

1 Safra Square, POB 775, Jerusalem, 91007, Israel, Tel. 02-297997, Fax. 02-296014

ميدان سفرا ١، ص.ب. ٧٧٥، اورشليم-القدس ٩١٠٠٧، هاتف ٢٩٧٩٩٧-٢، فاكس ٢٩٦٠١٤-٢.

TABLE OF CONTENTS

ACKNOWLEDGMENTS

Many dedicated people contributed to making this curriculum possible. First and foremost, ARZA salutes Dr. Betsy Dolgin Katz, the director of the Department of Reform Education for the Community Foundation for Jewish Education in Chicago and a skilled educator and writer, who was so excited by the project that she took upon herself the responsibility of writing the curriculum in half the time that would otherwise be standard. Dr. Katz is infused with love of Israel and is driven to find the most effective means of conveying this love to American Jews.

Additionally, this publication would not have been possible without hundreds of hours of expert editing and leadership by Alan D. Bennett, chair of the ARZA Jerusalem 3000 Committee, president of ARZA's Lake Erie Region, and master educator.

Special thanks are extended to Seymour Rossel, director of the UAHC Department of Education, who gave the manuscript its final form. We especially note the work of Stuart Benick of the UAHC Press for his sage counsel and expeditious and professional publishing of the manuscript. We are grateful to the Jewish Education Center of Cleveland for use of its facilities to produce the Teacher's Guide and Resource Book and to Helen Wolf, J.E.C.C.'s Israel Programs Director, for her gracious help in getting the manuscript through the computers. Ari Kelman worked hours and hours locating resources that formed the basis of the curriculum.

Lastly, from the ARZA staff, Jamie Rosenberg and Ilana Plutzer, together with Naomi Schorsch, worked long days and nights tying together thousands of logistical details, ensuring the timely publication of this curriculum.

The **Jerusalem 3000** curriculum originated as a dream that became a joint proposal of ARZA and the UAHC Department of Education. For the original proposal, and for willing the dream to reality, thanks go to Seymour Rossel and to Rabbi Ammiel Hirsch.

PREFACE

For three thousand years Jews have turned toward Jerusalem as the symbol of our civilization. Conquered by King David around 1000 BCE, Jerusalem became more than the capital of the ancient kingdom. Jerusalem became the center of our faith; the very heart of the Jewish body. While other faiths have holy sites, for the Jews, Jerusalem itself is holy. Not only a city of bricks and mortar, it is the very gateway to heaven. For as tradition emphasized, *Yerushalayim Shel Matah*—the earthly Jerusalem—is a bridge to *Yerushalayim Shel Ma-alah*—the heavenly Jerusalem, the center of a more perfect world.

Despite their plundering of the earthly Jerusalem, the nations could never destroy the heavenly city, for it lives in the hopes and prayers of generations of Jews. God too was in exile, said the Talmud, and would return only when the earthly city was redeemed. Judaism thus *required* that Jerusalem be restored. There was never a shred of doubt in the believer's mind. Like a migrating bird drawn to its nest, the Jews knew that one day they would be lifted "on wings of eagles" and returned home.

As in the past, so today, a Jew says "Jerusalem" and means Judaism itself: the very embodiment of the faith, culture, history, and destiny of the Jewish people. To experience Jerusalem is to penetrate the mystery of Jewish existence. After two millennia of bitter exile, the Jews have returned. All of the other nations of antiquity that lusted after the City of David are no more. Herein lies profound religious meaning. Explore this meaning. Awaken your Jewish senses. Drink deep from the wellsprings of our faith. As the Bible implores, "Set Jerusalem above your highest joy."

Do your best to complete the entire course, which includes a week of study in Jerusalem. You will find there the capital city of a thriving, modern Jewish state, which, within a generation, will be home to the majority of our people. In this era of Jewish independence, it is simply not possible to be a complete Jew without immersion in, and understanding of, the State of Israel.

If this curriculum awakens in you even a spark of Jewish awareness; if you begin to ponder the meaning of Jewish existence and our three-millennia love affair with the golden city on Zion's mount, then we will have accomplished our aim.

Next year in Jerusalem!
Rabbi Ammiel Hirsch
Executive Director, ARZA

INTRODUCTION

THE OCCASION FOR THIS ADVENTURE

About three thousand years ago King David unified the tribes of Israel, captured Jerusalem from the Jebusites, and proclaimed this already distinctive settlement the capital of Israel. David's son, King Solomon, built the Bet HaMikdash, God's Temple in Jerusalem. The growing city became the religious and national center of the Jewish people. Jerusalem is so today.

Jerusalem 3000 is a wonderful opportunity to become familiar with this special city, which has never been far from our hearts and minds. Throughout our nearly two millennia of exile from the Promised Land, Jerusalem was in our prayers and dreams. We break a glass at a wedding to remind us of the destruction of the Temple. We build our synagogues with the most important wall facing Jerusalem. In earlier days, homes remained partly unfinished because we were separated from our spiritual home.

Jerusalem is not only of our past. Since 1948, when Israel was reborn as a modern nation, the "City of Peace" has been its capital. It has been targeted by the armies of Arab countries and by terrorists. At the same time, it has witnessed tremendous advances in industry, science, agriculture, and education. As the capital of a democratic religious state, Jerusalem plays a vital role in Middle East and world politics. It lives up to its promise to provide an open-door home to Jews form all over the world. Whether they arrive from the east or the west, Jews are welcome and integrated into its multifaceted society. Jerusalem is Israel; Israel is Jerusalem.

This complicated, bewildering, miracle-producing, infuriating city is ours. To be a Jew is to feel its past, understand its streets and stones, and dream about its future. Jerusalem's three-thousandth anniversary affords an opportunity to study its literature and history, contemplate its beauty, sing its songs, and wrestle with its internal and international politics. It provides an incentive to get to know a city that is as much a part of us as the city in which we were born. All Jews have roots in Jerusalem. All of Jerusalem's stories are our stories.

WHAT YOU WILL STUDY

Part of the excitement and the mystery of Jerusalem is its double personality. Books, articles, poetry, and stories marvel at *Yerushalayim Shel Ma-alah* and *Yerushalayim Shel Matah*, the holy and profane Jerusalems, the heavenly and the earthly, the sacred and the secular, the spiritual and the physical, the spirit and the stones. The curriculum presents both Jerusalems although it is sometimes difficult to ascertain where one ends and the other begins. For the same reason, the curriculum units on geography, topography, history, people, and faith overlap and blend into one another.

To compress three thousand years of history, literature, art, music, people, and places into thirteen group sessions and a week of study in Jerusalem is a daunting task. Therefore, the curriculum presents only what fits in the context of this special study and travel and attempts to provide, at the same time, a stimulating learning experience. The curriculum also links information with Jewish observance, thereby emphasizing Jerusalem's religious significance. Finally, the curriculum explores a variety of political issues. In the rapidly changing terrain of politics, some of the content was rewritten almost daily and may require further emending as study proceeds.

HOW THE CURRICULUM IS ORGANIZED

Each unit is divided into chapters containing sections such as *Background*, *Time Lines*, *Additional Possibilities*, *In Summation*, and *Pertinent Sites to Visit in Israel*. The sources—primary and secondary—are Jewish classical texts, historical documents, newspaper articles, letters, journal entries, maps, time lines, poetry, literature, art, and music. A special feature called *Deepening the Sources* poses questions and issues for discussion and often suggests techniques for study groups to follow.

What is totally unique about the approach of the *Or Hadash* curriculum is the close-knit association of what is studied to the sights and sounds of Jerusalem itself. Having discussed the sources, having gained a sense of the meaning of Jerusalem's many aspects, one's actual visit to Jerusalem becomes more than a photo opportunity. It becomes a path to deeper identification—with Jerusalem, with our heritage, with that part of our personal center that always remains a part of the Holy City, the City at the Center of the World.

JERUSALEM 3000

OR HADASH

LET A NEW LIGHT SHINE

JERUSALEM
OF STONE
AND MOUNTAIN

CHAPTER 1

ANCIENT JERUSALEM

BACKGROUND

Jewish claims to Jerusalem go back three thousand years to the beginning of our history as a Jewish nation. Before David unified the country and proclaimed Jerusalem its capital, Jerusalem was a small, mountaintop Canaanite settlement. It was conquered alternately by the competing armies of Assyria and Egypt. The first written reference to Jerusalem, called Urushamem, is found on a piece of nineteenth-century BCE Egyptian document pottery.

The name Jerusalem was thought to be derived from two Hebrew words, *ir* and *shalom*, giving it the meaning of "City of Peace." More recently, some scholars maintain the origin of the name to be from the words *yard*, meaning "founded," and *salem*, the name of a local god.

Even before David claimed the city, it already had religious associations. It is mentioned in the Bible when Abraham meets Melchi-zedek, King of Salem. It is also referred to in the time of Joshua as the Jebusite city ruled by Adoni-zedek.

When David came to power, he managed to unite the scattered, warring tribes of Israel and defeat their common foe, the Philistines. He secured the frontier and defeated the only remaining, internal, unconquered site, Jerusalem, then called Jebus. Jerusalem was strategically located for defending Israel against the Philistines and was politically neutral, not having been in the territory of either the northern or southern tribes. Under David, Jerusalem became the political and military capital of Israel. When David brought the Ark of the Law into the city, it likewise became the

spiritual capital, laying the groundwork for Solomon's construction of the Temple.

Once Jerusalem became the spiritual center for Jews, it remained so for all time. The City of Gold has been glorified in song, poetry, and fiction and is still a source of inspiration to poet and pilgrim, storyteller and sight-seer. Although the Temple as the site for offerings marking important occasions in Jewish life is long gone, our prayers, holidays, and life events lead us back to the site of the Temple, to Jerusalem.

CELEBRATING THE *SHALOSH REGALIM* AS A LINK TO JERUSALEM

You shall rejoice before Adonai your God with your son and daughter, your male and female slave, the Levite in your communities, and the stranger, the orphan, and the widow in your midst, at the place where Adonai your God will choose to establish God's name. Bear in mind that you were slaves in Egypt, and take care to obey these laws. After the ingathering from your threshing floor and your vat, you shall hold the Feast of Booths for seven days. You shall rejoice in your festival, with your son and daughter, your male and female slave, the Levite, the stranger, the fatherless, and the widow in your communities. You shall hold festival for Adonai your God seven days, in the place that Adonai will choose; for Adonai your God will bless all your crops and all your undertakings, and you shall have nothing but joy. Three times a year—on the Feast of Unleavened Bread, on the Feast of

Weeks, and on the Feast of Booths—all your males shall appear before Adonai your God in the place that God will choose.

—Deuteronomy 16:11–17

All the towns in the (priestly) district gather in the principal town. They spend the night in the town square and do not enter the houses. Early the next morning the person in charge would say: "Let us arise and go up to Zion to (the house of) Adonai, our God." The (nearby) farmers bring figs and grapes, and the distant ones bring dried figs and raisins. The ox precedes them with its horns gilded in gold and a crown of olive (branches) atop its head. The drum (or flute) beats before them until they approach Jerusalem. When they get close by they send (messengers) before them and decorate their first-fruits. The priestly officials and treasurers come out to greet them according to their stature. Likewise, all the craftspeople of Jerusalem would stand before them and greet them, saying: "People of Such-and-such a place, come in peace."

—Mishna, Bikkurim 3:2–3

Deepening the Sources

Deuteronomy 16:1–17: Name/describe the Shalosh Regalim, the Three Pilgrimage Festivals. What is "the place where Adonai your God will choose?" How were the festivals observed?

Mishna, Bikkurim 3:2–3: What additional information is provided? What are bikkurim? *Describe the procession into Jerusalem. How were people welcomed?*

NOTE: Discuss the alternate use of Jerusalem *and* Zion. *In Jewish tradition, the words are synonymous. Jerusalem and Zion both came to mean the land of Israel as a whole as well as the city. The word* Zion *is the basis of the modern word* Zionism. *The national movement took its name from the word that was both the country and the city.* Jerusalem *and* Zion *are geographical terms that go beyond mere geography.*

REGULATIONS IN ANCIENT JERUSALEM

Our ancestors point out the regulations practiced in Jerusalem in the olden days for the benefit of the inhabitants and the pilgrims:

"That peddlers selling spicery be allowed to travel about in the towns, for the purpose of providing toilet articles for the women so that they should not be repulsive in the eyes of their husbands . . .

"That neither beams nor balconies should be allowed to project there [the commentator explains that this is so as not to harm the pilgrims visiting the Holy City].

"That no dunghill should be made there, on account of reptiles.

"That no kilns should be kept there, on account of the smoke [which would blacken the buildings of the town and its walls].

"That neither gardens nor orchards should be cultivated there, with the exception, however, of rose gardens that existed from the day of the former prophets.

"That no fowls should be reared there [on account of the smell].

"That no dead person be kept there overnight—this is known by tradition."

It has already been said: "Never did serpent or scorpion do harm in Jerusalem, and no one said to another: The place is too strait for me that I should lodge in Jerusalem."

—Baba Kama 82B, Mishna Avot 5:5, Avot de Rabbi Natan A-35, from Zev Vilnay, *Legends of Jerusalem*, JPS: Philadelphia 1973

Deepening the Sources

What do the regulations reveal about concerns for health, happiness, and safety? How did the presence of the Temple in Jerusalem and the Pilgrimage Festivals affect the city and the pilgrims' perceptions of Jerusalem as the religious center of the nation?

HOW JERUSALEM BECAME THE POLITICAL AND SPIRITUAL CAPITAL OF THE JEWISH PEOPLE

David was thirty years old when he became king, and he reigned forty years. In Hebron he reigned over Judah seven years and six months, and in Jerusalem he reigned over all Israel and Judah thirty-three years.

The king and his men set out for Jerusalem against the Jebusites who inhabited the region. David was told, "You will never get in here! Even the blind and the lame will turn you back." (They meant: David will never enter here.) But David captured the stronghold of Zion; it is now the City of David. On that occasion David said: "Those who attack the Jebusites shall reach the water channel and [strike down] the lame and the blind, who are hateful to David." That is why they say: "No one who is blind or lame may enter the House."

David also occupied the stronghold and renamed it the City of David; David also fortified the surrounding area, from the Millo inward. David kept growing stronger, for Adonai, the God of Hosts, was with him.

—II Samuel 5:4–10

David and all Israel set out for Jerusalem, that is Jebus, where the Jebusite inhabitants of the land lived. David was told by the inhabitants of Jebus, "You will never get in here!" But David captured the stronghold of Zion; it is now the City of David. David said, "Whoever attacks the Jebusites first will be the chief officer"; Joab son of Zeruiah attacked first, and became the chief.

David occupied the stronghold; therefore it was renamed the City of David. David also fortified the surrounding area, from the Millo roundabout, and Joab rebuilt the rest of the city. David kept growing stronger, for the God of Hosts was with him.

—I Chronicles 11:4–9

Deepening the Sources

How old is the Jewish presence in Jerusalem? According to several reliable contemporary sources (Gilbert, Greenstein), David conquered Jerusalem in 1004 BCE.

How was Jerusalem conquered? Why was Jerusalem difficult to conquer? What advantage did it have being the only unconquered city?

For an excellent explanation of the puzzling record of the conquest of Jerusalem, see Jerusalem, Sacred City of Mankind, *Teddy Kollek and Moshe Pearlman, pp. 27–30.*

Of David. A psalm.

The earth is God's, and all that it holds,
   the world and its inhabitants.
For God founded it upon the ocean,
   set it on the nether-streams.

Who may ascend the mountain of Adonai?
Who may stand in God's holy place?—
Those who have clean hands and pure hearts,
   who have not taken a false oath by My life
   or sworn deceitfully.
They shall carry away a blessing from Adonai,
   a just reward from God, their deliverer.
Such is the circle of those who turn to God,
   Jacob, who seek Your presence.

O gates, lift up your heads!
Up high, you everlasting doors,
   so the Sovereign of glory may come in!
Who is the King of glory?—
   Adonai, mighty and valiant,
   Adonai, valiant in battle.
O gates, lift up your heads!
Lift them up, you everlasting doors,
   so the Sovereign of glory may come in!
Who is the Sovereign?—
   Adonai of hosts,
Adonai is the Sovereign of glory.

—Psalm 24

Then Solomon assembled the elders of Israel, and all the heads of the tribes, the chief of the fathers of the people of Israel, before King Solomon in Jerusalem, that they might bring up the ark of the covenant of Adonai from the City of David, which is Zion. And all the people of Israel assembled themselves to King Solomon at the feast in the month Ethanim, which is the seventh month. And all the elders of Israel came, and the priests took up the ark. And they brought up the ark of

Adonai, and the tabernacle of the congregation, and all the holy utensils that were in the tabernacle, those did the priests and the Levites bring up. And King Solomon, and all the congregation of Israel, who were assembled before him, were with him before the ark, sacrificing sheep and oxen, that could not be told nor numbered for multitude. And the priests brought in the ark of the covenant of Adonai to God's place, to the sanctuary of the house, to the most holy place, under the wings of the cherubim. For the cherubim spread out their two wings over the place of the ark, and the cherubim covered the ark and its poles above. And they drew out the poles, so that the ends of the poles were seen out in the holy place before the sanctuary, and they were not seen outside; and there they are to this day. There was nothing in the ark save the two tablets of stone, which Moses put there at Horeb, when God made a covenant with the people of Israel, when they came out of the land of Egypt. And it came to pass, when the priests came out of the holy place, that the cloud filled the house of God, And that the priests could not stand to minister because of the cloud; for the glory of Adonai had filled the house of God. Then spoke Solomon, Adonai said that God would dwell in the thick darkness. I have surely built you a house to dwell in, a settled place for you to abide in forever. And the king turned his face around, and blessed all the congregation of Israel; and all the congregation of Israel stood; And he said, Blessed be Adonai, God of Israel, who spoke with God's mouth to David my father, and has with God's hand fulfilled it, saying, Since the day when I brought forth my people Israel out of Egypt, I chose no city from all the tribes of Israel to build a house, that my name might be in there; but I chose David to be over my people Israel. And it was in the heart of David my father to build a house for the name of Adonai God of Israel. And Adonai said to David my father, Because it was in your heart to build a house to my name, you did well that it was in your heart. Nevertheless you shall not build the house; but your son who shall come forth from your loins, he shall build the house to my name. And Adonai has performed God's word that God spoke, and I have risen in place of David my father, and I sit on the throne of Israel, as Adonai promised, and I have built a house for the name of Adonai God of Israel.

And I have set there a place for the ark, where the covenant of Adonai is, which God made with our fathers, when he brought them out of the land of Egypt. And Solomon stood before the altar of Adonai in the presence of all the congregation of Israel, and spread out his hands toward heaven; And he said, Adonai God of Israel, there is no God like you, in heaven above, or on earth beneath, who keeps covenant and mercy with your servants who walk before you with all their heart; Who have kept with your servant David my father what you promised him; you spoke also with your mouth, and have fulfilled it with your hand, as it is this day. Therefore now, Adonai God of Israel, keep with your servant David my father what you promised him, saying, There shall not fail you a person in my sight to sit on the throne of Israel; so that your children take heed to their way, that they walk before me as you have walked before me. And now, O God of Israel, let your word, I pray you, be confirmed, which you spoke to your servant David my father. But will God indeed dwell on the earth? Behold, the heaven and heaven of heavens cannot contain you; how much less this house that I have built? Yet have regard for the prayer of your servant, and for his supplication, O Adonai my God, to listen to the cry and to the prayer, which your servant prays before you today; That your eyes may be open toward this house night and day, toward the place of which you have said, My name shall be there; that you may listen to the prayer which your servant shall make toward this place. And listen to the supplication of your servant, and of your people Israel, when they shall pray toward this place; and hear you in heaven your dwelling place; and when you hear, forgive. If any people trespasses against their neighbor, and an oath is laid upon them to cause them to swear, and the oath comes before your altar in this house; Then hear you in heaven, and do, and judge your servants, condemning the wicked, to bring their way upon their head; and justifying the righteous, to give them according to their righteousness. When your people Israel are stuck down before the enemy, because they have sinned against you, and shall turn again to you, and confess your name, and pray, and make supplication to you in this house; Then hear you in heaven, and forgive the sin of your people Israel, and bring them again to the land which you gave to their ancestors. When heaven is closed, and there is no rain, because they have sinned against you; if they pray toward this place, and acknowledge your name, and turn from their sin, when you afflict them; Then hear you in heaven, and forgive the sin of your servants, and of your people Israel, and teach them the good way where they should walk,

and give rain upon your land, which you have given to your people for an inheritance. If there is in the land famine, if there is pestilence, blasting, mildew, locust, or if there is caterpillar; if their enemy besiege them in the land of their cities; whatever plague, whatever sickness there might be; Whatever prayer and supplication is made by any person, or by all your people Israel, who shall know every person the plague of their own heart, and spread out his hands toward this house; Then hear you in heaven your dwelling place, and forgive, and do, and give to every one according to their ways, whose heart you know; for you, you only, know the hearts of all people; That they may fear you all the days that they live in the land which you gave to our fathers. And also concerning a stranger, who is not of your people Israel, but comes from a far country for your name's sake; For they shall hear of your great name, and of your strong hand, and of your stretched-out arm; when they shall come and pray toward this house; Hear you in heaven your dwelling place, and do according to all that the stranger calls to you for; that all people of the earth may know your name, to fear you, as do your people Israel; and that they may know that this house, which I have built, is called by your name. If your people go out to battle against their enemy, wherever you shall send them, and shall pray to Adonai toward the city which you have chosen, and toward the house that I have built for your name; Then hear you in heaven their prayer and their supplication, and maintain their cause. If they sin against you, for there is no person who does not sin, and you are angry with them, and deliver them to the enemy, so that they carry them away captive to the land of the enemy, far or near; Yet if they take thought in the land where they were carried captive, and repent, and make supplication to you in the land of them that carried them captive, saying, We have sinned, and have done perversely, we have committed wickedness; And

so return to you with all their heart, and with all their soul, in the land of their enemies, who led them away captive, and pray to you toward their land, which you gave to their ancestors, the city which you have chosen, and the house which I have built for your name; Then hear you their prayer and their supplication in heaven your dwelling place, and maintain their cause, And forgive your people who have sinned against you, and all their transgressions where they have transgressed against you, and give them compassion before those who carried them captive, that they may have compassion on them; For they are your people, and your inheritance, whom you brought forth out of Egypt, from the midst of the furnace of iron; That your eyes may be open to the supplication of your servant, and to the supplication of your people Israel, to listen to them in all that they call for to you. For you did set them apart from among all the people of the earth, to be your inheritance, as you spoke by the hand of Moses your servant, when you brought our ancestors out of Egypt, O Adonai God. And it was so, that when Solomon had finished praying all this prayer and supplication to Adonai, he arose from before the altar of Adonai, from kneeling on his knees with his hands spread up to heaven. And he stood, and blessed all the congregation of Israel with a loud voice, saying, Blessed be Adonai, who has given rest to the people Israel, according to all that God promised; there has not failed one word of all God's good promise, which God promised by the hand of Moses God's servant. Adonai our God be with us, as God was with our ancestors; let God not leave us, nor forsake us; That God may incline our hearts to God, to walk in God's ways, and to keep God's commandments, and God's statutes, and God's judgments, which God commanded our ancestors. And let these my words, with which I have made supplication before Adonai, be near to Adonai our God day and night, that God maintain the cause of God's servant, and the cause of God's people Israel at all times, as each day may require; That all the people of the earth may know that Adonai is God, and that there is no one else. Let your heart therefore be perfect with Adonai our God, to walk in God's statutes, and to keep God's commandments, as at this day. And the king, and all Israel with him, offered sacrifice before Adonai. And Solomon offered a sacrifice of peace offerings, which he offered to Adonai, twenty-two thousand oxen, and a hundred and twenty thousand sheep. And the king and all the people of Israel dedicated the house of God. The same day did the king hallow the middle of the court that was before the house of God for there he offered burnt offerings, and meal offerings, and the fat of the peace offerings; because the bronze altar that was before Adonai was too small to receive the burnt offerings, and meal offerings, and the fat of the peace offerings. And at that time Solomon held a feast, and all Israel with him, a great congregation, from the entrance to Hamath to the brook of Egypt, before Adonai our God, seven days and seven days, fourteen days. On the eighth day he sent the people away; and they blessed the king, and went to their tents joyful and glad of heart for all the goodness that Adonai had done for David God's servant, and for Israel God's people.

—I Kings:8

Deepening the Sources

Psalm 24 and I Kings: 8 describe the ark's journey to Jerusalem. What emotions are expressed? What do the verses reveal about how people felt about Jerusalem and the ark?

When King Solomon got ready to build the great Temple, he remembered that the sages had said it would be built "in a field of brotherly love." But first he had to find that field.

Solomon strode out of the palace and walked toward Mount Zion. He remembered that a fertile field stretched across Mount Zion, but there was nothing special about the field that he could call to mind. The field had been left to two brothers. Each lived in a house built at opposite ends of the field. The first brother was married and the father of four children; the second brother lived alone. Together, they tilled and tended the field, and when the harvest was in, they divided the wheat equally between them.

When Solomon reached Mount Zion, he saw only the brothers' two houses, pale in the moonlight. Except for the crickets chirping, the night was silent.

While the king waited in the silent field, the brothers were tossing on their beds, unable to sleep, worrying about each other. The first brother said to himself, "How fortunate I am! I have a wife and children, and when I am old, my children will care for me. But my brother has no one. I must bring part of my wheat to him, so he will have something to save for his future."

The second brother, in his house, thought to himself, "Here I am, with only myself to feed. But my poor brother has a wife and children to care for. In all fairness, my brother should have a larger share of the wheat than I. I shall bring part of my wheat to him, secretly, in the night."

The two brothers got out of bed and each went to the granary where he stored his crops. Stealing across the field in the light of the full moon, their arms filled with sheaves of wheat, each was too busy to see the other or to notice Solomon in the distance. But the king saw them.

Each brother left his gift of wheat in the others granary, then hurried back for more. But when they reached their own granaries, they were amazed to find that there was still as much wheat as there had been in the beginning. Again they carried sheaves across the field, and when they returned home, again they found that they had as much wheat as in the beginning.

All night they went back and forth, and when the sun rose, the two brothers met at last in the middle of the field. For a moment they only stared at each other. Then as they began to realize what had happened and why their stores of wheat were not diminished, they threw their arms about each other and laughed aloud.

Then King Solomon knew he had found the place he sought. And when King Solomon built the great Temple, he built it in the middle of the field on Mount Zion, where two brothers, walking in opposite directions, had met in love and concern at dawn.

—"The Field of Brotherly Love" by
Kelly Cherry, in Jules Harlow, ed.,
Lessons from Our Living Past,
NY: Behrman House, 1972

And Gad came that day to David, and said to him, Go up, erect an altar to Adonai in the threshing floor of Araunah the Jebusite. And David, according to the saying of Gad, went up as God commanded. And Araunah looked, and saw the king and his servants coming on towards him; and Araunah went out, and bowed before the king on his face upon the ground. And Araunah said, Why has my lord the king come to his servant? And David said, To buy the threshing floor from you, to build an altar to Adonai, that the plague may be averted from the people. And Araunah said to David, Let my lord the king take and offer up what seems good to him; behold, here are oxen for a burnt sacrifice, and threshing instruments and other instruments of the oxen for wood. All these things did Araunah, a king, give to the king. And Araunah said to the king, Adonai your God accepts you. And the king said to Araunah, No; but I will surely buy it from you at a price; nor will I offer burnt offerings to Adonai my God of that which costs me nothing. So David bought the threshing floor and the oxen for fifty shekels of silver. And David built there an altar to God, and offered burnt offerings and peace offerings. So Adonai was entreated for the land, and the plague was averted from Israel.

—II Samuel 24:18–25

Deepening the Sources

Discuss the folktale of the two brothers for another dimension on the choice of Jerusalem as the site of the Temple. Note the possible connection between the folktale and II Samuel 24. Note also that the Temple Mount, considered to be the mountain in Moriah referred to in Genesis, was the site where, according to tradition, the Akedah, *the binding of Isaac, took place.*

THE CENTRALITY OF JERUSALEM

A Song of Maalot of David. I was glad when they said to me, Let us go into the house of God. Our feet shall stand inside your gates, O Jerusalem. Jerusalem is built as a city which is bound firmly together; There the tribes go up, the tribes of Adonai, as was decreed for Israel, to give thanks to the name of God. For thrones of judgment were set there, the thrones of the house of David. Pray for the peace of Jerusalem; those who love you shall prosper. Peace be within your walls, and prosperity within your palaces. For my siblings' and companions' sakes, I will now say, Peace be within

you. Because of the house of Adonai our God I will seek your good.

—Psalm 122

God's world is great and holy. Among the holy lands in the word is the Holy Land of Israel. In the Land of Israel the holiest city is Jerusalem. In Jerusalem, the holiest place was the Temple, and in the Temple the holiest spot was the Holy of Holies.

There are seventy peoples in the world. Among these holy peoples are the People of Israel. The holiest of the people of Israel is the tribe of Levi. In the tribe of Levi the holiest are the priests. Among the priests, the holiest was the high priest.

There are 354 days in the year. Among these the holidays are holy. Higher than these is the holiness of the Sabbath. Among Sabbaths the holiest is the Day of Atonement, the Sabbath of Sabbaths.

There are seventy languages in the world. Among the holy languages is the holy language of Hebrew. Holier than all else in this language is the holy Torah, and in the Torah the holiest part is the Ten Commandments. In the Ten Commandments the holiest of all words is the name of God.

And once during the year, at a certain hour, these four supreme sanctities were joined with one another. That was on the Day of Atonement, when the high priest would enter the Holy of Holies and there utter the name of God. And because this hour was beyond measure holy and awesome, it was the time of utmost peril not only for the high priest but for the whole of Israel. For if, in this hour, there had, God forbid, entered the mind of the high priest a false or sinful thought, the entire world would have been destroyed.

Every spot where people raise their eyes to heaven is a holy of holies. Every person, having been created by God in God's own image and likeness, is a high priest. Every day of a person's life is a day of Atonement, and every word that a person speaks with sincerity is the Name of God.

—Folk tale adapted from a version in *The Dybbuk* by Saul Anski

Deepening the Sources

Psalm 122 and the folktale on the Holy of Holies both emphasize the centrality of Jerusalem. Ex-

plore the references to "going up/aliyah," "the gates," and "peace/shalom" in Psalm 122, traditional elements that remain unchanged.

NOTE: There will be opportunities in future discussions to learn more about the Temple Mount.

IN SUMMATION

- Jerusalem became the spiritual center of the ancient Jewish world, is our center today, and will be so for all time.
- During the three pilgrimage festivals, the *Shalosh Regalim*, people crowded into Jerusalem and offered sacrifices at the Temple.
- Going up to Jerusalem, *aliyah*, occurred also on *Rosh Chodesh*, *Rosh Hashana*, and on less-known occasions as when Jews were commanded to bring wood offerings to the Temple nine times a year.
- Jerusalem was conquered by King David and designated as the political and military capital of the Jewish people. His son, Solomon, was named by God to be the builder of the Temple.
- Poets celebrate Jerusalem's beauty and storytellers and teachers tell of its mystical charm.

ADDITIONAL LEARNING POSSIBILITIES

1. The group may desire a mini-lesson on Jewish literary history. Discuss briefly the nature and development of *Tanach*, Talmud, and Midrash to enhance the use of the primary sources. A useful guide for a concise presentation can be found in *Our Sacred Texts* by Ellen Singer with Bernard Zlotowitz, UAHC Press.
2. View Neot Kedumim's slide presentation, *Seven Species*, emphasizing the presence today of the same flora known in Temple times. These plants will be seen in and around Jerusalem today.

PERTINENT SITES TO VISIT IN ISRAEL

- City of David
- Gihon Spring
- Siloam Tunnel/Hezekiah's Tunnel
- Temple Mount
- Flora and fauna in Jerusalem
- Mt. Zion
- Neot Kedumim

CHAPTER 2

GEOGRAPHY OF JERUSALEM

BACKGROUND

Ten measures of beauty came down to earth; nine were taken by Jerusalem and one by the rest of the world.

—Talmud

An important part of feeling at home in Jerusalem is knowing its hills and valleys, its streets and neighborhoods. Unlike many modern cities created in gridlike patterns almost in protest against the terrain, Jerusalem's pattern of growth was shaped by its natural environment, the land contours, and the location of its water supply. Walls encircling the city provided dwellings and defense up until the last century and also shaped its growth and history. Only extreme conditions at the end of the last century caused people to move beyond the walls that had enclosed Jerusalemites for almost three thousand years.

What God and nature provided and what people built have produced what is considered to be among the most uniquely beautiful cities in the world. Even the sunlight's colors, shadows, and movement are unlike light anywhere else in the world. Perhaps this has endowed Jerusalem with the mystical quality that has made it a spiritual center for the major religions.

Because Jerusalem lies on one of the major land routes of this part of the world, caravans, armies, and wandering tribes have approached and entered its walls. Others have come seeking the gifts Jeru-salem has to offer; others came to flee discrimination and oppression. When groups arrived, they chose to live in proximity to people from their countries of origin and established communities within the city. Some of these ethnic communities are still evident.

THE WALLS OF JERUSALEM: AN HISTORICAL OVERVIEW

And Hiram king of Tyre sent his servants to Solomon; for he had heard that they had anointed him king in place of his father; for Hiram had always loved David. And Solomon sent to Hiram, saying, You know how that David my father could not build a house to the name of Adonai his God on account of the wars which were around him on every side, until Adonai put them under the soles of his feet. But now Adonai my God has given me rest on every side, so that there is neither adversary nor evil hindrance. And, behold, I intend to build a house to the name of Adonai my God, as Adonai spoke to David my father, saying, Your son, whom I will set upon your throne in your place, he shall build a house to my name. And therefore command that they cut me cedar trees from Lebanon; and my servants shall be with your servants; and to you will I pay wages to your servants according to what you shall set; for you know that there is not among us any who can skillfully cut timber like the Sidonians. And it came to pass, when Hiram heard the words of Solomon, that he rejoiced greatly, and said, Blessed be Adonai this day, who has given to David a wise son over this great people. And Hiram sent to Solomon, saying, I have considered the things which you sent to me for; and I will do all you wish concerning the timber of cedar, and concerning the timber of cypress. My servants shall bring them down from Lebanon to the sea; and I will convey them by sea in floats to the place that you shall tell me, and will have them discharged there, and you shall receive them; and you shall meet my wishes by providing food for my household. And Hiram gave Solomon cedar trees and cypress trees according to all his wishes. And Solomon gave Hiram twenty thousand measures of wheat for food for his household, and twenty measures of pure oil; thus gave Solomon to Hiram year by year. And Adonai gave Solomon wisdom, as God promised him; and there was peace between Hiram and Solomon; and the two made a covenant together. And King Solomon raised a levy from all Israel; and the levy was thirty thousand people. And he sent them to Lebanon, ten thousand a month by turns; a month they were in Lebanon, and two months at home; and Adoniram was over the levy. And Solomon had seventy thousand people who carried burdens, and eighty thousand stone cutters in the mountains; Beside the chiefs of Solomon's officers who supervised the work, three thousand and three hundred, who ruled over the people who did the work. And the king commanded, and they brought great stones, costly stones, to lay the foundation of the house with dressed stones.

—I Kings 5:15–31

And it came to pass in the four hundred and eightieth year after the people of Israel came out of the land of Egypt, in the fourth year of Solomon's reign over Israel, in the month Ziv, which is the second month, that he began to build the house of Adonai. And the house which King Solomon built for Adonai, its length was sixty cubits, and its breadth twenty cubits, and its height thirty cubits. And the vestibule before the temple of the house, twenty cubits was its length, according to the breadth of the house; and ten cubits was its breadth before the house. And for the house he made windows wide outside and narrow inside. And against the wall of the house he built a side structure

around the walls of the house, both of the temple and of the sanctuary; and he made chambers around; The lowest chamber was five cubits broad, and the middle was six cubits broad, and the third was seven cubits broad; for outside around the wall of the house he made narrowed rests around, that the beams should not be fastened into the walls of the house. And the house, when it was being built, was built of stone prepared before it was brought there; so that there was neither hammer nor ax nor any tool of iron heard in the house, while it was being built. The door for the middle chamber was in the right side of the house; and they went up with winding stairs into the middle chamber, and out of the middle into the third. And he built the house, and finished it; and covered the house with beams and boards of cedar. And then he built the side structure against all the house, five cubits high; and they rested on the house with timber of cedar. And the word of the Adonai came to Solomon, saying, Concerning this house which you are building, if you will walk in my statutes, and execute my judgments, and keep all my commandments to walk in them; then will I perform my word with you, which I spoke to David your father; And I will dwell among the people of Israel, and will not forsake my people Israel.

—I Kings 6:1–13

Then Solomon began to build the house of Adonai at Jerusalem in Mount Moriah, where Adonai appeared to David his father, in the place that David had prepared in the threshing floor of Ornan the Jebusite. And he began to build in the second day of the second month, in the fourth year of his reign. And these are the foundations which Solomon laid for the building of the house of God. The length by cubits, according to the old measure, was sixty cubits, and the breadth twenty cubits. And the length of the vestibule that was in the front of the house was according to the breadth of the house, twenty cubits, and the height was a hundred and twenty; and he overlaid it inside with pure gold. And the greater house he covered with cypress wood, which he overlaid with pure gold, and set on it palm trees and chains. And he garnished the house with precious stones for beauty; and the gold was gold of Parvaim. He overlaid also the house, the beams, the posts, and its walls, and its doors, with gold; and engraved kerubim on the walls. And he made the most holy house, its length was according to the breadth of the house, twenty cubits, and its breadth twenty cubits; and he overlaid it with fine gold, amounting to six hundred talents. And the weight of the nails was fifty shekels of gold. And he overlaid the upper chambers with gold. And in the most holy place he made two kerubim of image work, and overlaid them with gold. And the wings of the kerubim were twenty cubits long; one wing of the one kerub was five cubits, reaching to the wall of the house; and the other wing was likewise five cubits, reaching to the wing of the other kerub. And one wing of the other kerub was five cubits, reaching to the wall of the house; and the other wing was five cubits also, joining to the wing of the other kerub. The wings of these kerubim spread themselves forth twenty cubits; and they stood on their feet, and their faces were inward. And he made the veil of blue, and purple, and crimson, and fine linen, and worked kerubim on it. Also he made before the house two pillars of thirty-five cubits high, and the capital that was on the top of each of them was five cubits. And he made chains in the inner sanctuary, and put them on the heads of the pillars; and made a hundred pomegranates, and put them on the chains. And he set up the pillars before the temple, one on the right hand, and the other on the left; and called the name of that on the right hand Jachin, and the name of that on the left Boaz.

And he made an altar of bronze, its length twenty cubits, and twenty cubits its breadth, and ten cubits its height. Also he made a molten sea of ten cubits from brim to brim, it was round, and five cubits its height; and a line of thirty cubits encircled it. And under it were figures of an oxen, which surrounded it; ten in a cubit, encircling the sea. Two rows of oxen were cast with it, when it was cast. It stood upon twelve oxen, three facing north, and three facing west, and three facing south, and three facing east; and the sea was set upon them, and all their hinder parts were inward. And the thickness of it was a handbreadth, and the brim of it like the work of the brim of a cup, with flowers of lilies; and it received and held three thousand bats. He made also ten basins, and put five on the right hand, and five on the left, to wash in them; such things as they offered for the burnt offering they washed in them; but the sea was for the priests to wash in. And he made ten

lampstands of gold according to their form, and set them in the temple, five on the right hand, and five on the left. He made also ten tables, and placed them in the temple, five on the right side, and five on the left. And he made a hundred basins of gold. And he made the court of the priests, and the great court, and doors for the court, and overlaid the doors of them with bronze. And he set the sea on the right side of the east end, opposite the south. And Huram made the pans, and the shovels, and the basins. And Huram finished the work that he did for King Solomon for the house of God: The two pillars, and the bowls, and the capitals which were on the top of the two pillars, and the two wreaths to cover the two bowls of the capitals which were on top of the pillars; And four hundred pomegranates on the two wreaths; two rows of pomegranates on each wreath, to cover the two bowls of the capitals which were on top of the pillars. He made also bases, and basins made he upon the bases; One sea, and twelve oxen under it. The pots also, and the shovels, and the forks, and all their instruments, made Huram-Aviv of bright bronze for King Solomon for the house of Adonai. In the plain of Jordan the king cast them, in the clay ground between Succoth and Zeredah. Thus Solomon made all these utensils in great abundance; so that the weight of the bronze could not be valued. And Solomon made all the utensils that were for the house of God, the golden altar also, and the tables on which the bread of display was set; And the lampstands with their lamps, that they should burn according to the prescribed form before the inner sanctuary, of pure gold. And the flowers, and the lamps, and the tongs, made he of gold, of purest gold; And the lamp snuffers, and the basins, and the spoons, and the censers, of pure gold; and the entrance of the house, the inner doors for the most holy place, and the doors of the house of the temple, were of gold.

Thus all the work that Solomon made for the house of Adonai was finished; and Solomon brought in all the things that David his father had consecrated; and the silver, and the gold, and all the instruments, put he among the treasures of the house of God. Then Solomon assembled the elders of Israel, and all the heads of the tribes, the heads of the ancestors' houses of the people of Israel, to Jerusalem, to bring up the ark of the covenant of Adonai from the city of David, which is Zion. And all the people of Israel assembled themselves before the king at the feast which is in the seventh month. And all the elders of Israel came; and the Levites took up the ark. And they brought up the ark, and the Tent of Meeting, and all the holy utensils that were in the tabernacle, these did the priests and the Levites bring up. Also King Solomon, and all the congregation of Israel who were assembled to him before the ark, sacrificed sheep and oxen, which could not be told nor numbered for multitude. And the priests brought the ark of the covenant of Adonai to his place, to the inner sanctuary of the house, into the most holy place, under the wings of the kerubim; For the kerubim spread out their wings over the place of the ark, and the kerubim covered the ark and its poles above. And they drew out the poles of the ark, so that the ends of the poles were seen from the ark before the inner sanctuary; but they were not seen outside. And there it is till this day. There was nothing in the ark save the two tablets which Moses put in at Horeb, when Adonai made a covenant with the people of Israel, when they came from Egypt. And it came to pass, when the priests came out of the holy place; for all the priests who were present were sanctified, and did not then keep to their duty watches; Also the Levites who were the singers, all of them of Asaph, of Heman, of Jeduthun, with their children and their siblings, clothed in white linen, having cymbals and lyres and harps, stood at the east end of the altar, and with them a hundred and twenty priests sounding with trumpets; It came to pass, as the trumpeters and singers were as one, sounding a note in unison, in praise and thanksgiving to Adonai, lifting their voice with the trumpets and cymbals and instruments of music, praising God, saying, For God is good, for God's loving kindness endures forever, that then the house, the house of Adonai, was filled with a cloud; And the priests could not stand to minister because of the cloud; for the glory of Adonai had filled the house of God.

Then said Solomon, Adonai has said that God would dwell in the thick darkness. And I have built a house of habitation for you, and a place for your dwelling forever. And the king turned his face, and blessed the whole congregation of Israel; and all the congregation of Israel stood. And he said, Blessed be Adonai God of Israel, who has with God's hands fulfilled that which God spoke withGod's mouth to

my father David, saying, Since the day that I brought forth my people from the land of Egypt I chose no city among all the tribes of Israel to build a house in, that my name might be there; nor did I choose any person to be a ruler over my people Israel; And I have chosen Jerusalem, that my name might be there; and have chosen David to be over my people Israel. And it was in the heart of David my father to build a house for the name of Adonai God of Israel. And Adonai said to David my father, Whereas it was in your heart to build a house for my name, you did well in that it was in your heart; Nevertheless you shall not build the house; but your son who shall come forth from your loins, he shall build the house for my name. Adonai therefore has performed the word that God has spoken; for I am risen up in the place of David my father, and am set on the throne of Israel, as God promised, and have built the house for the name of Adonai God of Israel. And in it have I put the ark, where inside is the covenant of Adonai, that God made with the people of Israel. And he stood before the altar of Adonai in the presence of all the congregation of Israel, and stretched out his hands; For Solomon had made a bronze scaffold, of five cubits long, and five cubits broad, and three cubits high, and had set it in the midst of the court; and upon it he stood, and kneeled down upon his knees before all the congregation of Israel, and stretched out his hands toward heaven, And said, O Adonai God of Israel, there is no God like you in heaven or in earth; who keeps the covenant, and shows loving kindness to your servants, who walk before you with all their hearts; You who have kept with your servant David my father that which you had promised him; and have spoken with your mouth, and have fulfilled it with your hand, as it is this day. Now therefore, O Lord God of Israel, keep with your servant David my father that which you have promised him, saying, There shall not fail you a person in my sight to sit upon the throne of Israel, if only your children would take heed to their way, to walk in my Torah, as you have walked before me. Now then, O Adonai God of Israel, let your word be confirmed, which you have spoken to your servant David. Will God indeed dwell with people on the earth? Behold, heaven and the heaven of heavens cannot contain you; how much less this house which I have built! Have regard therefore to the prayer of your servant, and to his supplication, O Adonai my God, to listen to the cry and the prayer which your servant prays before you; That your eyes may be open upon this house day and night, upon the place about which you have said that you would put your name there; to listen to the prayer which your servant prays toward this place. Listen to the supplications of your servant, and of your people Israel, which they shall make toward this place; hear from your dwelling place, from heaven; and when you hear, forgive. If people sin against their neighbor, and an oath is laid upon them to make them swear, and the oath comes before your altar in this house; Then hear you from heaven, and do, and judge your servants, by requiting the wicked, by rewarding their way upon their own head; and by justifying the righteous, by giving him according to their righteousness. And if your people Israel are defeated by the enemy, because they have sinned against you; and shall return and confess your name, and pray and make supplication before you in this house; Then hear you from the heavens, and forgive the sin of your people Israel, and bring them back to the land which you gave to them and to their ancestors. When the heaven is shut up, and there is no rain, because they have sinned against you; yet if they would pray toward this place, and confess your name, and turn from their sin, when you afflict them; Then hear you in heaven, and forgive the sin of your servants, your people Israel, when you have taught them the good way, in which they should walk; and send rain upon your land, which you have given to your people as an inheritance. If there should be famine in the land, if there should be pestilence, if there should be blight, or mildew, locusts, or caterpillars; if their enemies should besiege them in the cities of their land; whatever plague, whatever sickness should be; Then whatever prayer, whatever supplication, shall be made by any person, or by all your people Israel, when every one shall know their own affliction and their own grief, and shall stretch out their hands in this house; Then hear from heaven your dwelling place, and forgive, and render to all people according to all their ways, whose heart you know; for only you know the hearts of people; That they may fear you, to walk in your ways, that they should live in the land which you gave to our ancestors. And also, concerning the foreigner, who is not of your people Israel, but has come from a far country for your great name's sake, and your mighty hand, and your stretched-out arm; if they come and pray in this house; Then hear you from the heavens, from your dwelling place, and do according to all that the foreigner calls to you for; that all the peoples of the earth may know your name, and fear you, as does your people Israel, and may know that this house which I have built is called by your name. If your people go out to war against their enemies by the way that you shall send them, and they pray to you toward this city which you have chosen, and the house which I have built for your name; Then hear you from the heavens their prayer and their supplication, and maintain their cause. If they sin against you, for there is no perrson who does not sin, and you are angry with them, and deliver them over before their enemies, and they carry them away captives to a land far or near; Yet if they take thought in the land where they are carried captive, and turn and pray to you in the land of their captivity; saying, We have sinned, we have done amiss, and have dealt wickedly; If they return to you with all their heart and with all their soul in the land of their captivity, where they have carried them captives, and pray toward their land, which you gave to their fathers, and toward the city which you have chosen, and toward the house which I have built for your name; Then hear you from the heavens, from your dwelling place, their prayer and their supplications, and maintain their cause, and forgive your people who have sinned against you. Now, my God, let, I beseech you, your eyes be open, and let your ears be attentive to the prayer that is made in this place. Now therefore arise, O Lord God, into your resting place, you, and the ark of your strength; let your priests, O Adonai God, be clothed with salvation, and let your pious ones rejoice in goodness. O Adonai God, turn not away the face of your anointed; remember the mercies of David your servant.

—II Chronicles 3–6

Deepening the Sources

Read I Kings 5:15–31, 6:1–13, and II Chronicles 3–6 on the building of the Temple, its magnificence, and its dedication ceremony. Note particularly the Chronicles reference to Jerusalem.

Following are selected maps from Carta's Historical Atlas of Jerusalem.

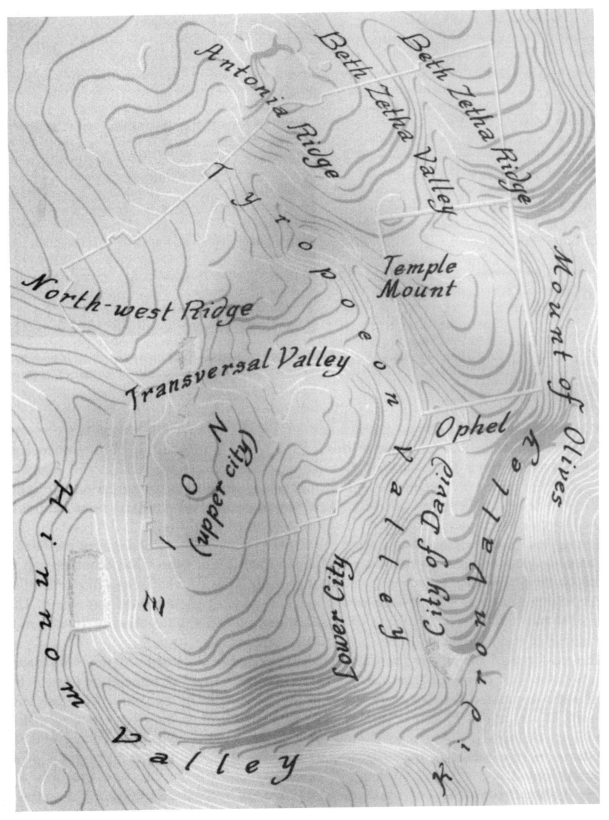

Figure 1A.   The topography of Jerusalem, 1000 BCE–587 BCE.

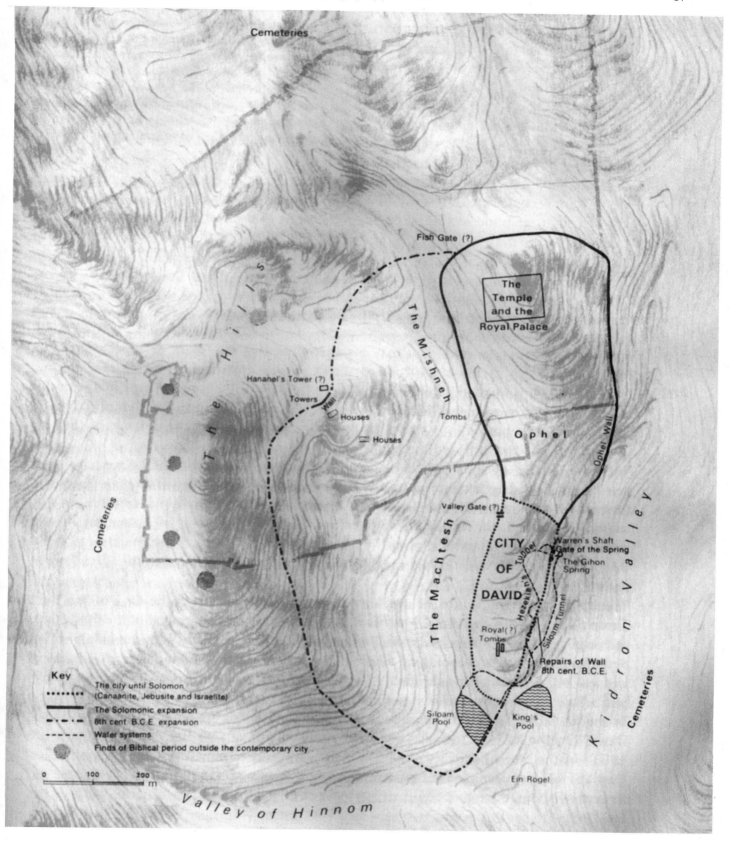

Figure 1B. The city of Jerusalem during the reign of King David and King Solomon, 1000 BCE–587 BCE.

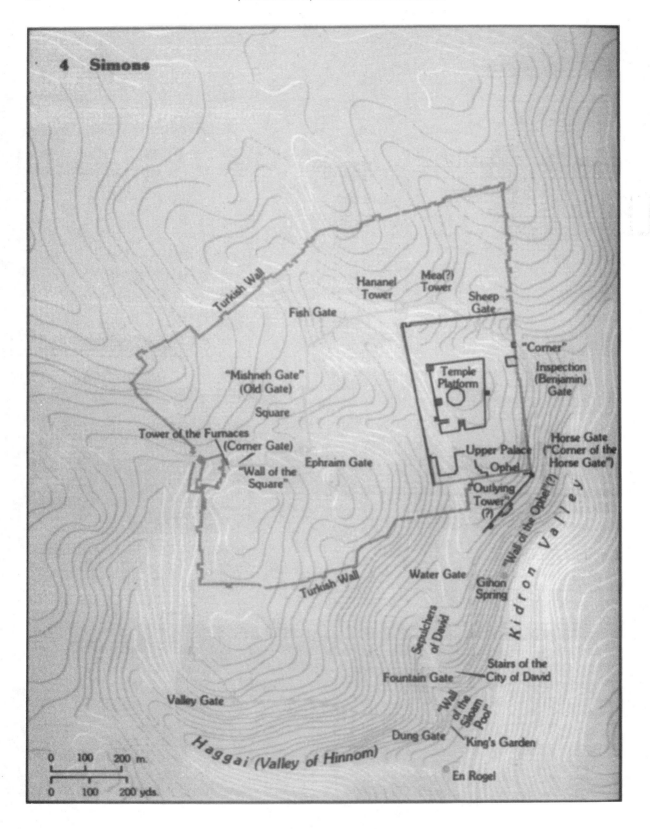

Figure 2.   Jerusalem as it was rebuilt under Nehemiah, 435 BCE.

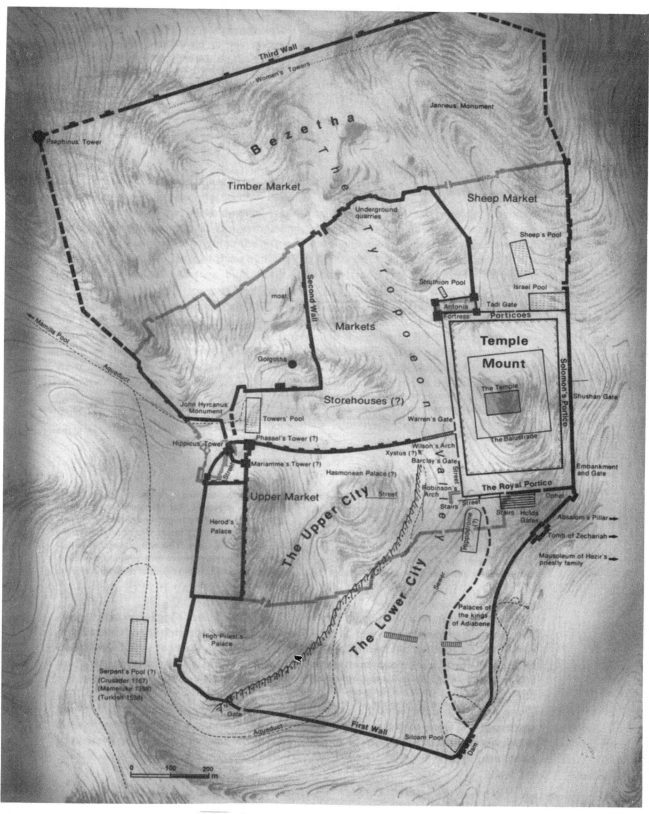

Figure 3. Jerusalem after extensive construction during the days of King Herod in the Second Temple Period, 34 BCE.

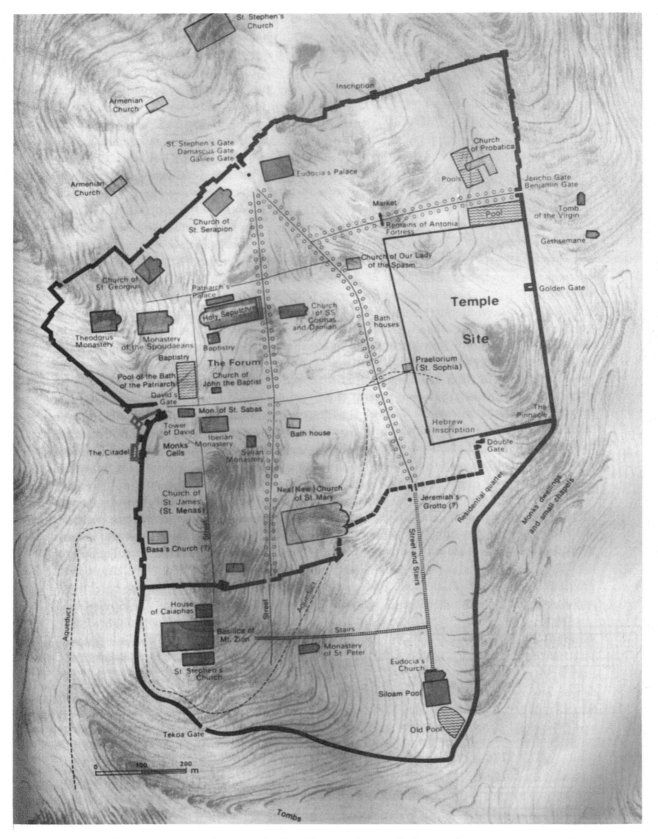

Figure 4.   Jerusalem experienced a period of building and growth during the Byzantine Period, 324–638 CE.

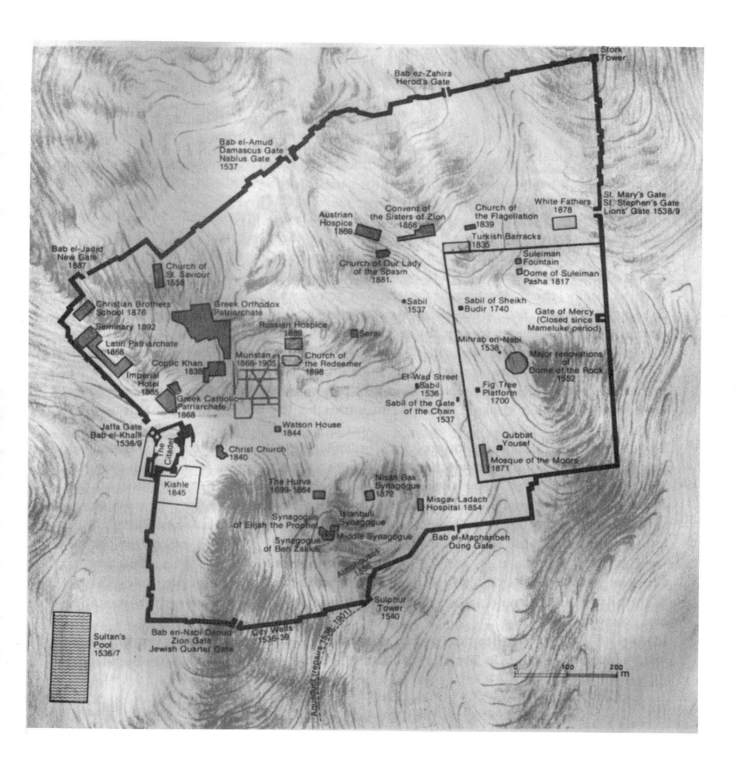

Figure 5. Restoration of Jerusalem occurred during the Turkish Period, 1540 CE, under the rule of Suleiman the Magnificent.

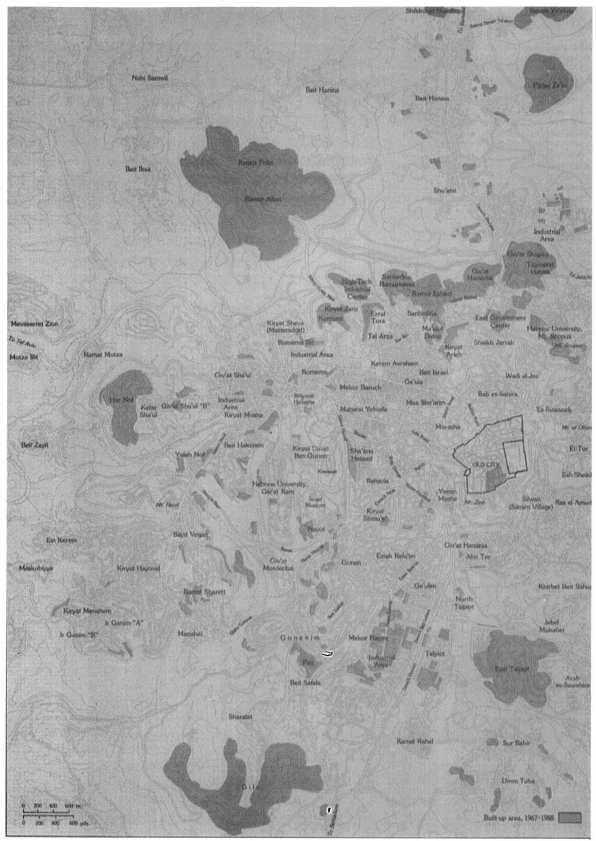

Figure 6. The city of Jerusalem as it is today.

Deepening the Sources

Look at the maps depicting the building, destruction, and rebuilding of the walls of the city of Jerusalem. A complete history course could be taught based on what has happened to the stones of this city. Glance at the maps now, and we will consider them again when we learn about the history of the city. The purpose of this exercise is to gain a sense of the waxing and waning of the population and the ambitions of the leaders and the people of Jerusalem at various points in history.

MAPS 1A and 1B: JERUSALEM TOPOGRAPHY AND THE PERIOD OF DAVID AND SOLOMON, 1000 BCE–587 BCE: Why did David locate his city where he did? It is easily defended because it is surrounded on three sides by deep valleys and on the fourth by a somewhat defendable saddle. The main consideration is the water supply. How does the location of Solomon's Temple relate to the City of David? Note the addition of new areas north of the City of David, the Temple Mount and the Ophel. How did these help in the defense of the City? Where are they relative to the walls of the Old City today?

MAP 2: NEHEMIAH'S JERUSALEM, 435 BCE: When requesting permission to leave Persia to rebuild Jerusalem after its destruction by the Assyrians, Nehemiah describes it by saying, "the city; the place where my fathers are buried, lies waste, its gates consumed by fire." Nehemiah was granted permission to return and rebuild the city walls, its gates, and its towers. The city was, however, much reduced in size, smaller than it had been since the time of Solomon.

MAP 3: HEROD'S JERUSALEM, 34 BCE: During the days of King Herod many magnificent walls, towers, and fortresses were built and the Temple was reconstructed to make it even more beautiful. Jerusalem's population had spread to the area known as the Upper City where there were said to be a monument at the tomb of King David, mansions of the high priests, and more palaces. Josephus describes the largest territory yet encompassed by massive walls and defensive towers. The extraordinary splendor of Herod's Jerusalem came to a tragic end when the Roman general, Titus, destroyed all of Jerusalem except one outer wall of the Temple that was kept in order to protect the Tenth Roman Legion remaining in Jerusalem after the city was razed.

MAP 4: BYZANTINE PERIOD, 324–638 CE: On becoming the religious center of the Christian world, Jerusalem experienced a period of building and growth. Within the general outline of the walls as they had been rebuilt during the time of Roman emperor Hadrian, great churches, roads, and other religious structures were built. We know much about this period from the writings of pilgrims and from the Jerusalem section of the sixth-century Madaba Map, the first real map of Jerusalem.

MAP 5: TURKISH PERIOD, 1540 CE: The Moslems did much to increase the beauty of the most beautiful city in the world, which they also considered to be sacred. From the seventh century until the twentieth, with the interruption of the Crusades during which time burning, destruction, and pillaging marred the land, the Moslems would periodically refurbish a city that easily fell into decay. It was the Turks, however, under Suleiman the Magnificent, who refortified Jerusalem, repaired aqueducts and fountains, and attempted to make the city secure and livable. In spite of Suleiman's efforts, Jerusalem fell into decay once again and was ravaged by invading forces, fires, and internal skirmishing.

MAP 6: JERUSALEM TODAY: As you will see, the walls of Jerusalem remain very much as they were at the beginning of this century. However, the expansion outside the walls that began with a trickle of settlers in the middle of the last century has exploded across the Judean hillside. Suburban sprawl is as much a part of Jerusalem as it is a part of any other modern city! Discuss what this reveals about the population growth and about the ambitions of the leadership and people of this era.

THE BIRTH OF THE NEW CITY
Russian and Greek Orthodoxy

Russian activity in Jerusalem during the second part of the nineteenth century was connected mainly with the growing number of Russian pilgrims. One of the chief reasons for this growth was the evolution of the means of transportation and the opening of Jerusalem to the foreign world. Until the 1830s, only sailing boats had reached the coasts of Palestine. In the 1840s the first steamboats started to come in, although regular shipping lines did not as yet exist. In the early 1850s steamboats started to arrive in Jaffa port regularly. About that time, in 1856, a company was founded in Russia—"The Russian Society for Shipping and Commerce"—whose objective was to compete with, and push out, other foreign companies who were making good profits transporting Russian pilgrims from the Black Sea to Palestine.

In order to provide accommodation for the many Russian pilgrims, the Russians purchased land in Jerusalem in the late 1850s. Later they started to build on a large tract of land, called the Russian Compound, that contained many buildings and constituted a sort of separate quarter that could accommodate at first many hundreds, and later even many thousands, of pilgrims. This area contained the Russian consulate, a Russian cathedral, a hospital, the palace of the Russian Ecclesiastical Mission and the Russian bishop, hospices for pilgrims, and residential buildings.

The Russian activity increased in the 1880s. In 1881, a decision was made to establish the "Imperial Russian Pravoslav Society in Palestine," which set for itself several goals: a) to extend help to the local eastern congregations; b) to take care of the pilgrims; c) to conduct scientific explorations of the Holy Land.

Pilgrims' reports from that period testify to a considerable improvement in the accommodation arrangements for Russians in Jerusalem. The pilgrims received much help from Russian bodies. The route from Russia to Jerusalem became easier and cheaper, owing to agreements signed between the Russian Imperial Society and shipping and railway companies in Russia, by which the pilgrims could get special tickets for reduced prices. The company also guaranteed convenient and safe transportation for the pilgrims from Jaffa to Jerusalem. For this purpose they kept coaches, horses, and camels and also provided protection. The company laid roads by which the pilgrims could reach the very doorsteps of the Russian hospices.

The extensive Russian activity and the considerable growth in the number of Russian pilgrims to Jerusalem induced the Russians to acquire more lands and build more intensively. In 1886 the Society bought a piece of land north of the Russian Compound for building a new hospice. The building was completed in 1890 and contained bedrooms, dormitories, dining rooms, laundry, and storerooms. Later, public baths were added, which were an essential commodity for the pilgrims who had come a long way. Repairs were done also in the old part of the Russian Compound. Medical services were improved and given free of charge.

The Russians also built on Mount of Olives and in Gethsemane. In 1870 they started to build a chapel and a home for pilgrims on Mount of Olives. This work was interrupted by the outbreak of war between Russia and Turkey, resumed in 1883, and finished in 1887. In 1888, Czar Alexander III built in Gethsemane the fine and rich church of Maria Magdalene, in memory of the Mother Czarina—Maria Alexandrova. The church was constructed along the lines of the Great Church of Moscow and had seven domes.

The First World War and the Communist Revolution put an end to Russian activity in Jerusalem.

The Christian community that the Russians supported and that was the biggest in Jerusalem was the Eastern community of the Greek-Orthodox.

The Greek-Orthodox is one of the oldest Christian communities in Palestine, dating back to the pre-Muslim period, when the country was still ruled by Christians. At the beginning of the nineteenth century, this church owned the major part of the Holy Sepulchre, as well as the great Greek convent, twelve more convents and small churches in the city itself, and several more footholds in the area outside the walls—in the "Monastery of the Cross," "Virgin's Tomb," the ruins of the "Ascension Church" on Mount of Olives, and more. Thousands of Greek pilgrims used to come from all over the empire to Jerusalem, their primary purpose being a visit to the Church of the Holy Sepulchre; they mostly timed their visits around Easter, when religious ceremonies were held there. These pilgrims found accommodations in the many convents owned by the Greek church.

Mishkenot Sha'ananim

Like the other pioneer projects outside the walls, the establishment of Mishkenot Sha'ananim was bound up with prior developments within the Old

City. It was also connected with earlier activities of Sir Moses Montefiore in Jerusalem.

Several visits to the country had acquainted Montefiore with the plight of the Jews of Jerusalem and convinced him of the need to provide them with a source of livelihood. In the first volume of this study we described his efforts in this respect as far as they concerned the Old City.

Montefiore decided to extend his operations beyond the Old City walls, and on his fourth visit to Jerusalem, in 1855, he purchased a plot of land west of the Sultan's Pool. The money for this project came from the legacy of Judah Touro, a wealthy New Orleans Jew whose estate was administered by Montefiore and whose name was originally attached to the new neighborhood, which later came to be known as Mishkenot Sha'ananim (Hebrew for "tranquil dwellings"). Since at that time it was forbidden for a foreign national to purchase land in Palestine, Montefiore had to obtain a special dispensation from the authorities. The total area of the "Moses and Judith Vineyard," later the two adjacent neighborhoods of Mishkenot Sha'ananim and Yemin Moshe, was 38,150 square meters acquired at a price of 1,000 pounds.

Montefiore set aside one parcel of land in the southeastern corner of the area for a hospital, for he had observed the high morality rate due to the epidemics that occasionally broke out in Jerusalem and the depressingly low state of health of Jerusalem's poor. It soon transpired, however, that this part of the plan was doomed to failure: the patients feared the dangers that lurked in the "wilderness" outside the walls, and besides, the Rothschild family had in the meantime built a hospital inside the Old City. Montefiore decided, therefore, to build residential houses, as well as a windmill that was to provide a source of livelihood for the settlers. He hoped that the mill would supply flour at a lower price than that exacted by the Arab millers (who at that time enjoyed a monopoly) and would thus ease the plight of the poor people of Jerusalem. All the construction equipment was sent to Jerusalem from London. At first, the mill was operated by millers from Canterbury, England; when the homes had been built, it was leased to a Joseph Rosenthal. In the course of time the machinery broke down; but in any case, since steam-driven flour mills soon appeared in Jerusalem,

Montefiore's windmill became obsolete and the equipment fell into disuse.

A unique piece of equipment, installed for the first time in Mishkenot Sha'ananim, was a small iron pump used to draw water from the neighborhood well. The pump was then considered a veritable technological wonder, and people came from far and wide to view it in action.

As to the actual construction, it seems that the first building to go up was the windmill, in 1857, followed by the first two homes and, in 1860, by twenty more. Other sources claim that the first stage consisted of twenty-four houses.

Half of the houses that had been built by 1860 were allocated to Sephardim, the other half to Ashkenazim. A stone plaque fixed in the neighborhood gate recorded for posterity Montefiore's initiative and the contribution from Judah Touro's will.

In 1869 Sir Moses decided to build another four houses in the "Moses and Judith Vineyard," bringing the total number of houses in the neighborhood to seventy-six.

Montefiore maintained constant contact with the residents of Mishkenot Sha'ananim and assisted them occasionally. In particular, he would see to it that they were fully provided for during religious festivals. In 1875 he arranged for necessary repairs to be made to the houses, the well, and the stone wall surrounding the neighborhood. He also had a gate built, hired a guard, and had gardens planted next to the houses. All the work was performed by Jewish laborers.

The mode of construction—fortress-style, to provide protection from bandits and wild beasts—was apparently dictated by the security conditions then prevailing in the country. For this reason, too, the new neighborhood was built in close proximity to the Old City: two elongated structures, one above the other, on the western slope of the Ben-Hinnom Valley. The walls were about one meter thick; the doors and windows all faced east, looking out on the Old City. The doors were reinforced with iron strips and the windows had the additional protection of iron bars, specially imported from England. The parapet along the edge of the roof was crenellated, presenting an appearance strikingly similar to that of the battlements atop the wall of the Old City across the valley, to facilitate defense in the event of an attack. All the apartments opened into a covered veranda, which extended along the entire length of the building, its roof supported by a row of ornate iron pillars. Each home comprised two rooms, a kitchen, and a pantry, and in front of each a small plot of land was set aside for a garden. In addition to the residential apartments, two synagogues were erected, one for Ashkenazim and the other for Sephardim, as well as a ritual bath (mikvah)) and a bakery. Several cisterns provided water for the community. The heavy iron gates in the surrounding wall were locked each night.

Upon arrival in Mishkenot Sha'ananim, tenants were given a Book of Regulations whose provisions, which reflect the prevailing way of life in those days, were binding. The main regulations were the following:

1. The gatekeeper shall not open the gates to anyone, except by permission of the community's officers or by a letter of permission presented to the gatekeeper.
2. In the evening, at sundown, the gatekeeper shall shut the gates of Mishkenot Sha'ananim, and they shall not be reopened until sunrise the following morning, except in an emergency.
3. All visitors to Mishkenot Sha'ananim shall record their names in a register.
4. No stranger shall spend the night in these houses, prohibition covering even relatives of the tenants of Mishkenot Sha'ananim, except in an emergency.
5. Each and every resident of Mishkenot Sha'ananim shall instruct those who do his bidding to clean his home daily of all refuse and of every unclean thing, as well as to spray the floors of his home with clean water at least once daily.
6. Each and every resident of Mishkenot Sha'ananim shall instruct the members of his household not to cast any refuse in front of the house, to clean the area around his home, to cast all refuse into the container provided therefore, and immediately to replace the cover.
7. All cisterns and pools containing water shall remain covered at all times and shall not be opened except at such time as members of the household shall come there to draw water.

The keys shall be kept by the community officers.
8. Every day, following the study of a chapter of the Mishnah [Oral Law] someone shall recite kaddish derabbanan [special prayer recited after the study of sacred texts] for the soul of the departed benefactor Judah Touro, may he rest in peace. Moreover, on the anniversary of his death, a section of the Mishnah shall be studied in his memory, and a memorial prayer in his name shall be recited, as well as the kaddish.
9. The synagogue and the study house shall be cleaned twice daily, and water shall be poured on the floors at least once daily and before the worshippers arrive for services.
10. All monetary contributions collected by the officers—whether from residents of Mishkenot Sha'ananim or from visitors who come to review the homes—shall be reserved to provide for the needs of the synagogue and the study house, and for any repairs to the houses that may be required.
11. A box with a narrow opening shall be placed to the right of the entrance to the synagogue, so that any person who feels moved to do so may deposit there his contribution to Mishkenot Sha'ananim; and when the officers find that a large amount has been accumulated, they shall remove the money and spend it for the purposes mentioned.
12. The ritual bathhouse must be kept free from all dirt, and no mud or filth of any kind should be seen there.
13. The residents of Mishkenot Sha'ananim shall have no claim of hazakah (title) with regard to the homes of Mishkenot Sha'ananim, even after they have inhabited them regularly for three years, for hazakah to these homes cannot be acquired.

The Book of Regulations ends with a call to the residents:

Take heed not to transgress the fraternal covenant, so that no conflict and discord shall break out amongst you. See the welfare of your brethren wherever you go and in whatever you do, and you shall dwell safely in your domiciles.

Non-Jewish sources also have much to say about the establishment of Mishkenot Sha'ananim. Charles Warren, writing at the end of the 1860s, mentions the work of Judah Touro and Sir Moses Montefiore.

The peculiar shape of the elongated structure seems to have impressed people. Munk (1871) considers "the Jewish poorhouse" that had been built not long before one of the finest buildings in Jerusalem. It boasted a beautiful garden that had been wrested with much labor from the rocky ground. Not far from the houses, on slightly elevated ground, there was also a windmill made of stone. Lievin (1875) describes Mishkenot Sha'ananim, mentioning Montefiore and the allocation of the houses free of charge to Jewish poor; in his opinion it looked like an "industrial neighborhood."

The first Jewish attempt at settlement outside the Old City of Jerusalem was initiated, as we have seen, not by local Jews but rather by a Jew from abroad—Sir Moses Montefiore. Indeed, the Jews of Jerusalem at first hesitated to associate themselves with the enterprise, and it was only after much effort that they could be persuaded to do so. Nevertheless, the project made an impression in the city, and it played a notable role in subsequent progress outside the Old City. It opened up new prospects for the Jewish community in the Old City, which at that time was growing rapidly. And it was to be followed in later years by a whole series of Jewish neighborhoods outside the walls, established on the initiative of the Jewish leaders themselves.

Me'ah She'arim

The Me'ah She'arim Society was formed late in 1873, with the aim of building a new neighborhood. The portion of the Torah read during the week in which the society was founded was Toledot, in the book of Genesis, which includes the verse: "And Isaac sowed in that land, and found in the same year a hundred-fold (Me'ah She'arim), and Adonai blessed him" (Gen. 26:12); hence the name chosen for the projected neighborhood. The society's guiding principle was to enable anyone interested in doing so to build a home for himself on easy terms—with payments spread over a long period of time. The founding members had no outside sources of financing at their disposal. The

conditions under which prospective buyers could join the project were set forth in a book of rules and regulations (eleven in number).

Most of the members of the society—Jewish families from the Old City—lived on the halukkah ("distribution money," consisting of donations from Diaspora Jewry); as a rule, therefore, they were far from wealthy. This may have been the reason that they bought the property on the northern outskirts of Jerusalem, rather than near the main thoroughfare, Jaffa Road, to the west, where the cost of land was considerably higher.

The ground for the project was apparently purchased from Arab peasants living in Lifta, a village near Jerusalem. The area was called Kerem Kadkhod ("ruby vineyard"; see Isaiah 54:12)—probably a Hebrew rendition of the Arabic name. The land, comprising about eight acres, was purchased in three stages. The neighborhood's first account book, dated 1874, notes that the original purchase was for an area of 25,000 square cubits, acquired at a cost of 29,608 Turkish piasters. Later, a second parcel was bought for 12,261 piasters; the third and final parcel cost 12,040 piasters.

The land was to be registered in the name of five Jews of foreign nationality, but was ultimately registered in the name of Ben-Zion Leon, a wealthy merchant who was a British subject and who had invested in the project. The British consul assisted in the launching of the project: the contracts between the society and the contractors for the construction work and the digging of cisterns were arranged by the British consulate.

The newspaper *Ha-Levanon* of 25 November 1874 reports the completion by that date of the first ten houses and, with them, the first water cistern. The society, approaching the end of the first year of its existence, was said to number 177 members. The Book of Regulations confirms that by Hannukah 5635 (years end 1874), ten houses had been completed—about eight months after the laying of the cornerstone.

Toward the end of 1875 Moses Montefiore visited the neighborhood. Reporting this, *Ha-Levanon* says that Montefiore found twenty houses standing and another twenty-eight in the final stages of construction. From other sources we learn, too, that in 1875 construction began of a synagogue, a large house of learning ("Yeshu'ot

Ya'akov"), a Talmud Torah, a ritual bath, and a water cistern.

By about 1882, the society had finished building all the houses of the neighborhood—some 140 buildings all told. Later on, Me'ah She'arim was to become the hub of a whole complex of additional neighborhoods built around it.

In the early stages of construction, Christian experts were employed, since there were no suitable professionals among the Jews. The plan for the neighborhood, drafted by the German architect Conrad Schick, was substantially influenced by security considerations. The neighborhood was planned as a square, closed off by the exterior walls of the houses. At first the houses were built on three sides, and only some time later was the fourth side closed off. An area in the center of the complex was earmarked for public buildings. The entrances to the neighborhood were secured by iron gates, which were locked by night, again for security reasons. According to the records of Me'ah She'arim, these gates were named the Jerusalem Gate, the Beit David Gate, the Mill Gate, and the Lifta Gate. The gates were removed in 1915.

The regulations also reflect actions taken and arrangements made for the regular supply of water to the residents. In addition to supervising the digging of three public cisterns, the committee also encouraged residents to dig cisterns of their own in their private courtyards. Hence the regulations' insistence on keeping the streets and marketplaces clean at all times, as well as the drainpipes leading down from the roofs, "so that the water running into the cisterns might be clean." In years of drought, when the cisterns ran dry, water would be brought to Me'ah She'arim in leather containers by Arabs whose cisterns still held water, or who brought the water from the Lifta spring. In years of particular hardship, the "Committee of all the Kolelim" would bring water by pack animal and cart. A serious water shortage usually brought in its wake epidemics, to which many succumbed and died.

A number of regulations promulgated by the founders of the neighborhood were designed to serve its religious character. Thus, in Chapter 1 of the regulations, Paragraph 10, we read: "It is forbidden for anyone to make over their property, or part of it, not only to a non-Jew but even to one

[Jew] belonging to the sect of those violating the Words of our Sages." In Chapter 2, Paragraph 7, it is stressed that "it is forbidden to lease an apartment to one who is not held to be a good Jew." In other words, not every Jew was eligible for residence in the neighborhood.

Also included in the Book of Regulations are matters pertaining to education, health, and aid to the needy, as well as concern for new immigrants—refugees from persecution in various lands of the Diaspora. One may detect here a tendency to establish some measure of autonomy vis-à-vis the Jewish community in the Old City, through the development of parallel institutions, not only on the local level but also on a more general public level.

To prevent the penetration of "new ideas," especially in all that concerned the haskalah ("Enlightenment") movement, it was determined that these regulations should be observed in perpetuity, and were not to be changed.

First, who calls Me'ah She'arim a "voluntary ghetto," sums up the character of the neighborhood:

> Me'ah She'arim is not simply a religious congregation; from the outset, it took upon itself all the functions of any secular community, like any city or township (shtetl) that ever existed in Czarist Russia or Poland. (Nor did the Turkish authorities have any real control over what went on within Me'ah She'arim, since it came under British protection.) . . . It is the local administration of the neighborhood that deals with all its affairs, insofar as these touch on the life of its inhabitants and their needs: it paves and repairs streets, builds stores and markets . . . repairs cisterns, ritual baths and outhouses, registers properties in the government registry . . . . and, finally—and this is the main thing—ensures that peace, quiet and tranquillity shall prevail . . . .

First also cites the opinion of Brinker, who sees in Me'ah She'arim "a miniature sample of the Old City," though his own view is different:

> It has a character all its own. Those who built this neighborhood came here from Eastern Europe, and they purposely and delib-

erately built themselves a copy of the old shtetl, a real ghetto, closed off to the outside world and far removed from the main arteries of communication, completely self-isolated so that it should not become sullied through contact with others; these walls protected them, body and soul. . . .

Even Yisrael and Mishkenot Yisrael

The next neighborhood to rise in Jerusalem was Even Yisrael. Because of the severe shortage of housing in Jerusalem there was a surge in the construction of new neighborhoods. As early as 1874, *Ha-Lavanon* reported that the Kneset Yisrael Association, prompted by rising costs of apartments in Jerusalem, had established the Bonei Yerushalayim ("Builders of Jerusalem") Society, for the purpose of buying land and building homes. Over a year later we learn from the same newspaper that a new construction society, named Even Yisrael, had been founded. The society purchased a plot large enough to build fifty-three houses— whence its name (the numerical value of the Hebrew word "even" is 53).

According to the society's Book of Regulations, twenty-five houses had been built by 1878, "and the great lottery took place in the presence of most of the members of the society, the rabbis and the city's leading citizens, on Sunday, the 28th day of Sivan, 5635 (1875). Each of the winners received a deed written and signed by the neighborhood committee . . . ." (One of the twenty-five winners in that first lottery was Chief Rabbi Shemuel Salant, but he continued to reside in the Old City, in the "Hurva" of R. Yehuda Hasid, until his death in 1909.)

On the method of purchase, the Book of Regulations states:

> The title deed shall be made out in the names of three or five persons, to be chosen by secret ballot from among the members of the society. And each one of them shall present to the committee, or to someone chosen by the committee, a document certified by the court and by his consul that this is for the Even Yisrael Society.

The same source notes that, because of the location of the land on the main Jerusalem-Jaffa highway, it cost more than that purchased for Me'ah She'arim— 30 piasters per [square] cubit. The houses were built for Sephardim as well as Ashkenazim.

Among the founders of this neighborhood, too, we find Yosef Rivlin, the "Father of Jerusalems Neighborhoods"; and Yehoshua Yellin was also active in its construction. In her memoirs, Ita Yellin (wife of David Yellin), describes the neighborhood in the early days of the British Mandate (1920s):

> The old-new neighborhood is an open square, encompassed on all four sides by rows of houses. It is clean, and extends along the main street, Jaffa Road . . . . In the center of the neighborhood there is a large cistern. Most of the residents did not dare take apartments having more than two rooms—except for a few wealthy families, like the Pines family, who had four rooms. In front of the flat was a kind of covered corner that served as a dining-room. The floor of one of the rooms contained a trap-door that gave access to a cellar, used for the storage of coal, wine, sesame oil and the like . . . . Although the neighborhood was newly-built, the winter rains penetrated the houses.

The neighborhood had two main entrances— one to the north (on Jaffa Road) and one to the south (on Agrippas Road).

—Ben Arieh, *Jerusalem in the 19th Century*, NY: St. Martins Press, 1986

On the following pages are maps from Gilbert's *Jerusalem Illustrated History Atlas*

Deepening the Sources

It was not until the second half of the nineteenth century that citizens of Jerusalem moved outside of the security and community of what is today called the Old City. The population of the city increased dramatically, creating poor health conditions, overcrowding, and inadequate housing. Although it meant leaving the security of the walled city and moving outside of what was con-

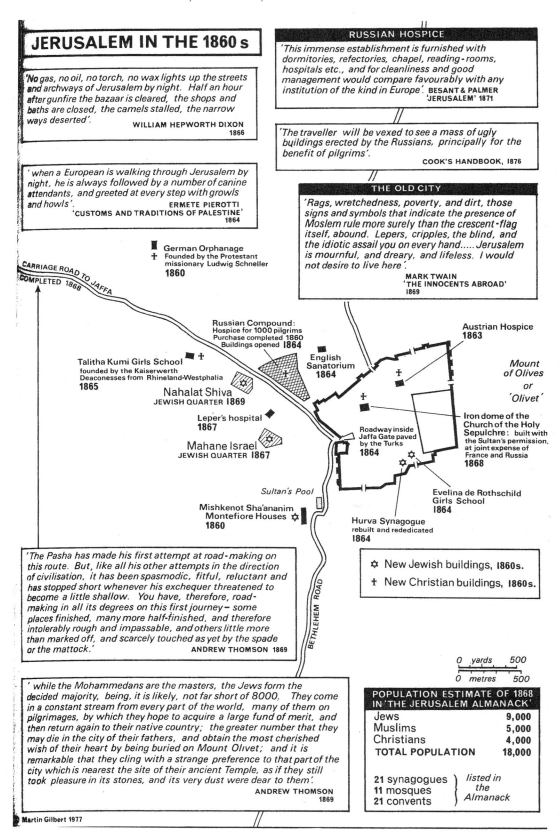

JERUSALEM IN THE 1860s

'No gas, no oil, no torch, no wax lights up the streets and archways of Jerusalem by night. Half an hour after gunfire the bazaar is cleared, the shops and baths are closed, the camels stalled, the narrow ways deserted'.
                              WILLIAM HEPWORTH DIXON
                                              1866

' when a European is walking through Jerusalem by night, he is always followed by a number of canine attendants, and greeted at every step with growls and howls'.
                              ERMETE PIEROTTI
              'CUSTOMS AND TRADITIONS OF PALESTINE'
                                              1864

RUSSIAN HOSPICE

'This immense establishment is furnished with dormitories, refectories, chapel, reading-rooms, hospitals etc., and for cleanliness and good management would compare favourably with any institution of the kind in Europe'. **BESANT & PALMER**
                                    'JERUSALEM' 1871

'The traveller will be vexed to see a mass of ugly buildings erected by the Russians, principally for the benefit of pilgrims'.
                              COOK'S HANDBOOK, 1876

THE OLD CITY

'Rags, wretchedness, poverty, and dirt, those signs and symbols that indicate the presence of Moslem rule more surely than the crescent-flag itself, abound. Lepers, cripples, the blind, and the idiotic assail you on every hand..... Jerusalem is mournful, and dreary, and lifeless. I would not desire to live here'.
                              MARK TWAIN
                      'THE INNOCENTS ABROAD'
                                    1869

■ German Orphanage
✝ Founded by the Protestant missionary Ludwig Schneller
1860

CARRIAGE ROAD TO JAFFA COMPLETED 1868

Talitha Kumi Girls School
founded by the Kaiserwerth Deaconesses from Rhineland-Westphalia
1865

Nahalat Shiva
JEWISH QUARTER **1869**

Leper's hospital
1867

Mahane Israel
JEWISH QUARTER **1867**

Russian Compound:
Hospice for 1000 pilgrims
Purchase completed 1860
Buildings opened **1864**

English Sanatorium
1864

Roadway inside Jaffa Gate paved by the Turks
1864

Austrian Hospice
1863

Mount of Olives or 'Olivet'

Iron dome of the Church of the Holy Sepulchre: built with the Sultan's permission, at joint expense of France and Russia
1868

Evelina de Rothschild Girls School
1864

Sultan's Pool

Mishkenot Sha'anim
Montefiore Houses
1860

Hurva Synagogue
rebuilt and rededicated
1864

✿ New Jewish buildings, 1860s.
✝ New Christian buildings, 1860s.

'The Pasha has made his first attempt at road-making on this route. But, like all his other attempts in the direction of civilisation, it has been spasmodic, fitful, reluctant and has stopped short whenever his exchequer threatened to become a little shallow. You have, therefore, road-making in all its degrees on this first journey— some places finished, many more half-finished, and therefore intolerably rough and impassable, and others little more than marked off, and scarcely touched as yet by the spade or the mattock.'
                              ANDREW THOMSON 1869

BETHLEHEM ROAD

```
0    yards    500
|——|——|——|——|——|
0   metres    500
```

' while the Mohammedans are the masters, the Jews form the decided majority, being, it is likely, not far short of 8000. They come in a constant stream from every part of the world, many of them on pilgrimages, by which they hope to acquire a large fund of merit, and then return again to their native country; the greater number that they may die in the city of their fathers, and obtain the most cherished wish of their heart by being buried on Mount Olivet; and it is remarkable that they cling with a strange preference to that part of the city which is nearest the site of their ancient Temple, as if they still took pleasure in its stones, and its very dust were dear to them'.
                              ANDREW THOMSON
                                              1869

POPULATION ESTIMATE OF 1868 IN 'THE JERUSALEM ALMANACK'	
Jews	9,000
Muslims	5,000
Christians	4,000
TOTAL POPULATION	**18,000**

21 synagogues ⎫ listed in
11 mosques   ⎬   the
21 convents   ⎭   Almanack

© Martin Gilbert 1977

Figure A.   The citizens of Jerusalem begin to settle outside of the Old City in the 1860s.

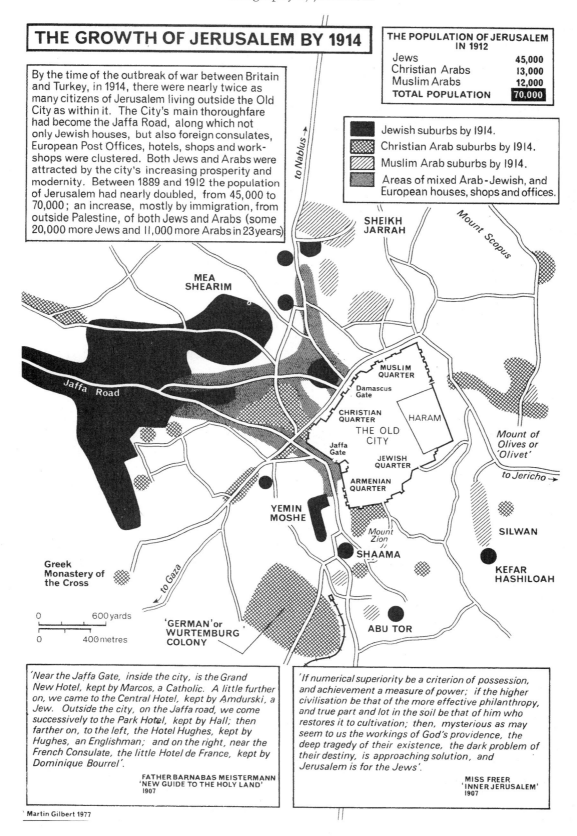

THE GROWTH OF JERUSALEM BY 1914

THE POPULATION OF JERUSALEM IN 1912	
Jews	45,000
Christian Arabs	13,000
Muslim Arabs	12,000
TOTAL POPULATION	70,000

By the time of the outbreak of war between Britain and Turkey, in 1914, there were nearly twice as many citizens of Jerusalem living outside the Old City as within it. The City's main thoroughfare had become the Jaffa Road, along which not only Jewish houses, but also foreign consulates, European Post Offices, hotels, shops and workshops were clustered. Both Jews and Arabs were attracted by the city's increasing prosperity and modernity. Between 1889 and 1912 the population of Jerusalem had nearly doubled, from 45,000 to 70,000; an increase, mostly by immigration, from outside Palestine, of both Jews and Arabs (some 20,000 more Jews and 11,000 more Arabs in 23 years)

- Jewish suburbs by 1914.
- Christian Arab suburbs by 1914.
- Muslim Arab suburbs by 1914.
- Areas of mixed Arab-Jewish, and European houses, shops and offices.

'Near the Jaffa Gate, inside the city, is the Grand New Hotel, kept by Marcos, a Catholic. A little further on, we came to the Central Hotel, kept by Amdurski, a Jew. Outside the city, on the Jaffa road, we come successively to the Park Hotel, kept by Hall; then farther on, to the left, the Hotel Hughes, kept by Hughes, an Englishman; and on the right, near the French Consulate, the little Hotel de France, kept by Dominique Bourrel'.

FATHER BARNABAS MEISTERMANN 'NEW GUIDE TO THE HOLY LAND' 1907

'If numerical superiority be a criterion of possession, and achievement a measure of power; if the higher civilisation be that of the more effective philanthropy, and true part and lot in the soil be that of him who restores it to cultivation; then, mysterious as may seem to us the workings of God's providence, the deep tragedy of their existence, the dark problem of their destiny, is approaching solution, and Jerusalem is for the Jews'.

MISS FREER 'INNER JERUSALEM' 1907

Martin Gilbert 1977

Figure B. The population of Jerusalem expands significantly by 1914.

sidered the holy city, small groups of people organized and financed in diverse ways began to populate the rocky hillsides beyond the gates.

Divide into four groups. Each group should read one of the four selections depicting the diverse communities built in the middle and late nineteenth century, the Russian Compound (1858), Mishkenot Sha'ananim (1857), Me'ah She'arim (1874), and Even Yisrael (1878). Each group should ask: Who made up the communities? Where are they located? What motivated their creation? How were they supported? Are there unique stories connected to their creation? Each group then reports back to the whole.

Refer to the maps illustrating nineteenth-century expansion. Compare the map of the 1860s to the 1914 map. How did the population change? Where did the Jewish neighborhoods develop? What was happening inside the Old City?

IN SUMMATION

- Jerusalem is a thriving, modern city built upon and around the timeless ruins of an ancient city.
- The natural environment of Jerusalem has influenced its development and its destiny.
- The City of Jerusalem outside of the walls is less than 150 years old in contrast to the nearly three thousand years of habitation within the changing walls of the Old City.
- The nature of the expansion of Jerusalem outside the city walls reflects the multifaceted nature of the people and their lifestyles.
-

NOTE: Ask members of the group to bring something to class next week that connects them to Jerusalem and is meaningful to them.

ADDITIONAL LEARNING POSSIBILITIES

1. THE STRATEGIC LOCATION OF JERUSALEM: Analyze the topographical map of Jerusalem and the map of ancient trade routes to determine the strategic power of a city located on the crest of a ridge of the Judean Mountain Range. Locate the Judean Mountain Range and its plateau, the Dead Sea, and the Judean Desert to the East and the Judean lowlands to the West. Caravans that traveled the length of the mountain ridge could not deviate from the route that led through Jerusalem without being stopped by ravines and canyons. People traveling east and west had to ascend to Jerusalem in order to cross the mountain range. Armies traveling through the Middle East passed through Jerusalem, sometimes leaving it unscathed but more often stopping to destroy and/or conquer. Jerusalem's position at this crossroad allowed it to dominate a considerable area in this part of the world, but also placed it in a strategic location advantageous to many conquering nations.

2. GATES OF JERUSALEM: Study the gates of Jerusalem, their construction, artistic qualities, history, and legends. The Board of Jewish Education of Greater New York's unit, B'Sha-araich Yerushalayim, In the Gates of Jerusalem, by Shoshana Glatzer, can be the basis of the study.

PERTINENT SITES TO VISIT IN ISRAEL

- Walk on Walls of the Old City
- City of David
- Archaeological sites in the Old City
- Southern Wall excavations
- Gates of the Old City
- Neighborhood tours: Russian Compound, Mishkanot Sha'ananim/Yemin Moshe, Me'ah She'arim

CHAPTER 3

FINDING OUR WAY

BACKGROUND

Next to one's hometown, a Jew should feel at home in Jerusalem more than anywhere else in the world. We should be drawn to that city in the same way that so many people of diverse faiths have in the past. When we walk its streets for the first time, we should feel as if we have been there before. We should leave it only reluctantly, as if leaving close family and friends. Part of that at-homeness is knowing what Jerusalem has meant to us. Another significant part is knowing our way around, becoming familiar with the streets, sights, sounds, and smells. When we visit Jerusalem, that will happen very easily. We should prepare ourselves so that our experience in Jerusalem will be as meaningful as possible. We can study and participate in activities that will pave the way for our full enjoyment and appreciation of the journey.

GETTING AROUND JERUSALEM
Deepening the Sources

Distribute maps and guidebooks of Jerusalem to the members of the group.

Present a bird's-eye view of Jerusalem, pointing out on the map key geographical, architectural, historical, and religious sites with a brief description about each. Use slides if available.

Begin by pointing out the modern-day locations of the neighborhoods introduced in Chapter 2. Show again how the modern city of Jerusalem has spread across the surrounding hills. In many cases, neighborhoods are homogeneous, reflecting the desire and need of people to create communities within the larger community.

In the 1992 census, the major population groups in Jerusalem were: Jews: 455,000, Moslems: 145,500, Christians:15,300, Others: 500.

Examine the city a little more closely by pointing out some of the most frequently visited sites:

Old City	*King David Hotel*
New City	*Hebrew Union College*
Gates of the Old City	*Beit Shmuel*
Western Wall	*Jaffa Road*
Dome of the Rock	*Zion Square*
Citadel	*Ben Yehuda Street*
Church of the Holy	*King George Road*
Sepulchre	*Independence Park*
Mt. Zion	*Hechal Shlomo*
Yemin Moshe,	*Liberty Bell Park*
Montefiore's Windmill	*Hebron Road*
YMCA	*Mahaneh Yehudah*
Kenesset	*Me'ah She'arim*
Israel Museum and	*Yad V'Shem*
Shrine of the Book	*Hadassah Hospital*
Mt. Scopus,	*Har Herzl*
Hebrew University	*Mount of Olives*

POETRY OF JERUSALEM OF TODAY

Jerusalem Is Full of Used Jews

Jerusalem is full of used Jews, worn out by history, Jews second-hand, slightly damaged, at bargain prices.

And *the eye yearns toward Zion* all the time. And
   all the eyes
of the living and the dead are cracked like eggs
on the rim of the bowl, to make the city
puff up rich and fat.

Jerusalem is full of tired Jews,
always goaded on again for holidays, for memorial
   days.
like circus bears dancing on aching legs.

What does Jerusalem need? It doesn't need a
   mayor,
it needs a ring-master, whip in hand,
who can tame prophecies, train prophets to gallop
around and around in a circle, teach its stones to
   line up
in a bold, risky formation for the grand finale.

Later they'll jump back down again
to the sound of applause and wars.

And the eye yearns toward Zion, and weeps.

—Yehuda Amichai

Jerusalem

Jerusalem is a lullaby that rocks me.
When I awake things happen to me during the day.
My days force me to open my eyes and remember
The face of every passer by: maybe he loves me,
Maybe he has placed a bomb wrapped and
Decorated as a gift of love. I see the
Weak points in the stone houses,
The hole through which electricity flows,
The cavity for the water,
The nakedness of telephone cables and the signing
   mouths.
I am a man of Jerusalem.
Swimming pools and their sounds
Are not part of my spiritual life. The dust is my
   consciousness
The stone—my subconsciousness
And all my memories are courtyards on a summer
   afternoon.

—Yehuda Amichai

Little Girl, Give Me Your Hand

Little girl, give me your hand
And we will see Jerusalem,
We'll pass by, and go near
Within and around.
We'll look at the flowers,
We'll walk on the Wall
We may meet angels
And other surprises.
Across from 'Ashpot Gate'
By the shade of the pines
We'll stop to observe
The goings-on.
We may even see God
At one site or another
Because God has been known
To be seen in Jerusalem.

—Moshe Ha-Naomi

Deepening the Sources

*Read the poem, "Jerusalem Is Full of Used Jews,"
by Yehudah Amichai. How does Amichai describe Jews? Why does Jerusalem need a ringmas-
ter and not a mayor? Note the three images of the
eyes. What does each one mean? What does the
image of the stones represent? How would you
characterize the mood of the poem? Point out the
phrases that represent irony within the poem.*

*Read Amichai's second poem, "Jerusalem."
What are the paradoxes and tensions in this poem?
What are the characteristics implied by what he
describes as his "spiritual life?"*

*Read "Little Girl, Give Me Your Hand." What
dimension of Jerusalem appears in this poem that
was absent in the Amichai poems?*

KEY IDEAS

- Jerusalem is a very complex city filled with an
  endless variety of people, places, and things.
- Jerusalem is both an historic city and a thriving
  modern city. Old and new exist side by side.
- Becoming familiar with the streets and the locations of key sites is a way to begin to feel at
  home in Jerusalem.

ADDITIONAL LEARNING POSSIBILITIES

1. Ask those who have been to Israel to show and describe their favorite slides of sites in Jerusalem. As they make their presentations, locate the sites on maps.

2. Use a commercial slide show or video to explore Jerusalem today. "Fifty Selected Slides of Jerusalem," Holy Views Ltd., Jerusalem, should be available in libraries and resource centers.

3. Build on the experiences of those who have been to Israel. Divide the group into pairs. Each pair is to design a one- to three-day tour of Jerusalem based on a specific interest or theme. Allow twenty minutes to design the program. The remaining class time will be devoted to presentations. Participants should locate the sites being described on their maps.

The following could be used as "topics" for the imaginary tours: Highlights of the Old City of Jerusalem; Museums of Jerusalem; Archaeological Tour of Jerusalem; Aliyah and Absorption: Past and Present Jerusalem Neighborhoods; Parks and Gardens in Jerusalem; Jerusalem: City of Prophets; Jerusalem: Center for Jew, Christian, and Moslem; Jerusalem: Center for Lifelong Learning; Peace and Security in Jerusalem; Synagogue Tour of Jerusalem.

PERTINENT SITES TO VISIT IN ISRAEL

- All of the above!!

JERUSALEM OF THE AGES

TIME LINE OF KEY EVENTS IN JERUSALEM

BCE	19th century	Jerusalem listed in Execration Texts—first recorded mention of the city
	18th–Mid-16th Century	**The Hyksos Period**
	1000–961 (reign)	King David established Jerusalem as Capital of United Kingdom of Israel
	961–922 (reign)	King Solomon—building of the First Temple
	922	Division of kingdom into Judah and Israel
	715–687 (reign)	Hezekiah successfully withstands Sennacherib's assault
		Tunnel built from Gihon spring to Siloam pool
	587	Destruction of Jerusalem and of the Temple by Nebuchadnezzar, and exile of Jews to Babylon
	537–332	**The Persian Period**
	537	Return of the Jews from Babylon
	515	Completion of Second Temple
	445	Nehemian arrives from Babylon and rebuilds the walls of Jerusalem
	about 435	Ezra the Scribe comes from Babylon and joins Nehemiah in rebuilding the community and the city of Jerusalem
	332–167	**The Hellenistic Period**
	332	Alexander the Great visits Jerusalem
	169	Seleucid king, Antiochus IV Epiphanes, plunders the Temple
	167–163 and 140–137	**The Hasmoneans (Maccabees)**
	167–141	Maccabean War of Liberation
	164	Reconquest of Temple Mount and rededication of Temple
	166–135	First Hasmonean leaders, sons of Mattathias

	63 BCE–CE 324	**The Roman Period**
	63	Pompeii captures Jerusalem
	37–34	King Herod the Great—builds Antonia Fortress, palace and towers, starts rebuilding Temple
CE	33	Crucifixion of Jesus
	66–70	The Great Revolt—The War of the Jews against Romans
	70	Fall of Jerusalem and destruction of the Second Temple by Titus
	132–35	Bar Kochba's war of freedom—Jerusalem again the Jewish Capital
	135	Emperor Hadrian's total destruction of Jerusalem and building new walls and new city renamed Aelia Capitolina
	324–638	**The Byzantine Period**
	326	Queen Helena visits Jerusalem, determines locations of events in Jesus' life
	614	Persian conquest of Jerusalem
	629	Recaptured by Byzantines
	638–1099	**The Moslem Period**
	638	Caliph Omar enters Jerusalem
	691	Dome of the Rock completed
	1099–1187	**The Crusader Period**
	1099	Crusaders capture Jerusalem
	end of 12th century	Visit of Rabbi Moshe Ben Maimon (Maimonides)
	1173	Visit of Benjamin of Tudela
	1187	Saladin captures Jerusalem
	1250–1517	**The Mameluke Period**
	1267	Rabbi Moshe Ben Nahman (Nachmanides) arrives from Spain
	1488	Rabbi Obadiah da Bertinoro settles in Jerusalem
	1517–1917	**The Ottoman Turkish Period**
	1515	Ottoman conquest of Jerusalem
	1538–1540	Sultan Suleiman rebuilds City walls
	1700	Rabbi Yehuda He'Hassid arrives, starts building Hurva Synagogue
	1836	First visit of Sir Moses Montefiore
	1838	First consulate (British) opened in Jerusalem
	1860	First settlements outside walls of the city
	1898	Visit by Dr. Theodor Herzl, founder of World Zionist Organization
	1917–1948	**The British Occupation and Mandatory Period**
	1917	British conquest and Allenby's entry into Jerusalem
	1918	Dr. Chaim Weizmann lays foundation stone of Hebrew University on Mount Scopus

CE	1920	Sir Herbert Samuel appointed first British High Commissioner and "Government House" established in Jerusalem
	1925	Hebrew University buildings inaugurated
	1947	United Nations Resolution recommending the partition of Palestine into Arab and Jewish States

1948–1967   **The Divided City**

14 May, 1948	British Mandate ends and State of Israel proclaimed
14 May, 1948–Jan. 1949	Israel's War of Liberation
28 May, 1948	New City of Jerusalem remains intact but Jewish Quarter in Old City falls
Feb. 1949	Dr. Chaim Weizmann elected first president of Israel
April 1949	Israel-Transjordan Armistice Agreement signed, whereby Jerusalem divided between the two countries
13 December 1949	New City declared capital of the State of Israel
Nov. 1956	Israel victorious in Sinai battle against Egyptian forces
April 1960	Discovery of Dead Sea Scrolls
May 1960	Eichman found and tried for crimes against the Jews
5 June 1967	Jordan shells New City of Jerusalem on the first day of the Six Day War
7 June 1967	Israeli troops capture Old City and Jerusalem reunited

1967–   **The United City**

6 Oct. 1973	Yom Kippur War begins as Syria and Egypt attack on two fronts
26 Mar 1979	Israel and Egypt sign Camp David Agreement, the first treaty between Israel and an Arab neighbor
6 June 1982	War in Lebanon, Operation Peace in the Galilee
1987	Beginning of Intifada
1994	Signing of Declaration of Principles with PLO
1994	Peace treaty with Jordan

CHAPTER 4

FROM KING DAVID (961 BCE) TO THE HASMONEANS (135 CE)

BACKGROUND

We have seen how King David unified the tribes and centralized religious activity by transforming Jerusalem from a Jebusite village into the capital of Israel. Solomon's construction of the Temple and development of foreign relationships turned the city into a thriving center of the ancient Near East.

The next five chapters deal with the history of Jerusalem. Each contains an overview of the chronological events, a time line, and an opportunity to examine some of the key occurrences through study of primary documents of the period.

As we will see, the greatness achieved in Solomon's time was not to last. At Solomon's death the kingdom was divided into the Southern Kingdom of Judah with Jerusalem as the capital and the Northern Kingdom of Israel with Samaria as the capital. Although Jerusalem remained the center of religious life for both kingdoms, there was warring between the two and both were attacked by outside forces.

In 720 BCE the Northern Kingdom was conquered by Assyria. Its citizens were exiled to various parts of the Assyrian Empire, and they subsequently disappeared. The Assyrians then attacked Judah and besieged Jerusalem. Although King Hezekiah was able to break the siege of Sennacherib and save Jerusalem, it ultimately fell to the Babylonians, the city was razed, and many Jews were taken captive to Babylonia. When Cyrus I, ruler of Persia, conquered Babylon, he allowed the Jews to leave Babylon and return to rebuild Zion. Not all Jews chose to return.

The Babylonian community, along with the Egyptian community, looked to rebuild Jerusalem as the center of Jewish life.

The period after the return and the rebuilding of the Temple and Jerusalem is called the Second Commonwealth. Ezra and Nehemiah are remembered for their role in the reconstruction of Jewish life and the Jewish city.

The Greeks brought the next great changes to Jerusalem. Two centuries after the return, Greek culture and values began to permeate Jewish life. It reached the point of the Greeks using the Temple for worshiping their pagan gods. Our Hanukkah celebration marks the victory of the Maccabees who fought against the Hellenization of Jewish life. They actually fought against assimilating Jews and, with victory, were able to liberate Jerusalem from Greek influence and to cleanse and rededicate the Temple.

A DIVIDED KINGDOM

And Jeroboam and all the people came to Rehoboam the third day, as the king had appointed, saying, Come to me again the third day. And the king answered the people roughly, forsaking the elders' counsel that they gave him; And spoke to them after the counsel of the young people, saying, My father made your yoke heavy, and I will add to your yoke; my father also chastised you with whips, but I will chastise you with scorpions. Therefore the king listened not to the people; for this was caused by Adonai, that God might perform this saying, which Adonai spoke by Ahijah the Shilonite to Jeroboam the son of Nebat. And when all Israel saw that the king listened not to them, the people answered the king, saying, What portion have we in David? We have no inheritance in the son of Jesse; to your tents, O Israel; Look now to your own house, David. And Israel departed to their tents. But as for the people of Israel who lived in the cities of Judah, Rehoboam reigned over them. Then king Rehoboam sent Adoram, who was over the forced labor; and all Israel stoned him with stones, and he died. Therefore king Rehoboam hurried to mount his chariot, to flee to Jerusalem. And Israel rebelled against the house of David to this day. And it came to pass, when all Israel heard that Jeroboam had returned, that they sent and called him to the congregation, and made him king over all Israel; there was none who followed the house of David, but the tribe of Judah only. And when Rehoboam came to Jerusalem, he assembled all the house of Judah, with the tribe of Benjamin, a hundred and eighty thousand chosen men, who were warriors, to fight against the house of Israel, to bring the kingdom back to Rehoboam the son of Solomon. But the word of God came to Shemaiah the man of God, saying, Speak to Rehoboam, the son of Solomon, king of Judah, and to all the house of Judah and Benjamin, and to the remnant of the people, saying, Thus said Adonai, You shall not go up, nor fight against your brothers the people of Israel; return all of you to your houses; for this thing is from me. They listened therefore to the word of Adonai, and turned and went their way, according to the word of God.

—I Kings 12: 12–24

And the priests and the Levites who were in all Israel resorted to him from all places where they lived. For the Levites left their pasture lands and their possessions, and came to Judah and Jerusalem; for Jeroboam and his sons had cast them off from performing the priest's duties to Adonai; And he ordained his own priests for the high places, and for the hairy goats, and for the calves which he had made. And those, from all the tribes of Israel, who had set their hearts to seek Adonai God of Israel, came to Jerusalem, to sacrifice to Adonai God of their ancestors. And they strengthened the kingdom of Judah, and made Rehoboam the son of Solomon strong, three years; for three years they walked in the way of David and Solomon.

—II Chronicles 11: 13–17

Deepening the Sources

After briefly reviewing the early history of Jerusalem, locate Israel and Judah and their capitals on the map of the divided kingdom. Read the passages on the Divided Kingdom and on the sustained contact between priests and Levites from Israel with the Temple in Jerusalem. What is the significance of the second passage? It strengthened the importance of Jerusalem in spite of the political division. It may have influenced thinking later in history when those in exile still looked to Jerusalem as the center of religious life rather than establishing a new center.

DEFENSE AGAINST SENNACHERIB

Then Isaiah the son of Amoz sent to Hezekiah, saying, Thus said Adonai God of Israel, That which you have prayed to me against Sennacherib king of Assyria I have heard. This is the word that Adonai has spoken concerning him; The virgin the daughter of Zion despises you, and laughs at you with scorn; the daughter of Jerusalem has shaken her head at you. Whom have you taunted and blasphemed? and against whom have you exalted your voice, and lifted up your eyes on high? Against the Holy One of Israel. By your messengers you have taunted Adonai, and have said, With the multitude of my chariots I have come up to the height of the mountains, to the sides of Lebanon, and will cut down their tall cedar trees, and their choice cypresses; and I will enter into its farthest lodges, and into the forest of his Carmel. I have dug and drunk strange waters, and with the sole of my feet

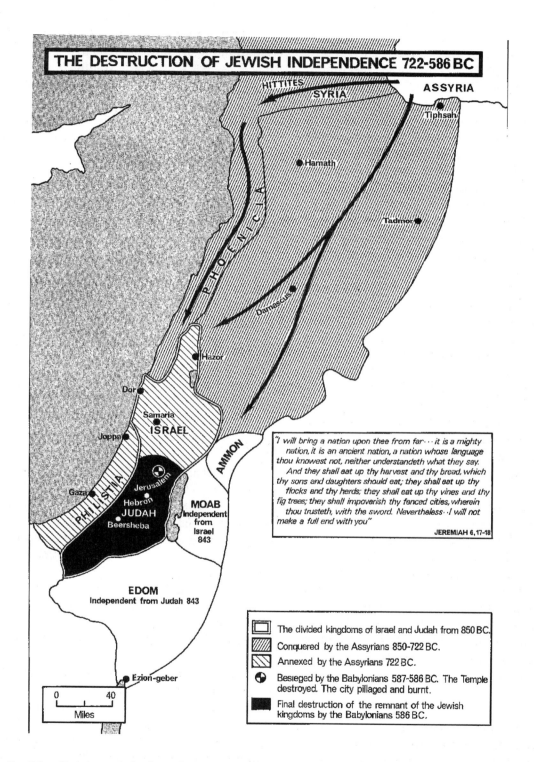

THE DESTRUCTION OF JEWISH INDEPENDENCE 722-586 BC

HITTITES
SYRIA
ASSYRIA
Tiphsah
Hamath
PHOENICIA
Tadmor
Damascus
Hazor
Dor
Samaria
ISRAEL
Joppa
AMMON
Gaza
Jerusalem
Hebron
JUDAH
Beersheba
MOAB
Independent from Israel 843
EDOM
Independent from Judah 843
Ezion-geber

"*I will bring a nation upon thee from far··· it is a mighty nation, it is an ancient nation, a nation whose language thou knowest not, neither understandeth what they say. And they shall eat up thy harvest and thy bread, which thy sons and daughters should eat; they shall eat up thy flocks and thy herds; they shall eat up thy vines and thy fig trees; they shall impoverish thy fenced cities, wherein thou trusteth, with the sword. Nevertheless··I will not make a full end with you*"

JEREMIAH 6, 17-18

The divided kingdoms of Israel and Judah from 850 BC.

Conquered by the Assyrians 850-722 BC.

Annexed by the Assyrians 722 BC.

Besieged by the Babylonians 587-586 BC. The Temple destroyed. The city pillaged and burnt.

Final destruction of the remnant of the Jewish kingdoms by the Babylonians 586 BC.

0   40
Miles

Figure C. The division of the kingdom, 850–568 BCE.

have I dried up all the canals of Mazor. Have you not heard long ago how I have done it, and of ancient times that I have formed it? Now have I brought it to pass, that fortified cities should be laid waste into ruinous heaps. Therefore their inhabitants were of small power, they were dismayed and confounded; they were as the grass of the field, and as the green herb, as the grass on the house tops, and as grain blasted before it has grown up. But I know your abode, and your going out, and your coming in, and your rage against me. Because your rage against me and your arrogance has come into my ears, therefore I will put my hook in your nose, and my bridle in your lips, and I will turn you back by the way by which you came.

—II Kings 19: 20–28

Therefore thus said Adonai concerning the king of Assyria, He shall not come to this city, nor shoot an arrow there, nor come before it with shield, nor cast up a mound against it. By the way that he came, by the same shall he return, and shall not come into this city, said Adonai. For I will defend this city, to save it, for my own sake, and for my servant David's sake. And it came to pass that night, that the angel of Adonai went out, and struck in the camp of the Assyrians a hundred and eighty five thousand; and when they arose early in the morning, behold, they were all dead corpses. And Sennacherib king of Assyria departed, and went and returned, and lived in Nineveh. And it came to pass, as he was worshiping in the house of Nisroch his god, that Adrammelech and Sharezer his sons struck him with the sword and they escaped to the land of Ararat. And Esar-Haddon his son reigned in his place.

—II Kings 19: 20–28

And the rest of the acts of Hezekiah, and all his might, and how he made a pool, and an aqueduct, and brought water to the city, are they not written in the Book of the Chronicles of the Kings of Judah?

—II Kings 20: 20

This same Hezekiah also plugged the upper watercourse of Gihon, and brought it straight down to the west side of the city of David. And Hezekiah prospered in all his works.

—II Chronicles 32: 30

Meanwhile, Hezekiah got to work on the physical strengthening of Jerusalem. The new Assyrian ruler, Sennacherib, was smashing his way even further southwards, and although Hezekiah could and did put off the confrontation by various alliances with kingdoms equally threatened by the Assyrians, he knew that eventually Jerusalem would be attacked.

It is evident from the Bible that he was much preoccupied with the water system, and from this ancient record—as well as from a remarkable archaeological discovery some ninety years ago—we know that he devised a plan to secure his own water supply and at the same time deny water to the enemy. However strong his fortifications, he would never withstand siege if his water ran out. By the same token, a besieger could not long maintain his pressure on the city if, in the arid surroundings in which his men would be encamped, the main local source of water were cut off.

Hezekiah accordingly 'made a pool, and a conduit, and brought water into the city' (II Kings 20, 20). He 'also stopped the upper watercourse of Gihon, and brought it straight down to the west side of the city of David' (II Chronicles 32, 30). Gihon, as we have seen, was at the foot of the eastern wall and was the main source of the city's water. What Hezekiah did, therefore, was to seal the Gihon cave in which the spring issued, thus denying it to an invader. At the same time, he cut a 600-yard tunnel (preserved to this day) which led the water under the southeastern part of the city and out to a reservoir or pool inside the city a point where the ground is lower. This is known as the pool of Siloam (or Shiloah).

In 1880, the biblical record was confirmed by the discovery in the rock wall of the lower entrance to the tunnel, south of the Temple area, of a Hebrew inscription on how the underground passage was excavated. The language is perfect classical Hebrew prose, its contents and script pointing to the reign of Hezekiah. The words were inscribed on a prepared surface of the wall, like the surface of a tablet, but the top part of the inscription was missing. Six lines alone remained, enough to tell the story of how the tunnel was dug by two teams of miners starting at opposite ends, working towards each other and meeting in the middle. It is known as 'The Siloam [or Shiloah] Inscription.' In its standard English translation, it reads as follows:

[when] (the tunnel) was driven through. And this was the way in which it was cut through:—while [. . .] (were) still [ ] axe (s), each man toward his fellow, and while there were still three cubits to be cut through, [there was heard] the voice of a man calling to his fellow, for there was an overlap in the rock on the right [and on the left]. And when the tunnel was driven through, the quarrymen hewed (the rock), each man toward his fellow, axe against axe; and the water flowed from the spring toward the reservoir for 1,200 cubits, and the height of the rock above the head(s) of the quarrymen was 100 cubits.

—Kollek & Perlman
Hezekiah's Tunnel, 1968

Deepening the Sources

Jerusalem endured attacks by numerous great powers of the world. It is a price paid for Jerusalem's location at a key crossroad of the Near East.

Strengthened by its prophets, who raised people's courage and faith, and by its kings, who built reliable defenses and knew what was necessary to sustain life, Judah persisted until 586 BCE.

With the destruction of the Northern Kingdom of Israel, many of its inhabitants sought refuge in Jerusalem. Measures had to be taken to defend and sustain the increased population.

Read the texts above. How did the measures described in these passages sustain life? What does the Bible present as the ultimate factor that saved Jerusalem?

EXILE AND RETURN

By the rivers of Babylon, there we sat down, we also wept, when we remembered Zion. We hung our lyres on the willows in its midst. For there those who carried us away captive required of us a song; and those who tormented us required of us mirth, saying, Sing us one of the songs of Zion. How shall we sing Adonai's song in a foreign land? If I forget you, O Jerusalem, let my right hand forget its cunning. If I do not remember you, let my tongue cleave to the roof of my mouth; if I do not set Jerusalem above my highest joy. Remember, O God, against the Edomites, the day of Jerusalem; who said, Raze it, raze it, to its foundation. O daughter of Babylon, you are to be destroyed! Happy shall the one be, who repays you for what you have done to us! Happy shall the one be, who takes your little ones and dashes them against the rock!

—Psalm 137

And these are the people of the province who went up from the captivity, of those exiles whom Nebuchadnezzar the king of Babylon had carried away to Babylon, and returned to Jerusalem and Judah, every one to their city; They came with Zerubbabel, Jeshua, Nehemiah, Seraiah, Reelaiah, Mordecai, Bilshan, Mizpar, Bigvai, Rehum, Baanah. The number of the people of the people of Israel;

—Ezra 2:1–2

The whole congregation together was forty two thousand three hundred and sixty, Beside their servants and their maids, of whom there were seven thousand three hundred and thirty seven; and there were among them two hundred singing men and singing women. Their horses were seven hundred and thirty six; their mules, two hundred and forty five; Their camels, four hundred and thirty five; their asses, six thousand seven hundred and twenty. And some of the chiefs of ancestors' houses, when they came to the house of Adonai which is in Jerusalem, offered freely for the house of God to set it up in its place; They gave, according to their ability, to the treasure of the work sixty one thousand drams of gold, and five thousand pound of silver, and one hundred priests' garments. So the priests, and the Levites, and some of the people, and the singers, and the gate keepers, and the temple servants, lived in their cities, and all Israel in their cities.

—Ezra 2: 64–70

And when the seventh month came, and the people of Israel were in the cities, the people gathered themselves together as one person in Jerusalem. Then stood up Jeshua the son of Jozadak, and his brothers the priests, and Zerubbabel the son of Shealtiel, and his brothers, and built the altar of the God of Israel, to offer burnt offerings on it, as it is written in the Torah of Moses, the person of God.

— Ezra 3:1-2

And when the builders laid the foundation of the temple of Adonai, the priests in their vestments came forward with trumpets, and the Levites, the sons of Asaph, with cymbals, to praise Adonai, according to the directions of David king of Israel. And they sang responsively in praising and giving thanks to Adonai: For God is good, for God's grace endures for ever towards Israel. And all the people shouted with a great shout when they praised Adonai, because the foundation of the house of Adonai was laid. But many of the priests and Levites and chiefs of the ancestors' houses, old people who had seen the first house, wept with a loud voice when the foundation of this house was laid before their eyes, though many shouted aloud for joy; And the people could not distinguish the sound of joyful shouting from the sound of people weeping, because the people shouted loudly, and the sound was heard from far away.

— Ezra 3:10–13

And after these things, in the reign of Artaxerxes king of Persia, Ezra the son of Seraiah, the son of Azariah, the son of Hilkiah, The son of Shallum, the son of Zadok, the son of Ahitub, The son of Amariah, the son of Azariah, the son of Meraioth, The son of Zerahiah, the son of Uzzi, the son of Bukki, The son of Abishua, the son of Phinehas, the son of Eleazar, the son of Aaron the chief priest; This Ezra went up from Babylon; and he was a scribe skilled in the Torah of Moses, which Adonai God of Israel had given; and the king granted him all that he asked, for the hand of God was upon him. And there went up also some of the people of Israel, and some of the priests, and the Levites, and the singers, and the gate keepers, and the temple servants, to Jerusalem, in the seventh year of Artaxerxes the king. And he came to Jerusalem in the fifth month, which was in the seventh year of the king. For on the first day of the first month he began to go up from Babylon, and on the first day of the fifth month he arrived to Jerusalem, for the good hand of his God upon him. For Ezra had set his heart to study the Torah of the Lord, and to do it, and to teach in Israel his statutes and judgments. And this is the copy of the letter that the king Artaxerxes gave to Ezra the priest, the scribe, learned in the words of the commandments of the Lord, and of his statutes to Israel. Artaxerxes, king of kings, to Ezra the priest, a scribe of the law of the God of heaven, perfect peace, I make a decree, that any of the people of Israel, and of his priests and Levites, in my kingdom, who wish of their own free will to go up to Jerusalem, go with you. For you are being sent by the king, and his seven counsellors, to make inquiries concerning Judah and Jerusalem, according to the law of your God which is in your hand; And to carry the silver and gold, which the king and his counsellors have freely offered to the God of Israel, whose habitation is in Jerusalem, And all the silver and gold that you can find in all the province of Babylon, with the freewill offering of the people, and of the priests, offering willingly for the house of their God which is in Jerusalem; That you may buy speedily with this money bulls, rams, lambs, with their meat offerings and their drink offerings, and offer them upon the altar of the house of your God which is in Jerusalem. (K) And whatever shall seem good to you, and to your brothers, to do with the rest of the silver and the gold, do that according to the will of your God. And the utensils that are given to you for the service of the house of your God, those deliver before the God of Jerusalem. And whatever else shall be needed for the house of your God, which you shall have occasion to provide, provide it from the king's treasure house. And I, Artaxerxes the king, issue a decree to all the treasurers who are beyond the river, that whatever Ezra the priest, the scribe of priest, the scribe of the law of the God of heaven, shall require of you, be done with all diligence. Up to one hundred talents of silver, and one hundred measures of wheat, and one hundred bats of wine, and one hundred bats of oil, and salt, without prescribing how much. Whatever is commanded by the God of heaven, let it be diligently done for the house of the God of heaven, lest God's wrath be against the realm of the king and his sons. We also notify you that it shall not be lawful to impose toll, tribute or custom upon any of the priests and Levites, singers, gate keepers, servants, or ministers of this house of God. And you, Ezra, according to the wisdom of your God, which is in your hand, appoint magistrates and judges, who may judge all the people who are beyond the river, all those who know the laws of your God; and teach those who do not know them. And whoever will not obey the law of your God, and the law of the king, let judgment be executed upon him strictly, whether for death, for banishment, for confiscation of goods, or for imprisonment. Blessed be Adonai God of our ancestors, who has put such a thing as this in the king's heart, to beautify the house of God which is in Jerusalem; And has extended loving kindness to me before the king, and his counsellors, and before all the king's mighty princes. And I was strengthened for the hand of Adonai my God was upon me, and I gathered leaders of Israel to go up with me.

—Ezra 7:1–28

And it came to pass in the month Nisan, in the twentieth year of Artaxerxes the king, that wine was before him; and I took up the wine, and gave it to the king. Now I had never been sad before in his presence. And the king said to me, Why is your face sad, seeing you are not ill? This is nothing else but sorrow of heart. Then I was very much afraid. And I said to the king, Let the king live for ever! Why should not my face be sad, when the city, the place of my ancestors' sepulchers, lies in ruins, and its gates have been consumed by fire? Then the king said to me, For what do you make request? So I prayed to the God of heaven. And I said to the king, If it pleases the king, and if your servant has found favor in your sight, that you would send me to Judah, to the city of my ancestors' sepulchers, that I may rebuild it. And the king said to me, the queen sitting by him, How long will your journey last? And when will you return? So it pleased the king to send me; and I set him a time. And I said to the king, If it pleases the king, let letters be given to me for the governors beyond the river, that they may convey me over till I come to Judah; And a letter to Asaph, the keeper of the king's forest, that he may give me timber to make beams for the gates of the fortress of the temple, and for the wall of the city, and for the house to which I go. And the king granted me, for the good hand of my God was upon

me. Then I came to the governors beyond the river, and gave them the king's letters. And the king had sent officers of the army and horseriders with me. When Sanballat the Horonite, and Tobiah the servant, the Ammonite, heard of it, it displeased them greatly that a person had come seeking the welfare of the people of Israel. So I came to Jerusalem, and was there three days. And I arose in the night, I and a few men with me; and I told no one what my God had put in my heart to do for Jerusalem. And there was no beast with me, but the beast on which I rode. And I went out by night by the Valley Gate, to the Well of the Crocodile, and to the Dung Gate, and viewed the walls of Jerusalem, which were broken down, and its gates had been consumed by fire. Then I went on to the Fountain Gate, and to the King's Pool; but there was no place for the beast that was under me to pass. Then I went up in the night by the brook, and viewed the wall, and turned back, and entered by the Valley Gate, and so returned. And the rulers did not know where I went, or what I did. And to the Jews, and to the priests, and to the rulers, and to the rest who would do the work, till then I had not told. Then I said to them, You see the distress that we are in, how Jerusalem lies in ruins, and its gates are burned by fire; Come, and let us build up the wall of Jerusalem, that we no longer should suffer insult. Then I told them of the hand of my God which had been good upon me; and also of words that the king had spoken to me. And they said, Let us rise up and build. So they strengthened their hands for this good work. But when Sanballat the Horonite, and Tobiah the servant, the Ammonite, and Geshem the Arab, heard of it, they laughed at us with scorn, and despised us, and said, What is this thing that you are doing? Are you rebelling against the king? Then I answered them, and said to them: The God of heaven will make us prosper, and we God's servants will arise and build; but you have no portion, no right, no memorial, in Jerusalem.

Then Eliashib the high priest rose up with his brothers the priests, and they built the Sheep Gate; they consecrated it, and set its doors; they consecrated it as far as the Tower of the Hundred, as far as the Tower of Hananeel. And next to him built the people of Jericho. And next to them built Zaccur the son of Imri. And the sons of Hassenaah built the Fish Gate, and also laid its beams, and set up its doors, its locks, and its bars. And next to them repaired Meremoth the son of Uriah, the son of Koz. And next to them repaired Meshullam the son of Berechiah, the son of Meshezabeel. And next to them repaired Zadok the son of Baana. And next to them the Tekoites repaired; but their nobles did not put their necks to the work of their God. And Jehoiada, the son of Paseah, repaired the Old Gate, and Meshullam the son of Besodeiah. They laid its beams, and set up its doors, and its locks, and its bars. And next to them repaired Melatiah the Gibeonite, and Jadon the Meronothite, the people of Gibeon, and of Mizpah, as far as the seat of the governor beyond the river. Next to him repaired Uzziel the son of Harhaiah, of the goldsmiths. Next to him repaired Hananiah, one of the perfumers, and they restored Jerusalem as far as the Broad Wall. And next to them repaired Rephaiah the son of Hur, the ruler of half the district of Jerusalem. And next to them repaired Jedaiah the son of Harumaph, opposite his house. And next to him repaired Hattush the son of Hashabniah. Malchiah the son of Harim, and Hashub the son of Pahath-Moab, repaired another section, and the Tower of the Ovens. And next to him repaired Shallum the son of Hallohesh, the ruler of half the district of Jerusalem, he and his daughters. Hanun repaired the Valley Gate, and the inhabitants of Zanoah; they rebuilt it, and set up its doors, its locks, and its bars, and a thousand cubits of the wall, as far as the Dung Gate. And Malchiah the son of Rechab, the ruler of the district of Beth-Hakerem, repaired the Dung Gate; he rebuilt it, and set up its doors, its locks, and its bars. And Shallun, the son of Colhozeh, the ruler of the district of Mizpah, repaired the Fountain Gate; he rebuilt it, and covered it, and set its doors, its bolts, and its bars, and the wall of the pool of Shiloah in the king's garden, as far as the stairs that descend from the city of David. After him repaired Nehemiah the son of Azbuk, the ruler of half the district of Beth-Zur, to a place opposite the sepulchers of David, as far as the one made pool, and as far as the house of the warriors. After him repaired the Levites, Rehum the son of Bani. Next to him Hashabiah, the ruler of half the district of Keilah, repaired his area. After him repaired their brothers, Bavai the son of Henadad, the ruler of half the district of Keilah. And next to him repaired Ezer the son of Jeshua, the ruler of

Mizpah, another section opposite the ascent to the armory at the corner. After him Baruch the son of Zabbai earnestly repaired another section, from the corner as far as the door of the house of Eliashib the high priest. After him repaired Meremoth the son of Uriah the son of Koz another section, from the door of the house of Eliashib to the end of the house of Eliashib. And after him repaired the priests, the men of the plain. After him repaired Benjamin and Hashub opposite their house. After him repaired Azariah the son of Maaseiah the son of Ananiah by his house. After him repaired Binnui the son of Henadad another section, from the house of Azariah to the turning of the wall, as far as the corner. Palal the son of Uzai, repaired opposite the corner, and the tower which projects out from the king's upper house, that was by the court of the guard. After him Pedaiah the son of Parosh, And the temple servants living in Ophel, repaired to the place opposite the Water Gate towards the east, and the projecting tower. After them the Tekoites repaired another section, opposite the great projecting tower, as far as the wall of Ophel. The priests repaired from above the Horse Gate, every one opposite his own house. After them repaired Zadok the son of Immer, opposite his own house. After him repaired also Shemaiah the son of Shechaniah, the keeper of the East Gate. After him repaired Hananiah the son of Shelemiah, and Hanun the sixth son of Zalaph, another section. After him repaired Meshullam the son of Berechiah opposite his chamber. After him repaired Malchiah the goldsmith's son as far as the place of the Temple servants and of the merchants, opposite the Hamiphkad Gate, and to the ascent of the corner. And the goldsmiths and the merchants repaired between the ascent of the corner and the Sheep Gate. And it came to pass, that when Sanballàt heard that we built the wall, he was angry, and greatly enraged, and he mocked the Jews. And he spoke before his brothers and the army of Samaria, and said, What are these feeble Jews doing? Will they restore things? Will they sacrifice? Will they finish up in a day? Will they revive the stones out of the heaps of rubbish which are burned? And Tobiah the Ammonite, who was next to him, said, Even a fox climbing up on what they build, shall break down their stone wall! Hear, O our God; for we are despised; and turn their taunt upon their own head, and give them for a prey in the land of captivity; And do not cover their iniquity, and do not let their sin be blotted out from before you; for they have provoked you to anger before the builders. So we built the wall; and all the wall was joined together to half its height; for the people had a mind to work.

—Nehemiah 2,3

Deepening the Sources

Jerusalem was able to withstand Sennacherib but was not able to defend against Nebuchadnezzar.

How did Nebuchadnezzar's policy on the treatment of conquered people change the course of our history? Unlike the Assyrians, who sent the inhabitants of the Northern Kingdom in many directions, the Babylonians took the masses of Jerusalemites into captivity where they continued to live as a community and mourn their separation from Jerusalem.

What are the poetic images in Psalm 137 that have made this echo powerfully throughout Jewish history? To what do Zion and Jerusalem refer?

Less than 50 years later Persia conquered Babylon. Persia's King, Cyrus, allowed Jews to return and rebuild their life and their Temple. Read passages from Ezra and Nehemiah. What did each contribute to the rebuilding process? Using the map from Chapter 2, locate the sites written about by Nehemiah.

THE FIRST HANUKKAH
THE CLEANSING OF THE TEMPLE AND REDEDICATION OF THE ALTAR

But Judas and his brothers said: "Now that our enemies have been crushed, let us go up to Jerusalem to cleanse the temple and rededicate it." So the whole army was assembled and went up to Mount Zion. There they found the temple laid waste, the altar profaned, the gates burnt down, the courts overgrown like a thicket or wooded hillside, and the priests rooms in ruin. They tore their garments, wailed loudly, put ashes on their heads, and fell on their faces to the ground. They sounded the ceremonial trumpets, and cried aloud to Heaven.

Then Judas detailed troops to engage the garrison of the citadel while he cleansed the temple. He selected priests without blemish, devoted to the law, and they purified the temple, removing to an unclean place the stones which defiled it. They discussed what to do with the altar of burnt-offering, which was profaned, and rightly decided to demolish it, for fear it might become a standing reproach to them because it has been defiled by the Gentiles. They therefore pulled down the altar, and stored away the stones in a fitting place on the temple hill, until a prophet should arise who could be consulted about them. They took unhewn stones, as the law commands, and built a new altar on the model of the previous one. They rebuilt the temple and restored its interior, and consecrated the temple courts. They renewed the sacred vessels and the lamp-stand, and brought the altar of incense and the table into the temple. When they had put the Bread of the Presence on the table and hung the curtains, all their work was completed.

Then, early on the twenty-fifth day of the ninth month, the month Kislev, in the year 148, sacrifice was offered as the law commands on the newly made altar of burnt-offering. In the anniversary of the day when the Gentiles had profaned it, on that very day, it was rededicated, with hymns of thanksgiving, to the music of harps and lutes and cymbals. All the people prostrated themselves, worshiping and praising Heaven that their cause had prospered.

They celebrated the rededication of the altar for eight days; there was great rejoicing as they brought burnt-offerings and sacrificed peace-offerings and thank-offerings. They decorated the front of the temple with golden wreaths and ornamental shields. They renewed the gates and the priests' rooms, and fitted them with doors. There was great merry-making among the people, and the disgrace brought on them by the Gentiles was removed.

Then Judas, his brothers, and the whole congregation of Israel decreed that the rededication of the altar should be observed with joy and gladness at the same season each year, for eight days, beginning on the twenty-fifth of Kislev.

At that time they encircled Mount Zion with high walls and strong towers to prevent the Gentiles from coming and trampling it down as they had done before. Judas set a garrison there; he also fortified Bethsura, so that the people should have a fortress facing Idumaea.

—I Maccabees 4:36–61

We give thanks for the redeeming wonders and the mighty deeds by which, at this season, our people was saved in days of old.

In the days of the Hasmoneans, a tyrant arose against our ancestors, determined to make them forget Your Torah, and to turn them away from obedience to Your will. But You were at their side in time of trouble. You gave them strength to struggle and to triumph, that they might serve You in freedom.

Through the power of Your spirit the weak defeated the strong, the few prevailed over the many, and the righteous were triumphant. Then Your children returned to Your house, to purify the sanctuary and kindle its lights. And they dedicated these days to give thanks and praise to Your great name.

—*Al Ha-Nissim*, from *Gates of Prayer*

Deepening the Sources

This period in Jerusalem's history is very familiar to most of us. Begin this segment with a verbal quiz on basic words associated with this era. Explain words as you proceed.

WHO, WHAT, OR WHERE?!!

Hellenization	*Antiochus*
Zeus (Desecration)	*Menorah*
Hassidim	*Modin*
Mattathias	*Maccabees*
Hasmoneans	*Judah, Jonathan, Simon*
Hanukkah— rededication	*Nes gadol haya sham (po)*
Alexander	*Seleucus*

"Not by might, and not by power, but by spirit alone will we all dwell in peace."

Read I Maccabees, IV, 59 and the Al ha-nissim *prayer. Discuss the significance of the military miracle over the miracle of the oil. Note the relationship between Hanukkah and Succot.*

ADDITIONAL LEARNING POSSIBILITIES

1. Look at the reasons behind the Talmud's story of the miracle of the oil and the significance of the eight-day observance as described in the Book of Maccabees. Discuss Hanukkah as a civil war of Jewish Hellenists against Hassidim. Elias Bickerman's *The Maccabees* is an excellent resource for this discussion.

2. For homework to be discussed briefly in class next time, or just for fun, suggest students read the chapter "In the Gymnasium" in James A. Michener's *The Source*.

PERTINENT SITES TO VISIT IN ISRAEL

- Old City
- Temple Mount
- Hezekiah's tunnel
- Solomon's Quarry
- Nehemiah's wall
- Hasmomean Tower
- Hasmonean remains, Southern Wall

CHAPTER 5

ROMAN PERIOD

BACKGROUND

Jewish life continued in Jerusalem under the Hasmoneans. The spread of the Roman Empire and the beginnings of Christianity, however, were constantly threatening clouds on the horizon. In 63 BCE the Romans conquered Jerusalem and put their own rulers in power. Herod, an Edomite convert to Judaism who married a Jewess, was a tyrant and a murderer. He rebuilt Jerusalem, including in it a breathtaking temple. He restored the city to a level of beauty it had not seen since the time of Solomon. Its magnificence came to an end when Titus, in 70 CE, razed the entire city while putting down a revolt against Roman rule.

Uprisings continued, including the Bar Kochba rebellion. Jews were subsequently prohibited from entering Jerusalem. Emperor Hadrian changed the name of the city to Aelia Capitolina and built an altar to Jupiter on the Temple Mount. Jerusalem was no longer a Jewish city. With Rome's adoption of Christianity, any new building or new groups in the city had Christian connections. A Jewish Jerusalem existed only in the prayers and dreams of Jews spread around the world.

HEROD

But besides that great advantage, as to the place where they were situated, it was also built very strong; because David, and Solomon, and the following kings were very zealous about this work. Now that wall began on the north, at the tower called Hippicus, and extended as far as the Xistus, a place so called, and then joining to the council-house, ended at the west cloister of the temple. But if we go to the other way westward, it began at the same place, and extended through a place called Bethso, to the gate of the Essene; and after that it went southward, having its bending above the fountain Siloam, where it also bends again towards the east at Solomon's pool, and reaches as far as a certain place which they called Ophlas, where it was joined to the eastern cloister of the temple. The second wall took its beginning from that gate which they called Genneth, which belonged to the first wall; it only encompassed the northern quarter of the city, and reached as far as the tower Antonia. The beginning of the third wall was at the tower Hippicus, whence it reached as far as the north quarter of the city, and the tower Psephinus, and then was so far extended till it came over against the monuments of Helena, which Helena was queen of Adiabene the mother of Izates: it then extended farther to a great length, and passed by the sepulchral caverns of the kings, and bent again at the tower of the corner, at the monument which is called Monument of the Fuller, and joined to the old wall at the valley called the Valley of Cedron. It was Agrippa who encompassed the parts added, to the old city with this wall, which had been all naked before; for as the city grew more populous, it gradually crept beyond its old limits, and those parts of it that stood northward of the temple, and joined that hill to the city, made it considerably larger, and occasioned that hill which is in number the fourth, and is called Bezetha, to be inhabited also. It lies over against the tower Antonia, but is divided from it by a deep valley, which was dug on

Figure D.   Model of Jerusalem of the Second Temple Period, located at the Holyland Hotel in Jerusalem.

purpose, and that in order to hinder the foundations of the tower of Antonia from joining to this hill, and thereby affording an opportunity for getting to it with ease, and hindering the security that arose from its superior elevation, for which reason also that depth of the ditch made the elevation of the towers more remarkable. This new built part of the city was called Bezetha, in our language, which if interpreted in the Grecian language, may be called The New City. Since, therefore, its inhabitants stood in need of a covering, the father of the present king, and of the same name with him, Agrippa, began that wall we spoke of: but he left off building it when he had only laid the foundations, out of the fear he was in of Claudius Caesar, lest he should suspect that so strong a wall was built in order to make some innovation in public affairs; for the city could no way have been taken, if that wall had been finished in the manner it was begun; as its parts were connected together by stones twenty cubits long and ten cubits broad, which could never have been either easily undermined by any iron tools, or shaken by any engines. The wall was, however, ten cubits wide, and it would probably have had an height greater than that, had not his zeal who began it been hindered from exerting itself. After this, it was erected with great diligence by the Jews, as high as twenty cubits, above which it had battlements of two cubits, and turrets of three cubits altitude, insomuch that the entire altitude extended as far as twenty-five cubits.

Now the towers that were upon it were twenty cubits in breadth, and twenty cubits in height; they were square, and solid as was the wall itself, wherein the niceness of the joints, and the beauty of the stones were no way inferior to those of the holy house itself. Now the third wall was all of it wonderful; yet was the tower Psephinus elevated above it at the north-west corner, and there Titus pitched his own tent: for being seventy cubits high, it both afforded a prospect of Arabia at sun-rising, as well as it did sea westward. These towers were for largeness, beauty, and strength, beyond all that were in the habitable earth. He built these after such an extraordinary manner, to gratify his own private affection, and dedicated these towers to the memory of those three persons who had been the dearest to him, and from whom he named them. They were his brother, his friend, and his wife. This wife he had slain out of his love, the other two he lost in war. Hippicus, so named from his friend, was square, its length and breadth were each twenty-five cubits, and its height thirty, and it had no vacuity in it. Over this solid building, which was composed of great stones untied together, there was a reservoir twenty cubits deep, over which there was an house of two stories; over which battlements of two cubits, and turrets all round of three cubits high. The second tower, which he named from his brother Phasaelus, had its breadth and its height equal, each of them forty cubits; over which a cloister went round about whose height was ten cubits, and it was covered from enemies by breast-works and bulwarks. There was also built over that cloister another tower, parted into magnificent rooms, and a place for bathing. It was also adorned with battlements and turrets. The third tower was Mariamne, for that was the queens name: it was solid as high as twenty cubits; its breadth and its length were twenty cubits, and were equal to each other: its upper buildings were more magnificent, and had greater variety than the other towers had; for the king thought it most proper for him to adorn that which was denominated from his wife, better than those denominated from men, as those were built stronger than this that bore his wife's name. The entire height of this tower was fifty cubits.

A Description of the Temple

Now this temple, as I have already said, was built upon a strong hill. At first the plain at the top was hardly sufficient for the holy house, and the altar, for the ground about it was very uneven, and like a precipice; but when King Solomon, who was the person that built the temple, had built a wall to it, on its east side, there was then added one cloister founded on a bank cast up for it, and on the other parts the holy house stood naked. But in future ages the people added new banks, and the hill became a larger plain. They then broke down the wall on the north side, and took in as much as sufficed afterward for the compass of the entire temple. And when they had built walls on three sides of the temple round about, from the bottom of the hill, and had performed a work that was greater than could be hoped for, (work long ages were spent by them, as well as all their sacred treasures were exhausted, which were still replenished by those tributes which were sent to God from the whole habitable earth;) they then encompassed their upper courts with cloisters, as well as they [afterward] did the lowest [court of the] temple . . . . they brought earth and filled up the valleys, as being desirous to make them on a level with the narrow streets of the city; wherein they made use of stones forty cubits in magnitude, for the great plenty of money they then had, and the liberality of the people, made this attempt of theirs to succeed to an incredible degree.

Now for the works that were above these foundations, these were not unworthy of such foundations: for all the cloisters were double, and the pillars to them belonging were twenty-five cubits in height, and supported the cloisters. These pillars were of one entire stone each of them, and that stone was white marble; and the roofs were adorned with cedar, curiously graven. The natural magnificence, and excellent polish, and the harmony of the joints in these cloisters, afforded a prospect that was very remarkable; nor was it on the outside adorned with any work of the painter or engraver. The cloisters [of the outmost court] were in breadth thirty cubits, while the entire compass of it was by measure six furlongs, including the tower of Antonia; those entire courts that were exposed to the air were laid with stones of all sorts. When you go through these [first] cloisters, unto the second [court of the] temple, there was a partition made of stone all round, whose height was three cubits, its construction was very elegant; upon it stood pillars, at equal distances from one another, declaring the law of purity, some in Greek, and some in Roman letters, that no foreigner should go within that sanctuary; for that second [court of the] temple was called the Sanctuary, and was ascended to by fourteen steps from the first court. This court was four square, and had a wall about it peculiar to itself; . . . Beyond these fourteen steps there was the distance of ten cubits: this was all plain; whence there were other steps, each of five cubits a-piece, that led to the gates, which gates on the north and south sides were eight, on each of those sides four, and of necessity two on the east. For since there was a partition built for the women on that side, as the proper place wherein they were to worship, there was a necessity for a second gate for them: this gate was cut out of its wall, over against the first gate. There was also on the other sides one southern and one northern gate, through which was a passage into the court of the women: for as to the other gates, the women were not allowed to pass through them: nor when they went through their own gate could they go beyond their own wall. This place was allotted to the women of our own country, and of other countries, provided they were of the same nation, and that equally; the western side of this court had no gate at all, but the wall was built entire on that side.

Now nine of these gates were on every side covered over with gold and silver, as were the jambs of their doors and their lintels: but there were one gate that was without the [inward court of] the holy house, which was of Corinthian brass, and greatly excelled those that were only covered over with silver and gold. Each gate had two doors, whose height was severally thirty cubits, and their breadth fifteen.

As to the holy house itself, which was placed in the midst [of the inmost court], that most sacred place of the temple, it was ascended to by twelve steps; and in front its height and its breadth were equal, and each an hundred cubits, though it was behind forty cubits narrower, for on its front it had what may be styled shoulders on each side, that passed twenty cubits farther. Its first gate was seventy cubits high, and twenty-five cubits broad: but this gate had no doors; for it represented the universal visibility of heaven, and that it cannot be excluded from any place. Its front was covered with gold all over, and through it the first part of the house, that was more inward, did all of it appear; which, as it was very large, so did all the parts about the more inward gate appear to shine

to those that saw them: but then, as the entire house was divided into two parts within, it was only the first part of it that was open to our view. Its height extended all along to ninety cubits in height, and its length was fifty cubits, and its breadth twenty. But that gate which was at this end of the first part of the house, was, as we have already observed, all over covered with gold, as was its whole wall about it: it had also golden vines above it, from which clusters of grapes hung as tall as a mans height. But then this house, as it was divided into two parts, the inner part was lower than the appearance of the outer, and had golden doors of fifty-five cubits altitude, and sixteen in breadth; but before these doors there was a veil of equal largeness with the doors. It was a Babylonian curtain, embroidered with blue, and fine linen, and scarlet and purple, and of a contexture that was truly wonderful. Nor was this mixture of colors without its mystical interpretation, but was a kind of image of the universe; for by the scarlet there seemed to be enigmatically signified fire, but the fine flax the earth, by the blue the air, and by the purple the sea; two of them having their colors the foundation of this resemblance; but the fine flax and the purple have their own origin for that foundation, the earth producing the one, and the sea the other. This curtain had also embroidered upon it all that was mystical in the heavens, excepting that of the [twelve] signs, representing living creatures.

When any persons entered into the temple, its floor received them. This part of the temple therefore was in height sixty cubits, and its length the same; whereas its breadth was but twenty cubits: but still that sixty cubits in length was divided again, and the first part of it was cut off at forty cubits, and had in it three things that were very wonderful and famous among all mankind, the candlestick, the table [of shew bread], and the altar of incense. Now the seven lamps signified the seven planets; for so many there were springing out of the candlestick. Now the twelve loaves that were upon the table signified the circle of the zodiac and the year; but the altar of incense, by its thirteen kinds of sweet smelling spices with which the sea replenished it, signified, that God is the possessor of all things that are both in the uninhabitable and habitable parts of the earth, and that they are all to be dedicated to his use. But the inmost part of the temple of all was of twenty cubits. This was also separated from the outer part by a veil. In this there was nothing at all. It was inaccessible and inviolable, and not to be seen by any; and was called the Holy of Holies. Now, about the sides of the lower part of the temple there were little houses, with passages out of one into another: there were a great many of them, and they were of three stories high; there were also entrances on each side into them from the gate of the temple. But the superior part of the temple had no such little houses any farther, because the temple was there narrower, and forty cubits higher, and of a smaller body than the lower parts of it. Thus we collect that the whole height, including the sixty cubits from the floor, amounted to an hundred cubits.

Now the outward face of the temple in its front wanted nothing that was likely to surprise either mens minds or their eyes; for it was covered all over with plates of gold of great weight, and at the first rising of the sun, reflected back a very fiery splendor, and made those who forced themselves to fine linen encompassed his head, which was tied by a blue ribband, about which there was another golden crown, in which was engraven the sacred name [of God]: it consists of four vowels. However, the high priest did not wear these garments at other times, but a more plain habit; he only did it when he went into the most sacred part of the temple, which he did but once a year, on that day when our custom is for all of to keep a fast to God. And thus much concerning the city and the temple; but, for the customs and laws hereto relating, we shall speak more accurately another time; for there remain a great many things thereto relating, which have not been here touched upon.

—Josephus, *The Wars of the Jews*

Deepening the Sources

Savage, merciless, and cunning, Herod, a convert to Judaism who was unfailingly loyal to Rome, was a brilliant administrator and a talented builder whose beautiful additions to Jerusalem can be seen today. Select and read a few passages from Josephus describing the palace and its towers, the Antonia Fortress, and the reconstructed Temple. What do the readings tell you about the wealth of Herod? The beauty of the construction? Why do you believe Herod invested so much in the rebuilding of Jerusalem? Look at the picture of the model of Jerusalem of the period of the Second Temple. In Jerusalem, visit the Citadel Museum, which tells the story of the many dwellers in the palace originally built by Herod and recounts the entire history of Jerusalem. Crusaders, Mamelukes, and Ottoman Turks all added to the structure and to its history. Note that the Western Wall, also called the "Wailing Wall," or the Kotel, remains sacred to the Jews until today. It is the western wall of the platform built by Herod to support his enlarged Temple.

In spite of his deeply evil acts, Herod is named in the Talmud. "He who has not set his eyes on the structure of Herod has not seen a structure of beauty in all his life."

DESTRUCTION OF JERUSALEM AND THE TEMPLE BY TITUS
The Destruction of the Temple

Titus proposed to these, that they should give him their advice what should be done about the holy house. Now some of these thought, "It would be the best way to act according to the rules of war, [and demolish it,] because the Jews would never leave off rebelling while that house was standing, at which house it was that they used to get all together." Others of them were of the opinion, That "in case the Jews would leave it, and none of them would lay their arms up in it, he might save it; but that in case they got upon it, and fought anymore, he might burn it; because it must then be looked upon not as an holy house, but as a citadel, and that the impiety of burning it would then belong to those that forced this to be done, and not to them." But Titus said, That "although the Jews should get upon that holy house, and fight us thence, yet ought we not to revenge ourselves on things that are inanimate, instead of the men themselves; and that he was not in any case for burning down so vast a work as that was, because this would be a mischief to the Romans themselves, as it would be an ornament to their government while it continued." So Fronto, and

Alexander, and Cerealis grew bold upon that declaration, and agreed to the opinion of Titus. Then was this assembly dissolved, when Titus had given orders to the commanders that the rest of their forces should lie still, but that they should make use of such as were most courageous in this attack. So he commanded that the chosen men that were taken out of the cohorts should make their way through the ruins, and quench the fire.

Now it is true, that on this day the Jews were so weary, and under such consternation, that they refrained from any attacks. But on the next day, they gathered their whole force together, and ran upon those that guarded the outward court of the temple, very boldly, through the east gate, and this about the second hour of the day. These guards received their attack with great bravery, and by covering themselves with their shields before, as if it were with a wall, they drew their squadron close together; yet it was evident that they could not abide there very long, but would be overborne by the multitude of those that sallied out upon them, and by the heat of their passion. However, Caesar seeing, from the tower of Antonia, that this squadron was likely to give way, he sent some chosen horsemen to support them. Hereupon the Jews found themselves not able to sustain their onset, and upon the slaughter of those in the forefront, many of the rest were put to flight. But as the Romans were going off the Jews turned back upon them, and fought them; and as those Romans came back upon them, they retreated again, until about the fifth hour of the day they were overborne, and shut themselves up in the inner [court of the] temple.

So Titus retired into the tower of Antonia, and resolved to storm the temple the next day, early in the morning, with his whole army, and to encamp around about the holy house. But as for that house, God had, for certain, long ago doomed it to the fire; and now that fatal day was come, according to the revolution of ages, it was the tenth day of the month Lous, [Av], upon which it was formerly burnt by the king of Babylon; although these flames took their rise from the Jews themselves, and were occasioned by them: for upon Titus's retiring, the seditious lay still for a little while, and then attacked the Romans again, when those that guarded the holy house, fought with those that quenched the fire that was burning the inner [court of the] temple; but these Romans put the Jews to flight, and proceeded as far as the holy house itself. At which time one of the soldiers, without staying for any orders, and without any concern or dread upon him at so great an undertaking, and being hurried only by a certain divine fury, snatched somewhat out of the materials that were on fire, and being lifted up by another soldier, he set fire to a golden window, through which there was a passage to the rooms that were round about the holy house, on the north side of it. As the flames went upward, the Jews made a great clamor, such as so mighty an affliction required, and ran together to prevent it; and now they spared not their lives any longer, nor suffered anything to restrain their force since that holy house was perishing, for whose sake it was that they kept such a guard about it.

And now a certain person came running to Titus, and told him of this fire, as he was resting himself in his tent, after the last battle: whereupon he rose up in great haste, and, as he was, ran to the holy house in order to have a stop put to the fire, after him followed all his commanders, and after them followed the several legions in great astonishment: so there was a great clamor and tumult raised, as was natural upon the disorderly motion of so great an army. Then did Caesar, both by calling to the soldiers that were fighting, with a loud voice, and by giving a signal to them with his right hand, order them to quench the fire. But they did not hear what he said, though he spake so loud, having their ears already dinned by a great noise another way: nor did they attend to the signal he made with his hand neither, as still some of them were distracted with fighting, and others with passion. But as for the legions that came running thither, neither any persuasions, nor any threatenings could restrain their violence, but each one's own passion was his commander at this time; and as they were crowding into the temple together, many of them were trampled on by one another, while a great number fell among the ruins of the cloisters, which were still hot, and smoking, and were destroyed in the same miserable way with those whom they had conquered: and when they were come near the holy house, they made as if they did not so much as hear Caesar's orders to the contrary, but they encouraged those that were before them to set it on fire. As for the seditious, they were in too great distress already to afford their assistance [towards quenching the fire:] they were everywhere slain, and everywhere beaten; and as for a great part of the people, they were weak and without arms, and had their throats cut wherever they were caught.

—Josephus, *The Wars of the Jews*

When the High Priest saw that the Temple was burning, he went up to the roof of the Sanctuary, accompanied by a platoon of apprentice Priests, carrying the keys of the Sanctuary.

They said to the Blessed Holy One:

"God of the Universe! Seeing that we have not proved to be worthy custodians for You, let the Keys of Your House be herewith returned to you!"

And they hurled the keys upward.

A hand appeared and received the keys.

—Talmud Bavli, *Taanit* 29a

The Destruction of Jerusalem by Titus

From the last hill that looks on thy once holy
*   dome*
I beheld thee, oh Sion! when render'd to Rome:
'Twas thy last sun went down, and the flames of
*   thy fall*
Flash'd back on the last glance I gave to thy wall.
I look'd for thy temple, I look'd for my home,
And forgot for a moment my bondage to come;
I beheld but the death-fire that fed on thy fane,
And the fast-fetterd hands that made vengeance
*   in vain.*
On many an eve, the high spot whence I gazed
Had reflected the last beam of day as it blazed;
While I stood on the height, and beheld the de-
*   cline*
Of the rays from the mountain that shone on thy
*   shrine.*
And now on that mountain I stood on that day,
But I mark'd not the twilight beam melting away;
Oh! would that the lightning had glared in its
*   stead,*
And the thunderbolt burst on the conqueror's
*   head!*

But the gods of the pagan shall never profane
The shrine where Jehovah disdain'd not to reign;
And scatter'd and scorn'd as thy people may be,
Our worship, oh Father! is only for thee.

—Lord Byron

Deepening the Sources

Read Josephus' account of the destruction of Jerusalem and the Temple by Titus' legions and the courageous strength of the defenders. Although the Jews were initially successful in their rebellion against Roman rule and established their independence for five years from the year 64 CE, internal conflict, hunger, and the military might of Titus, the son of the Emperor Vespasian, ultimately defeated them. The defense of Jerusalem and the Temple by Jewish Zealots as described by witnesses was superhuman. In the end, however, on the 9th of Av, the city was razed except for the three Herodian Towers and the Western Wall. Survivors were executed or taken captive. Titus returned to Rome in a triumphal procession commemorated on the Triumphal Arch of Titus. What is depicted on the Arch of Titus? What does it symbolize to the Romans? To the Jews?

Read the Aggadic passage on the destruction of the Temple and the poem by Lord Byron. What does each one say about responsibility for the event? What is the role of God and the role of people?

CONTINUATION OF JEWISH LIFE

Abba *Siqra* the head of the *biryoni* in Jerusalem, was the nephew of Rabban Yohanan ben Zakai. [The latter] sent to him saying, "Come to visit me privately." When he came he said to him, "How long are you going to carry on in this way and kill all the people by starvation?" He replied, "What can I do? If I say a word to them they will kill me." He said, "Devise some plan for me to escape. Perhaps I shall be able to save a little." He said to him, "Pretend to be ill and let everyone come to inquire about you. Bring something evil smelling and put it by you so that they will say you are dead. Let then your disciples get under your bed, but no others, so that they shall not notice that you are still light (since they know that a living being is lighter than a corpse)."

He [ben Zakai] did so, and Rabbi Eliezer went under the bier from one side and Rabbi Joshua from the other. When they reached the door some men wanted to put a lance through the bier. He said to them, "Shall [the Romans] say: "They have pierced their master?" They wanted to give it a push. He said to them, "Shall they say that they pushed their master?" They opened the town gate for him and he got out.

When he reached there [the Romans] he said, "Peace to you, O king; Peace to you, O king." He [Vespasian] said, "Your life is forfeit on two counts, one because I am not a king and you called me a king; and again, if I am a king, why did you not come to me before now?" He replied, "As for your saying that you are not a king, in truth you *are* a king, since[56b] if you were not a king, Jerusalem would not be delivered into your hand, as it is written: 'And Lebanon shall fall by a mighty one (Is. 10:34).' 'Mighty one' [is an epithet] applied only to a king, as it is written: 'And their mighty one shall be of themselves . . .(Jer. 30:12)' And 'Lebanon' refers to the sanctuary, as it says: ' . . . This goodly mountain and Lebanon (Deut. 3:25).'

"As for your question, 'Why if you are a king did I not come to you till now?' the answer is that the *biryoni* among us did not let me." He said to him, "If there is a jar of honey, 'round which a serpent is wound, would they not break the jar to get rid of the serpent?" He could give no answer. Rabbi Joseph (or some say Rabbi Akiva) applied to him the verse: ' . . .[God] turns wise people backward and makes their knowledge foolish (Is. 44:45).' He ought to have said to him, "We take a pair of tongs and grip the snake and kill it, and leave the jar [of honey] intact."

At this point a messenger came to him from Rome saying, "Up! For the emperor is dead and the notables of Rome have decided to make you head [of the state]." He had just finished putting on one boot. When he tried to put on the other he could not. He tried to take off the first, but it would not come off. He said, "What is the meaning of this?" Rabbi Yohanan said to him, "Do not worry—the good news has done it, as it says: 'Good tidings make the bone fat (Prov. 15:30).' "

He [Vespasian] said, "I am going now and will send someone to take my place. You can, however, make a request of me and I will grant it." He said to him, "Give me back Yavneh and its wise people and the family chair of Rabban Gamliel and physicians to heal Rabbi Zadoq." Rabbi Yoseph (or some say Rabbi Akiva) applied to him the verse: '[God] turns wise people backwards and makes their knowledge foolish.' He ought to have said to him: "Let them [the Jews] off this time." He, however, thought that so much he would not grant, and so even a little would not be saved.

—Rabbi Yohanan ben Zakkai,
Gittin 56a-b

Deepening the Sources

Jewish life continued in Judea after the destruction, but in an altered form. Emperor Hadrian considered the Jews' religious pursuits and nationalistic spirit a danger to the Roman Empire. When Bar Kochba successfully led a revolt in response to anti-Jewish edicts, Rome's military might was again called to Jerusalem to eliminate insurrection. With Bar Kochba's defeat, all remnants of Jewish Jerusalem were plowed under and Jews were forbidden to enter the city. A new city was built, Aelia Capitolina, whose walls are located very close to the walls that exist around the Old City of Jerusalem today. Jews continued to live outside of Jerusalem. They worshiped in the synagogues that had been established after the return from Babylon, giving up the sacrifices that had been restricted to the Temple in Jerusalem. Their teachers, rabbis, became their leaders not only in worship, but also in study and in the rapidly developing rules that governed daily life. Read the story of Yohanan ben Zakkai and discuss the significance of his decision to the survival of Jewish life.

PERTINENT SITES TO VISIT IN ISRAEL

- Model of Herod's Temple, Holyland Hotel
- Tower of David (Phasael Tower), Citadel Museum
- Rabbinic Tunnel
- Western Wall
- Excavations below the Temple Mount

- Christian sites from the life of Jesus
- Walls of the Old City
- View from Mount of Olives where Josephus viewed Jerusalem's fall
- Arch of Titus (Model in Diaspora Museum)
- High Priest's House
- Burnt House
- Siebenberg Museum

CHAPTER 6

MOSLEM AND CRUSADER PERIODS

BACKGROUND

Beginning in the seventh century and continuing into the twentieth, Jerusalem was controlled by Moslem powers. From the outset, the caliph Omar I permitted Jews to resettle in Jerusalem, restore the Temple Mount as a place of worship, and build academies of Jewish learning. The city, however, was in physical decline. In the eleventh century, when the Crusaders conquered Jerusalem, Jews and Moslems were massacred. Survivors were sold into slavery, and Jews were banned from living there. The Crusaders burned and pillaged the city until only ashes, rubble, and a few walls remained.

Moslems, under the leadership of Saladin of Egypt, regained control in 1187, rebuilt the city, converted churches to mosques, and welcomed Jews to Jerusalem once again.

The succeeding centuries, however, brought great suffering to Jerusalem as Crusaders regained control and were in turn conquered by Turks and a fanatical Arab nation, the Mamelukes. During the 267-year period of the Mamelukes, Jerusalem again became a center of Moslem learning and worship, but Jews were considered to be *dhimmis*, second-class citizens, and were discouraged from settling there. In 1488 a traveler in Jerusalem reported that there were only 70 Jewish families living in Jerusalem.

With the Ottoman Turks, who defeated the Mamelukes, came Suleiman the Magnificent. He constructed the walls that surround the city today. Once these walls were built, however, Jerusalem was abandoned and left to deteriorate. For the Turks, Constantinople was more important. For the Jews, Safed and Tiberias, centers of Kabbalah, became the centers for religious life. The few Jews in Jerusalem were impoverished and lived on their meager earnings and on the philanthropy of world Jewry. To seek better living conditions, Jews began to move outside the city walls, into the modern world.

The pictures of life in Jerusalem during this period are left to us by the many pilgrims who traveled to Jerusalem, which, in spite of its poverty, remained a holy city to Christians and Jews.

Deepening the Sources

Using the time line (pp.4-2 and 4-3) and the Background, review the history of Jerusalem during the periods of Moslem and Christian rule. Emphasize that Moslem, Christian, and Jewish pilgrims traveled to Jerusalem to visit holy sites. Some came peacefully; some with their swords and armor. Some left gifts; others took riches away. Many of them left personal records and reflections on their journeys. They are a treasure to those who want to go back in time and see Jerusalem as it was.

JERUSALEM THROUGH THE EYES OF ITS VISITORS

In the great wall which surrounds the city [of Jerusalem] Arculf counted eighty-four towers and

six gates, which are situated in this order around
the city: first, the Gate of David on the west side
of Mount Zion; second is the gate of the Fullers
Field; third is St. Stephen's Gate; fourth, the Gate
of Benjamin; fifth is a portula or "Little Gate"
from which one descends by stairway to the
Valley of Jehoshaphat; and the sixth is the Gate
of Tekoa.

This then is the order as one goes around the wall
connecting these gates and towers. From this Gate
of David it turns northwards and then to the east.
Though there are six gates in the wall, only three
are reckoned to be important as main thorough-
fares, the one on the west, the one on the north,
and the last on the east. Thus we see that one
section of the wall with its towers has no gates, the
section that extends across the northern edge of
Mount Sion (which overlooks the city from the
south), from the above mentioned Gate of David
as far as the face of the mountain which looks
eastward and ends in a cliff.

—French bishop Arculf (about 670) in
Peters, *Pilgrims View Jerusalem*,
Jerusalem, 1985 *(Arculf I, 1)*

We must speak briefly here of a very tall column
which stands in the middle of the city, where it is
seen by every passer-by coming northward from
the holy places. This column was set up in the
place where the Cross of the Lord was placed on a
dead man and he returned to life. At the summer
solstice when it is noon a marvelous event occurs.
When the sun reaches mid-heaven, the column
casts no shadow, but as soon as the solstice, that
is, the twenty-fourth of June, is past, and after three
days the day begins to get shorter, it first casts a
short shadow and then as the days pass a longer
one . . . . which demonstrates that the city of Jerusalem is situated in the center of the earth. This
explains why the Psalmist used these words to sing
his prophecy of the holy places of the Passion and
the Resurrection which are in this Aelia, "But God,
our King, before the ages worked salvation in the
midst of the earth," that is, in Jerusalem, which is
called the "Navel of the Earth."

—French bishop Arculf (about 670) in
Peters, *Pilgrims View Jerusalem*,
Jerusalem, 1985 *(Arculf I, 13)*

Each year on the fifteenth of the month of September a great crowd always comes to Jerusalem. They
come from almost every country and many nationalities to hold a fair, to buy and sell to each other.
Thus these crowds from various countries have
necessarily to spend some days in the inns of the
city, while a great many of their camels and horses,
asses and oxen, for their various baggages, cover
the city streets with their revolting dung. Not only
does the smell of this clogging filth cause a considerable nuisance to the citizens, but it even makes
walking about difficult.

—from Arculf I, 1

The Church of the Holy Sepulchre in A.D. 680

This is a very large church made entirely of stone
and built on a remarkable round plan. Three walls
rise from the foundations, and they have a single
lofty roof, with a broad pathway between one wall
and the next. There are also three altars arranged
in particular emplacements in the middle wall.
This lofty round church, with the above mentioned altars, one looking toward the south, another to the north, and a third on the west, rests on
twelve columns of remarkable size. It has eight
doors, or entries, in the three walls divided by the
width of a street. Four of them are on the northeast,
also called the Caecias wind, while the other four
are on the southeast.

In the center of the round space enclosed by this
church there is a small building cut out of a single
rock. Nine people can stand praying inside it, and
a man of ordinary height has one and a half feet
clearance between his head and its roof. The entrance to this small building faces east. Its whole
exterior is covered with choice marble, and the
roof is decorated on the outside with gold and
supports a large gold cross.

Inside this small building is the Lord's Tomb,
which has been cut into the same rock on the north
side. The pavement of this building is, however,
lower than the position of the Tomb, and the
distance between the floor and the edge of the
Sepulchre on the side is about three palms. This
information was given me by Arculf, who had

often been to visit the Lord's Tomb and measured it accurately.

—French bishop Arculf (about 670) in Peters, *Pilgrims View Jerusalem*, Jerusalem, 1985 *(Arculf I, 2-3)*

Further to the east has been built another very large church on the site which in Hebrew is called Golgotha. From the roof hangs a large bronze chandelier with lamps suspended from it by ropes. Below it stands a great silver cross, fixed in the same socket as the wooden cross on which the Savior of humankind once suffered. There is a cave in this same church, which has been cut into the rock below the place of the Lords Cross. Here there is an altar on which sacrifice is offered for the souls of certain specially honored persons. Their bodies are laid in the court in front of the door of this Church of Golgotha, until the Holy Mysteries for the dead are completed.

—French bishop Arculf (about 670) in Peters, *Pilgrims View Jerusalem*, Jerusalem, 1985 *(Arculf I, 6)*

This rectangular stone construction built on the site of Calvary has adjoining it on the east the stone basilica built with great reverence by King Constantine. It is also called the Martyrium, and people say it was built on the site where, by the permission of the Lord, after 233 years had gone by, the Cross of the Lord was discovered hidden underground, together with the two crosses of the thieves. Between these two churches comes the renowned spot where the patriarch Abraham set up an altar, and arranged a pile of wood on it, and took up his drawn sword to sacrifice his own son Isaac. Now a large wooden table stands there, on which the alms for the poor are offered by the people. I questioned Arculf further and he added: "There is a small court between the Anastasis, that is, the round church we have described above, and the Basilica of Constantine. It extends as far as the Church of Golgotha and lamps are burning continuously in it day and night."

—French bishop Arculf (about 670) in Peters, *Pilgrims View Jerusalem*, Jerusalem, 1985 *(Arculf I, 7-8)*

The buildings of the Holy City are of stone, and you will find nowhere finer or more solid constructions. And in no place will you meet with people more chaste. Provisions are most excellent here; the markets are clean, the mosque is among the largest, and nowhere are holy places more numerous. . . . In Jerusalem are all manner of learned people and doctors, and for this reason the heart of every person of intelligence yearns toward it. All the year round, never are its streets empty of strangers . . . . As to the saying that Jerusalem is the most illustrious of cities, is it not the one that unites the advantages of This World with those of the next? One who is of the children of This World and yet is ardent in the matters of the Next may find here a market for one's wares; while one who would be of those of the Next World, though his soul clings to the good things of This World as well, this one too may find them here . . . .

Truly Mecca and Medina have their superiority by reason of the Kaba and the Prophet—the blessings of God upon him and his family—but truly on the Day of Judgment they will both come to Jerusalem and the excellence of them all will be united there.

—Daniel the Pilgrim (1106) in Peters, *Pilgrims View Jerusalem*, Jerusalem, 1985 *(Muqaddasi 1896: 34–37)*

From Jerusalem come cheeses, cotton, the celebrated raisins of the species known as Aynuni and Duri, excellent apples, bananas—which is a fruit of the form of the cucumber, but the skin peels off and the interior is not unlike that of the watermelon, only finer flavored and more luscious—also pine nuts of the kind called "Quraysh-bite" and their equal is not to be found elsewhere; also mirrors, lamps, jars and needles.

—Daniel the Pilgrim (1106) in Peters, *Pilgrims View Jerusalem*, Jerusalem, 1985 *(Muqaddasi 1896: 69)*

Still [he continues], Jerusalem has some disadvantages. . . . You will not find anywhere baths more filthy than those in the Holy City; nor anywhere heavier fees for their use. Learned people are few, and the Christians numerous, and the latter are unmannerly in the public places. In the hostelries the taxes are heavy on all that is sold; there are guards at every gate, and no one is allowed to sell the necessities of life except in the appointed places. In this city the oppressed have no succor; the meek are molested, and rich are envied. Juris-consults remain unvisited, and erudite people have no renown; also the schools are unattended, for there are no lectures. Everywhere the Christians and Jews have the upper hand, and the mosque is void of either congregation or assembly of learned people.

—Daniel the Pilgrim (1106) in Peters,
Pilgrims View Jerusalem, Jerusalem,
1985 *(Muqaddasi 1896: 37)*

There is water in Jerusalem in plenty. Thus it is a common saying that "There is no place in Jerusalem where you cannot get water or hear the call to prayer," and few are the houses that have not cisterns, one or more. Within the city are three great birkehs [cisterns], namely the Birkeh of the Children of Israel, the Birkeh of Solomon, and the Birkeh Iyad. In the vicinity of each of these there are baths, and to them lead water channels from the streets. In the Haram area there are twenty underground cisterns of vast size, and there are few quarters in the city that have not public cisterns, though the contents of these last is only the rain water that drains into them from the streets. At a certain valley, about a stage from the city, they have gathered together the waters and made two pools into which the torrents of the winter rains flow. From these two reservoirs there are channels bringing the water to the city which are opened in the Spring in order to fill the cisterns in the Haram area and those in other places.

—Daniel the Pilgrim (1106) in Peters,
Pilgrims View Jerusalem, Jerusalem,
1985 *(Muqaddasi 1896: 39–41)*

Jerusalem . . . is a small city, fortified by three walls. It is full of people whom the Mohammadans call Jacobites, Syrians, Greeks, Georgians, and Franks, and of people of all tongues. In contains a dyeing-house, for which the Jews pay a small rent annually to the King, on condition that besides the Jews no other dyers be allowed in Jerusalem. There are about 200 Jews who dwell under the Tower of David in one corner of the city. The lower portion of the wall of the Tower of David, to the extent of about ten cubits, is part of the ancient foundation

set up by our ancestors, the remaining portion having been built by the Mohammadans. There is no structure in the whole city stronger than The Tower of David.

Jerusalem has four gates—The Gate of Abraham, the Gate of David, the Gate of Sion, and the Gate of Gushpat, which is the Gate of Jehoshaphat, facing our ancient Temple, now called the Templum Domini. Upon the site of the sanctuary Umar ibm al-Khattab erected an edifice with a very large and magnificent cupola, into which the Gentiles do not bring any image or effigy, but they merely come there to pray. In front of the place is the wall, which is one of the walls of the Holy of Holies. This is called the Gate of Mercy, and thither come all the Jews to pray before the wall of the court of the Temple. In Jerusalem, attached to the palace which belonged to Solomon, are the stables built by him, forming a very substantial structure composed of large stones, and the like of it is not to be seen anywhere in the world. There is also visible up to this day the pool used by the priests before offering the sacrifices, and the Jews coming thither write their names upon the wall. The Gate of Jehoshaphat leads to the Valley of Jehoshaphat, which is the gathering place of nations. Here is the pillar called Absolom's Hand and the sepulcher of King Uziah.

In front of Jerusalem is Mount Sion, on which there is no building, except a place of worship belonging to the Christians. Facing Jerusalem for a distance of three miles are the cemeteries belonging to the Israelites, who in the days of old buried their dead in caves, and upon each sepulcher is a dated inscription, but the Christians destroy the sepulchers, employing the stones thereof in building their houses. These sepulchers reach as far as Zelzah in the territory of Benjamin. Around Jerusalem are high mountains.

—Benjamin of Tudela (1173) in Peters,
Pilgrims View Jerusalem, Jerusalem,
1985 *(Benjamin of Tudela
1907: 21–23)*

On Mount Sion there are sepulchers of the House of David, and the sepulchers of the kings who ruled after him. The exact place cannot be identified, inasmuch as fifteen years ago a wall of the church of Mount Sion fell in. The patriarch commanded the overseer to take the stones of the old walls and restore therewith the church . . .

(Two workmen discovered a cave, however, and in it was the golden crown and scepter of David and Solomon and other kings.)

. . . So the men rushed forth in terror and they came unto the patriarch and related these things to him. Thereupon the patriarch sent for Rabbi Abraham al-Constantini, the pious recluse, who was one of the Mourners of Jerusalem, and to him he related all these things according to the report of the two men who had come forth. Then Rabbi Abraham replied, "These are the sepulchers of the House of David; they belong to the kings of Judah, and on the morrow let us enter, you and I and these men, and find out what is there." On the morrow they sent for the two men and found each of them lying on his bed in terror, and the men said, "We will not enter there for God doth not desire to show it to any man." Then the patriarch gave orders that the place be closed up and hidden from the sight of anyone unto this day. These things were told to me by the said Rabbi Abraham.

—Benjamin of Tudela (1173) in Peters,
Pilgrims View Jerusalem, Jerusalem,
1985 *(Benjamin of Tudela
1907: 24–25)*

Jerusalem is for the most part desolate and in ruins . . . it is not surrounded by walls. Its inhabitants, I am told, number about four thousand families. As for Jews, about seventy families of the poorest class . . . there is scarcely a family that is not in want of the commonest necessaries; one who has bread for a year is called rich . . . . When I came to Jerusalem there was a dreadful famine in the land. . . . I was told that the famine was less severe than it was at the beginning of the year. Many Jews died of hunger . . . . Many lived on grass, going out like stags to look for pasture. . . . Now, the wheat harvest being over, the famine is at an end, and there is once more plenty . . . .

The synagogue here is built on columns; it is long, narrow and dark, the light entering only by the door. There is a fountain in the middle of it. In the court of the synagogue, quite close to it, stands a mosque. The court [also] . . . contains many houses, all of them buildings devoted by the Ashkenasim [the reference here is to western Jews] to charitable purposes, and inhabited by Ashkenasi widows . . . .

The Jews' street and the houses are very large; some of them [Jews] dwell also on [Mount] Zion. At one time they had more houses, but these are now heaps of rubbish and cannot be rebuilt, for the law of the land is that a Jew may not rebuild a ruined house without permission, and the permission often costs more than the whole house is worth. The houses in Jerusalem are of stone, not of wood or plaster.

—Rabbi Obadiah da Bertinoro (1488)
in Kollek & Perlman, 1968

As for the view of Jerusalem from afar, filled with brilliance and beauty, it is one of the famous wonders. The most attractive view is that which one enjoys from the eastern side, from the Mount of Olives. Likewise from the south. But from the west and the north you can see only a small part of the city because of the mountains that conceal it. The cities of Jerusalem and Hebron are in effect situated on steep and rocky mountains where travel is difficult and round-about. The mountains that surround these two cities extend for nearly three days march, calculating with a pack animal, in width and breadth. Nonetheless, when God grants the pilgrims the favor of arriving at the solemn al-Aqsa shrine and the prayer station venerated by Abraham, they experience an indescribable feeling of joy and well-being and forget the pains and troubles they had endured. The poet Ibn Hujr improvised the following verses to precisely that point when he came on pilgrimage to Jerusalem:

"We came to Jerusalem with the hope of gaining pardon for our sins from a generous Master.

"For love of Him we have passed through Hell, but after Hell, there is nothing but Paradise."

—Mujir Al Din (1496) in Peters,
Pilgrims View Jerusalem, Jerusalem,
1985 *(Mujir 1876: 183–184)*

Jerusalem is a great city, solid in its construction, situated between mountains and valleys, with one part built on a height and the other resting down in a valley. The buildings built on the height dominate the lower sections beneath. The major streets of the city are either flat or sloped. In the greater number of the buildings you can find underground ancient constructions upon which the recent ones were raised. The houses are so crowded together that if they were to be spaced out in the way they are in most cities in the Islamic world, Jerusalem would occupy more than twice the space that it does now. The city has many cisterns designed to collect water since the citys water supply comes from rainfall . . . . The buildings of Jerusalem are extremely solid, all of them dressed stone and vaulted. There is no brickwork in the construction and no wood in the roofing. Travelers attest to the fact that there is no place in the empire with more solid buildings or indeed better looking that Jerusalem. Hebron is similar, but the buildings of the Holy City have greater strength and solidity. Those of Nablus come close, and the solidity of the buildings of these three cities arise from the fact that they are all situated in mountainous areas where there is a good deal of stone and it is easily quarried.

> —Mujir Al Din (1496) in Peters,
> *Pilgrims View Jerusalem*, Jerusalem,
> 1985 (Mujir 1876: 170–171, 183)

This is the great street, which begins at the gate of the Haram known as the Gate of the Chain and goes to the Gate of the Prayer Niche [of David], and this is the famous city gate now known as the Gate of a-Khalil [or the Friend of God, the normal honorific given to Abraham; this was the major entry from Hebron].

The street is divided into various segments, each of which has its own proper name. From the Haram to the Salamiyya Quran House it is called the Goldsmiths' Bazaar. From the entry of the Salamiyya as far as that of the Sharf quarter, the Straw Bazaar. From there to the Charcoal Khan as the Bazaar of the Bleachers. From the entry of the khan to the Arcade of al-Jubayli, as the Charcoal Bazaar. The section between the Arcade of al-Jubayli and the Stairway of the Rabble, it is known as the Bazaar of the Cooks. The Bazaar of the Cooks in Jerusalem was constructed with vaulted arcades covering the shops. The work was begun in the month of Rajab of the year 878 [A.D. 1471–1472]. Previous to this time the roofs of the shops consisted of palm branches, a very poor covering in winter by reason of the mud and the rain that fell down from the roof. The construction took place

from the Stairway of the Rabble as far as the Arcade of al-Jubayli. [To continue] from the Cooks' Bazaar to the entry of the Jewish quarter, as the Street of the Warehouse. This warehouse is a large khan whose income was endowed for the support of the Aqsa Mosque and is rented for four hundred dinars a year. All kinds of merchandise are sold there. From the entry to the Jewish quarter to the Khan of the Exchange, the street is known as the Bazaar of the Silk Merchants. From there to the city gate it is known as the Street of the Place of the Cereals.

There are a number of places in Jerusalem remarkable for their solid construction, and among them is the Market of the Cotton Merchants, near the western gate of the Haram. It is a bazaar remarkable for its solidity and height, and there are many cities where one cannot find its equal. Again, there are three suqs situated next to each other near the Western Gate or the Gate of al-Khalil; their construction goes back to Roman days. They run from south to north and connect with each other. The first, on the west, is the Druggists' Bazaar, whose income Saladin made an endowment for the Madrasa Salahiyya. The next or middle bazaar is used for the sale of vegetables. The next, on the east, is used by the textile merchants. The latter two bazaars are endowed for the upkeep of the Aqsa Mosque.

On the testimony of visitors, there are no bazaars anywhere that are the equal of these latter three in arrangement and architecture. They are one of the beautiful things that make Jerusalem distinctive.

It is reported . . . that the caliph [Umar], when he had conquered the Holy City, stopped at the entry of the bazaar, at its highest point. "Who owns this file [of shops]?" he asked, pointing to the row of the bazaar of the cereal sellers. "The Christians," he was told. "And the western row, where the bath of the market is?" he continued. "The Christians," they told him again. "So that this one is theirs and this one is theirs," he said, pointing with his hand. "But this section belongs to us." He was referring to the middle section between the other two rows, that is, the great bazaar with the "Lead Dome."

To return, it seems likely that the three markets being referred to are the ones which actually exist today, but that the older designations have given way to the newer constructions that one sees today. God knows best however.

—Mujir Al Din (1496) in Peters,
Pilgrims View Jerusalem, Jerusalem,
1985 (Mujir 1876: 171–172)

Jerusalem is on one mountain; across from it is the Mount of Olives, and there is a narrow valley between them, the Valley of Jehoshaphat. I went down into it, and at one end there is a large hole which looks like a kind of cave. They say that the mouth of Gehenna is there for the time to come, when Gog comes. Below this there are graves of Jews on the whole slope of the mountains, and a few on the incline of the mountain of Jerusalem. Half a mile below them are the waters of Siloam, and on the plain there are many beautiful gardens watered by those waters. It goes out from the mountain of Jerusalem, and no one knows from where it flows. On the visible end, there is a building which was once beautiful, with domes. They say that Solomon, may he rest in peace, minted coins there.

At the bottom of the Mount of Olives I saw the cave of Zachariah the Prophet, which is very lovely: it is all carved as one piece—the mountain is around it—and it is made into twelve columns, and its top is pointed, also all of one piece. Near it is a pit called the "Pit of the Daughters." They say that the daughters of Israel threw themselves into it at the time of the Destruction. There are two fine caves there, one made into niches all around, and one of fingers. Under them is a wide tower pointed at the top, which is Absaloms monument mentioned in the book of Samuel [2 Sam. 18:18].

Above, near the top of the mountain, is the cave of Haggai the Prophet, may he rest in peace, and below are caves large in width and circumference. Above the caves is the cave of Haggai, and below are the caves of his students and others besides. At the top of the Mount of Olives there is a large building, and there in a beautiful pavillion is Huldah the Prophetess in a marble grave. Also, one must pay an Ishmaelite guard there four dirhams to enter, and contribute oil for lighting, for there are perpetual lamps there.

—Rabbi Moses of Basola (1520) in
Peters, *Pilgrims View Jerusalem*,
Jerusalem, 1985 (Rabbi Moses Basola)

In Jerusalem I rented a room in a large house called the House of Pilate. I lived on an upper story, and from there I could see the whole Temple enclosure, into the courtyard. There is no house in Jerusalem from which as much can be seen; God has brought it about for me. There, every morning at dawn, I recited the prayer facing the Temple before going to the synagogue. Blessed be God who has found me worthy of this.

When one stands at the top of the Mount of Olives and looks across to Jerusalem, one sees the whole Temple, the courts and gardens. On that side, the eastern, the Temple has two closed iron gates whose ends are embedded in the earth. They call this the Gates of Mercy [the Golden Gate]. They say that bridegrooms entered through one and mourners through the other. Near the Temple on the south side is a building called Solomon's Academy [the Aqsa Mosque].

Outside Jerusalem on the south side is Mount Sion; the Nagid, may his Rock and Creator preserve him, told me that the place of the Jews also went from Mount Sion up to the Temple; and it stands to reason. And that is the true interpretation of the verse: "Sion, in the far north" [Ps. 48:3] On Mount Sion there is a place for [Christian] priests, like the conventi of Italy. Adjoining it is an iron door; they say that David and Solomon are buried there. The Ishmaelites never allowed anyone to enter these two places. On that side is a well-fortified citadel: they call it David's Tower. The tomb of Jesus is in Jerusalem, to the west: two churches, one opposite the other; a market passes between them, and there is a small square in front of one of the churches.

There is only one synagogue in Jerusalem. It is beautiful, with four columns in a row; it is sixty-three feet long and twenty-eight wide. In front of the Ark is a room with Torah scrolls all around—there are more than sixty. They pray towards the east, facing the Temple. The synagogue has no light except from the entrance, which is on the west, and there is a small window over it. They also use the lamps that they light all about for light during the day.

The congregation [in Jerusalem] is of all kinds. There are fifteen Ashkenazi householders, but the majority are Spanish; and there are Arabized [Jews], who are Moorish, long-ago natives of that country, and "westerners" who come from Barbary. In all there are about three hundred householders, excluding widows, who number more than six hundred, and who are well provided for in Jerusalem, for they do not pay any tax or levy. The community is financed because of them, for when they die it receives everything if there is no heir, and from this most public works have been done. Those who receive charity number more than two hundred souls. The Askenazi poor are not included in this category because their support comes from Venice.

—Rabbi Moses of Basola (1520) in
Peters, *Pilgrims View Jerusalem*,
Jerusalem, 1985 *(Rabbi Moses Basola)*

The land which to that point had preserved some greenery grew naked, the slopes of the mountains grew steeper and took on an appearance that was at the same time more grand and more barren. Soon all vegetation ceased and even the moss disappeared. The mountains all round took on a burning red color. We climbed for an hour in this desolate landscape to reach a high pass that we spied before us. Once come to this pass, we journeyed for another hour across a naked plain strewn with boulders. Suddenly, at the end of this plain I saw a line of gothic walls flanked with square towers and behind them rose the peaks of the buildings. At the foot of this wall appeared a camp of Turkish cavalry, in all its oriental splendor. The guild cried out: "Al Quds! the Holy City," and went off at a great gallop.

Then I understood what the historians and travelers reported of the surprise of the Crusaders and pilgrims at their first sight of Jerusalem. I am certain that whoever has had the patience, as I did, to read nearly two hundred modern accounts of the Holy Land, the rabbinic collections, and the passages of the ancients on Judea, would still understand nothing. I stood there, my eyes fixed on Jerusalem, measuring the height of its walls, recalling all the memories of history from Abraham to Godfrey of Bouillon, reflecting how the entire world was changed by the mission of the Son of Man, and seeking in vain the Temple, on which "not a stone rests upon a stone." If I were to live a thousand years, never would I forget this wilderness which still seems to breathe with the grandeur of Jehovah and the terrors of death.

—Chateaubriand (1806) in Peters,
Pilgrims View Jerusalem, Jerusalem,
1985 *(Chateaubriand)*

Seen from the Mount of Olives on the other side of the Valley of Jehoshaphat, Jerusalem is laid out on a terrain that descends from west to east. A crenellated wall fortified with towers and a gothic castle encloses the city in its entirety, presently leaving outside only part of Mount Sion, which it once enclosed. Toward the west and center of the city, in the vicinity of Calvary, the houses are in close rows, but toward the east, all along the Kedron Valley, there appear open spaces, among others the zone around the mosque built on the ruins of the Temple and the almost deserted terrain where once rose the castle Antonia and second palace of Herod.

The houses of Jerusalem are heavy square masses, quite low without passages and without windows. They are finished on top with either flat terraces or domes, and they resemble prisons or sepulchers. The city would present itself to the eye on a single level if the church towers, the minarets of mosques, and the tops of some cypresses did not break the uniformity. At the sight of these stone houses enclosed in a landscape of stone, one asks oneself if these are not the scattered monuments of a cemetery in the midst of a desert.

When you enter the city you find no consolation for the sadness of its exterior. You wander in the tiny unpaved streets which rise and descent over the uneven terrain and you walk amidst clouds of dust and over slippery gravel. The cloths thrown between one house and the other add to the darkness of this labyrinth; vaulted and filthy bazaars succeed in banning the light from the desolate city. Some wretched shops summon only misery to the eyes and often these shops are closed in fear of the passing by of a qadi. There is no one on the streets, no one at the gates of the city; only here and there a peasant slips through the shadows, hiding beneath his clothes the fruits of his labors lest it be stripped from him by a soldier. In a remote corner an Arab butcher disembowels some beast suspended by its hoofs from a ruined wall, and the worn and ferocious look of the man, his bloody arms, make you think he is about to slay another like himself rather than to slaughter a lamb. The only noise in the city of deicide is the occasional clatter of the hooves of the desert cavalry: it is a janissary carrying the head of a bedouin or riding off to pillage the fellahin.

—Chateaubriand (1806) in Peters,
Pilgrims View Jerusalem, Jerusalem,
1985 (Chateaubriand)

Deepening the Sources

Assign individuals to read the journal entries and diaries included in this chapter. Each person will summarize the descriptions and commentaries of the writers, reading aloud passages of interest. Locate the time the visit was made on the time line (pp. 4-2 and 4-3). Locate any sites mentioned on the map of Jerusalem. Take note of any features of the pilgrim records that reveal the nature of Jerusalem's citizens and the quality of life in Jerusalem at the time.

THE PEN VS. THE CAMERA
The Jewish Quarter

No landscape exists that is more tiresome to the eye than that which bounds the approaches to Jerusalem. The only difference between the roads and the surrounding country, perhaps, is that there are rather more rocks in the roads than in the surrounding country.

At last, away in the middle of the day, ancient bits of walls and crumbling arches began to line the way—we toiled up one more hill, and every pilgrim and every sinner swung their hat on high! Jerusalem!

Perched on its eternal hills, white and domed and solid-massed together and hooped with high gray walls, the venerable city gleamed in the sun. So small! Why, it was no larger than an American village of four thousand inhabitants, and no larger than an ordinary Syrian city of thirty thousand. Jerusalem numbers only fourteen thousand people.

We dismounted and looked, without speaking a dozen sentences, across the wide intervening valley for an hour or more; and noted those prominent features of the city that pictures make familiar to all people from their schooldays till their death. We could recognize the Tower of Hippicus, the Mosque of Omar, the Damascus Gate, the Mount of Olives, the Valley of Jehosaphat, the Tower of David, and the Garden of Gethsemane—and dating from these landmarks could tell very nearly the localities of many others we were not able to distinguish.

I record it here as notable but not discreditable that not even our pilgrims wept. I think there was no individual in the party whose brain was not teeming with thoughts and images and memories invoked by the grand history of the venerable city that lay before us, but still among them was no "voice of them that wept."

There was no call for tears. Tears would have been out of place.

—Mark Twain/Samuel Clemens,
Innocents Abroad, 1869 (Adapted)

Jerusalem, October 31

When I remember thee in days to come, O Jerusalem, it will not be with delight.

The musty deposits of two thousands of inhumanity, intolerance, and foulness lie in your reeking alleys. The one person who has been present here all this while, the lovable dreamer of Nazareth, has done nothing but help increase the hate.

If Jerusalem is ever ours, and if I were still able to do anything about it, I would begin by cleaning it up.

I would clear out everything that is not sacred, set up workers' houses beyond the city, empty and tear down the filthy rat-holes, burn all the non-sacred ruins, and put the bazaars elsewhere. Then, retaining as much of the old architectural style as possible, I would build an airy, comfortable, properly sewered, brand new city around the Holy Places. . . .

I am firmly convinced that a splendid New Jerusalem can be built outside the old city walls. The old Jerusalem would still remain Lourdes and Mecca and Yerushalayim. A very lovely beautiful town could arise at its side.

I would cordon off the old city with its relics, and keep out out all ordinary traffic; only places of worship and philanthropic institutions would be allowed to remain inside the old ramparts. And on the ring of encircling hillsides, which our labor would clothe with greenery, there would gradually rise a glorious New Jerusalem. The elite from every part of the world would travel the road up to the Mount of Olives. Loving care can turn Jerusalem into a jewel.

Everything holy enshrined within the old walls, everything new spreading round about it.

—Theodor Herzl (1898)

MODEH ANI

Thank you Lord for having me awaken
To become a witness to the birthday of the sun
Someone gently shook me from my sleep
As I dreamed I visited Jerusalem again.
And I walked (still half asleep) to watch
The city shake its sandy head awake
Robed in a royal cape
Of orange and swirling mist.
From my lookout on the roof I saw
The Magen-David flag
Wave in the distant wind
Bathed in the cloudy red
Of early morning sunshine.
How the birds and silent streets remind me
Of growing up in Arlington!
How the panorama called to mind
Toledo in El Grecos mystic eyes!
And I was full alive above the New Yerushalayim.

I go to sleep again, my Lord,
To speak of holiness in quiet different words
to mix the milk of Israel's morning
With the honey of a simple Pilgrim's dream.

My God! The sun above the Hills of Moab
A million million miles away!

—Danny Siegel, *Poems from*
Yerushalayim

PERSONAL PREFERENCE

I think
(now that I look back)
I'd rather drive a taxi
In Jerusalem
Than be the King

Of all of South Dakota
Or the cantor
In the Great and Ancient Synagogue
Of West Rangoon

I don't know why
(to be sure)

Here the sun sets red
And there the sun sets red

Here the trees sway with infinite grace
And there the breeze moves the leaves
With equally gentle fingers

I don't know why
I'd rather drive a taxi in Jerusalem

But neither have I come to know
why the seed becomes a daffodil
And not a rose

—Danny Siegel, *Poems from*
Yerushalayim

BLOWIN' IN THE WIND

Tsettelach
    people's simple-story notes to God
    stuffed in the cracks of the Wall
    on anything worth writing on
    El Al stationery
    backs of envelopes tickets to a show
        pencil ballpoint pen
            tears

        anything
        to tell Him how it is
    down here between the dust and dances

Falling to the ground
        in an inauspicious breeze

Do you read the Tsettelach of sorrow
        Lord
            even in the garbage can?

—Danny Siegel, *Poems from*
Yerushalayim

THE RAINY SEASON

Jerusalem has changed
With the drizzle of the rain
Before Sukkot
Robed in a regal raincoat
She sits wet and majestic
On her Judean throne
Reigning in slippery peace
The drops dazzle the streetlamps
And the headlights
Of an Egged bus
Announce that Torah
Once again
Goes forth from Zion
Come let us not go up
To the Mount of God
And dance in the Holy Rain

—Danny Siegel, *Poems from
Yerushalayim*

JERUSALEM: the face visible yet hidden, the sap and the blood of all that makes us live or renounce life. The spark flashing in the darkness, the murmur rustling through shouts of happiness and joy. A name, a secret. For the exiled, a prayer. For all others, a promise. Jerusalem: seventeen times destroyed yet never erased. The symbol of survival. Jerusalem: the city which miraculously transforms man into pilgrim; no one can enter it and go away unchanged . . . .

Here is the Valley of Jehoshaphat, where one day the nations will be judged. The Mount of Olives, where one day death will be vanquished. The citadel, the fortress of David, with its small turrets and golden domes where suns shatter and disappear. The Gate of Mercy, heavily bolted: let anyone other than the Messiah try to pass and the earth will shake to its foundations.

And higher than the surrounding mountains of Moab and Judea, here is Mount Moriah, which since the beginning of time has lured man in quest of faith and sacrifice. It was here that he first opened his eyes and saw the world that henceforth he would share with death; it was here that, maddened by loneliness, he began speaking to his Creator and then to himself. It was here that his two sons, our forefathers, discovered that which links innocence to murder and fervor to malediction. It was here that the first believer erected an altar on which to make an offering of both his past and his future. It was here, with the building of the Temple, that man proved himself worthy of sanctifying space as God had sanctified time.

—Eli Wiesel, *Beggars in Jerusalem*,
New York: Random House, 1970.

Deepening the Sources

Discuss the value of journal writing for travelers. What advantages does it have over slides and videos? The camera can be a barrier between the traveler and Jerusalem. It also does not encourage reflection as writing does. The art of journal writing persists. Contemporary visitors have recorded their observations and reactions to Jerusalem's sites, sounds, and people. Some of them are skilled authors; others write to savor the experience and preserve it for themselves. Either way, their writings are treasures for all who read them. Read the contemporary accounts of visits to Jerusalem.

ADDITIONAL LEARNING POSSIBILITIES

1. Ask those in the group who have traveled to Jerusalem and recorded their experiences to bring them to class to share.
2. Present each member of the class planning to go to Israel with a journal to keep in preparation for the study tour and while in Israel.

PERTINENT SITES TO VISIT IN ISRAEL

- Dome of the Rock
- Crusader ruins
- Church of the Holy Sepulchre
- Madaba Map (Cardo, or Jordan, or YMCA)
- Lion's Gate
- Nea Church
- Walls and Gates of Old City: Particularly Damascus Gate, Golden Gate, Nablus Gate (Shechem), Zion Gate, New Gate
- Mount Zion
- Russian Compound
- Yemin Moshe
- Even Moshe, Mishkenot Yisroel, Mazkeret Moshe, Ohel Moshe Exhibits in Diaspora Museum

CHAPTER 7

FROM ZIONISM TO MANDATE TO STATE

BACKGROUND

At the end of the nineteenth century and the beginning of the twentieth, the Jewish population of Jerusalem grew to a new high. Jerusalem within the walls remained crowded and living conditions were poor. Most citizens lived on the generosity of the world Jewish community.

Jerusalem outside of the walls continued to expand. Jews had become a majority of the population in the 1830s with an influx from Safed, which had suffered serious damage from an earthquake. At this time, also, Jews touched by persecution in Eastern and Central Europe, and by the "return to Zion" movement that was spreading throughout the world, came streaming into Jerusalem. Some became pioneers outside Jerusalem, but Jerusalem was the center for the return. Non-Jews also came: pilgrims and settlers from France, Russia, and Germany changed the skyline of the city as well as the population numbers.

During World War I the Turks joined with the German forces. Ottoman rule ended when Britain's General Allenby conquered Jaffa, cut off Turkish communication lines, and marched unchallenged into Jerusalem. Earlier, the British government had issued the Balfour Declaration, looking with favor on the establishment of a national home in Palestine for the Jewish people. Under the British Mandate Jerusalem flourished on an administrative, technical level.

Although initially the Arab world had supported the establishment of a Jewish state, hostility toward the Jews in Palestine developed rapidly, prompting the British to pursue policies sympathetic to Arab pressures. The British failed to intervene as violence increased. This prompted the strengthening of the Haganah, the underground Jewish defense force that saved hundreds of lives when the Jewish-Arab conflict erupted in the '30s and continued into the '40s.

In November 1947, when the British announced they were no longer able to maintain the Mandate, the United Nations General Assembly adopted by a two-thirds majority the Partition Resolution, creating an Arab state and a Jewish state, to take effect in May 1948. Rejecting the resolution, the Arabs, who far outweighed the Jews in size and power, attacked with the goal of driving the Jews into the sea. Jerusalem was placed under siege. Against tremendous odds, the Haganah managed to get supplies to the city and protect its population. When the war ended, however, the Jewish Quarter of the Old City had been lost, with much of it destroyed by the Arab Legion. In spite of an agreement to the contrary, the Jews were not allowed access to their holy sites. Jerusalem was a divided city.

POETRY OF ZIONISM
Jerusalem

From the summit of Mount Scopus,
I bow me down before thee,

From the summit of Mount Scopus,
Jerusalem, I greet thee,
A hundred generations I have dreamt of thee,
Hoping once more thy face to see.

Jerusalem, Jerusalem,
Shine forth upon thy son!
Thy ruins, O Jerusalem,
I will rebuild, each one.

From the summit of Mount Scopus,
Jerusalem, I greet thee,
Thousands of exiles from afar.
Lift up their eyes to thee.
A thousand blessings we will sing,
City and Temple of our King.

Jerusalem, Jerusalem,
I will not stir from here!
Jerusalem, Jerusalem,
Come, O Messiah, come near!

—Avigdor Hameiri

From Mount Scopus

I say Jerusalem from Mount Scopus,
and she was perfect and whole,
little, yet limitless, within her borders
contained and not contained.

Eastward, the hills of Judah,
wrapped in white and blue,
are ministering priests, and silently
they meditate blessing and burn the snail-shell
     incense.

Westward stretches the barren desert,
a monotone whose colors vary.
And the silence, is the silence
of a world shrouded with wastes and stones.

And on the hillsand pits
the embers still whispering burn,
as if spice were being perfumed there in the twilight
by the roasting of the sun's coals on censers of
     shadows.

And all Jerusalem was for me
like a single coal, kept on the altar,

that each nation and guardian might come
and brighten it with tongs, and take from it an ember.

—Yehuda Karni

Libi B'Mizrach (My Heart Is in the East)

My heart is in the East and I am at the edge
of the West. Then how can I taste what I
eat, how can I enjoy it? How can I fulfill
my vows and pledges while Zion is in the
domain of Edom, and I am in the bonds of
Arabia? It would be easy for me to leave
behind all the good things of Spain; it
would be glorious to see the dust of the
ruined Shrine.

—Yehuda Halevi

El Hatzipor (To a Bird)

Greetings! Peace to you, returning
Lovely bird, unto my window
From a warmer clime!
How my soul for songs was yearning
When my dwelling you deserted
In the winter-time!

Chirping, singing, dearest birdling,
Tell the wonders of that distant
Land from which you came.
In that fairer, warmer climate
Are the troubles and the trials
Multiplied the same?

Do you bring me friendly greetings
From my brothers there in Zion
Brothers far yet near?
Oh the happy! O the blessed!
Do they guess what heavy sorrows
I must suffer here?

Does your singing bring me greeting
From the land, its glens and valleys,
Mountain height and cleft?
Has her God compassioned Zion?
Is she still to graves deserted,
Only ruins left?

And the laborers, my brothers—
Have not these who sowed with weeping
Reaped with song and psalm?
Oh, that I had wings to fly with,
Fly unto the land where flourish
Almond tree and palm!

—Chaim Nahman Bialik

Ahavat Hadassah (Love of Hadassah)

The love of Hadassah is entwined upon my heart
While I am within the *golah*, my steps heavy laden.
If I but had permission I would ascend and get
  myself there
Withing the gates of Zion that are so glorious.

—Shalom Shabazi

Deepening the Sources

Begin by singing or playing Me'al Pisgat Har Ha-Tsofim, *the song which takes its lyrics from A. Hameiri's poem, "Jerusalem." Read the three additional selections of poetry and prose that express the deep longing for Jerusalem that was part of the Zionist movement at the end of the nineteenth century and the beginning of the twentieth century. Here are a few suggested questions for each of the poems:*

"Jerusalem" by Avigdor Hameiri: 1) What emotion is expressed by the poet? 2) What is the dominant image in the last two lines? Why is it so appropriate for Jerusalem? 3) Why did the poet consider himself exiled?

"From Mt. Scopus" by Yehuda Karni: 1) What is the view described? 2) What effect do the pilgrims have on Jerusalem? 3) How does Jerusalem affect the pilgrims?

"My Heart Is in the East" by Yehuda Halevi: 1) How is the theme of separation from Zion expressed? 2) How is Zion described? 3) How does the poet express the extent to which he desires to be in Zion?

"To a Bird" by Chaim Nahman Bialik: 1) From where does Bialik imagine the bird has returned? 2) What are the physical images of Zion? 3) How are brothers "far but near?" 4) Why does Bialik want to be like the bird?

"Love of Hadassah" by Sholom Shabazi: 1) How are exile (golah) and desire for Zion expressed? 2) What is the significance of the words "ascend" and "gates?"

MOUNT SCOPUS

Figure E. A View of Mt. Scopus Across Jerusalem

Deepening the Sources

Using the background information and the time line (pp. 39–41), give a fifteen-minute overview of the major events of the period although it is impossible to convey this period even in a full lesson. Dozens of shelves are devoted to the subject as are hundreds of movies and videotapes.

For the rest of this chapter we will attempt to view these years from the vantage point of Mount Scopus, some of the time looking down on Jerusalem below, some of the time reporting on events that took place on this mountain. Begin by looking at the photograph of Mount Scopus. Mount Scopus, and the Mount of Olives to its south, have frequently been the perches from which pilgrims, scholars, and tourists have viewed the city of Jerusalem. As one stands with one's back to the Judean desert, with the Dead Sea and Jordanian Mountains to the east, there is a breathtaking view of the Old City below and the New City of Jerusalem extending beyond its walls as far as one can see to the west. When one prays on Mount Scopus, one faces west. Why?

The View from Scopus

On December 11 the Commander in Chief, General Allenby, made his formal entry into Jerusalem. The great general rode on horseback as far as the Jaffa Gate. The gate had been closed for some time. Before the visit to Jerusalem of Kaiser Wilhelm II of Germany in 1898, the Turks, fearing the narrow gate would obstruct traffic, had made a breach in the old rampart wall so that carriages could enter the city. The Kaiser had entered on a white charger wearing the gorgeous white Uhlan uniform with the dazzling and burnished helmet surmounted by the German eagle, but even that was not spectacular enough for him. Whatever uniform His Majesty put on was the signal for the rest of his military entourage to copy; but as some of his suite were more imposing in stature than he was, he had made himself unique by wearing a white-and-gold keffiyeh gathered under the spreading eagle, and over his white uniform was a white silk abayah with gold threads running through that sparkled in the sunlight. The Emperor was not only an artist in his choice of costume to impress his oriental audience, but also an actor.

How different was the solemn and dignified entrance of General Allenby, who, to do honor to his Master, walked into the Holy City as a pilgrim.

First in the procession came Colonel Barton, postmaster general of Cairo, who had hurriedly come to Jerusalem to be the first military governor.

The commander in chief, preceded by his aide-de-camp, had on his right the commander of the French detachment and on his left the commander of the Italian detachment. Following were the Italian, French, and American military attachés and a few members of the General Staff. The American military attaché was Colonel Edward Davis. Guards of honor marched in the rear.

The procession entered the Jaffa Gate, walked past the Grand New Hotel, which was our hospital, turned to the right toward Zion, and on the steps of the citadel in the shadow of the Tower of David, part of which dates from Davids time, and the proclamation was read.

This proclamation, which was read in English, French, Arabic, Hebrew, Greek, Russian, and Italian, announced that order would be maintained in all the sacred sites of the three great religions which would be carefully guarded for the full use of the worshipers—it assured the people that they might pursue their lawful business without interruption.

Throughout the ceremony no Allied flag was flown. After the short ceremony the chief notables and ecclesiastics of the different communities who were in Jerusalem were presented to General Allenby. In a photograph of this ceremony the Chief Rabbi stands beside the Grand Mufti. After the reception the commander in chief left Jerusalem by the Jaffa Gate. Outside the gate he mounted his horse and rode away. Our American colony photographer took pictures of all. The photographs showing General Allenby leaving Jerusalem on a horse, with the city wall as a background, had difficulty in passing the censor, but it was finally released because the rampart wall at his back proved he was leaving the city, not entering.

Palestine had a so-called Christian government for the first time since the Crusaders were driven out by Saladin. As soon as the inhabitants were confident of the stability of the British occupation they expressed their gratitude for being delivered from the Ottoman yoke. Church bells rang in acknowledgment and officers were met with flowers thrown into their cars.

During the ceremony I was on the balcony of the Grand New Hotel. John Whiting touched me on my shoulder and asked whether I would mind giving my place to James McBey. Of course I minded, but I could not refuse the official artist a good place to make the sketches for his famous painting of the historical entry of General Allenby. I looked over his shoulder, and I knew I was fortunate indeed to be witnessing one of the great events in history. I realized that the whole Christian world outside of Germany and Austria was jubilant. People in the streets were crying at their deliverance. I saw a Jew embrace a Greek priest, and his tall clerical hat went askew in the exuberance of fraternal feeling. Truly we could sing with the Psalmist, "Then were our mouths filled with laughter and our tongue with smiling ... Adonai hath done great things for us, therefore we are glad."

I never recall this day without remembering John Finley's words:

The earth's free nations now will bring
Their genius to its glorying,
And they who sat in darkness sing
Fore'er of thee, O Allenby!

—from Bertha Spafford Vester,
An American Family
in the Holy Land, 1881–1949
from Eisenberg 1971 pp. 327–29

[*On July 24, 1918, when the Allied and Turkish armies were still locked in battle and the sound of cannons was still heard in the distance, Dr. Chaim Weizmann laid the cornerstone of what was to be the world-renowned Hebrew University. Following are excerpts from his address on that historic occasion.*]

It seems at first sight paradoxical that in a land with so sparse a population, in a land where everything still remains to be done, in a land crying out for such simple things as plows, roads, and harbors, we should begin by creating a center of spiritual and intellectual development. But it is no paradox for those who know the soul of the Jew. . . . We Jews know that when the mind is given fullest play, when we have a center for the development of Jewish consciousness, then coincidentally we shall attain the fulfillment of our material needs. In the darkest ages of our existence we found protection and shelter within the walls of our schools and colleges, and in devoted study of Jewish science the tormented Jew found relief and consolation. Amid all the sordid sqalor of the Ghetto there stood schools of learning where numbers of young Jews sat at the feet of our rabbis and teachers. Those schools and colleges served as large reservoirs where there was stored up during the long ages of persecution an intellectual and spiritual energy which on the one hand helped to maintain our national sages of Babylon and Jerusalem, Maimonides and the Gaon of Wilna, the lens polisher of Amsterdam and Karl Marx, Heinrich Heine and Paul Ehrlich, are some of the links in the long, unbroken chain of intellectual development.

A Hebrew University! I do not suppose that there is any one here who can conceive of a university in Jerusalem being other than a Hebrew one. The claim that the university should be a Hebrew one rests upon the values the Jews have transmitted to the world from this land. Here in the presence of adherents of the three great religions of the world, which amid many diversities built their faith upon the Lord who made Himself known unto Moses, before this world which has founded itself on Jewish law, has paid reverence to Hebrew seers, has acknowledged the great mental and spiritual values the Jewish people have given to it, the question is answered. The university is to stimulate the Jewish people to reach further truth. Am I too bold if, here today in this place among the hills of Ephraim and Judah, I state my conviction that the seers of Israel have not utterly perished, that under the aegis of this university there will be a renaissance of the Divine power of prophetic wisdom that once was ours? The university will be the focus of the rehabilitation of our Jewish consciousness not so tenuous, because it has become so world-diffused. Under the atmospheric pressure of this Mount our Jewish consciousness can become diffused without becoming feeble, our consciousness will be rekindled and our Jewish youth will be reinvigorated from Jewish sources.

The Hebrew University, though intended primarily for Jews, will, of course, give an affectionate welcome to the member of every race and creed. "For my house will be called a house of prayer for all the nations." Besides the usual schools and institutions which go to form a modern university, there will be certain branches of science which it will be peculiarly appropriate to associate with our university. Archeological research, which has revealed so much of the mysterious past of Egypt and Greece, has a harvest still to be reaped in Palestine, and our university is destined to play an important part in this field of knowledge. . . .

Side by side with scientific research the humanities will occupy a distinguished place. Ancient Jewish learning, the accumulated, half-hidden treasurers of our ancient philosophical, religious, and juridic literature, are to be brought to light again and freed from the dust of ages. They will be incorporated in the new life now about to develop in this country, and so our past will be linked up with the present.

May I be allowed, before concluding, to point to one very important aspect of our university? The university, while trying to maintain the highest scientific level must, at the same time, be rendered accessible to all classes of people. The Jewish workman and farm laborer must be enabled to find there is a possibility of continuing and completing their education in their free hours. The doors of our libraries, lecture rooms, and laboratories must be opened widely to them all. Thus the university will exercise its beneficial influence on the nation as a whole. . . .

Manifold are the preparations yet to be made. Some of them are already in progress; some, like the actual building, must necessarily be postponed until the happy day of peace arrives. But from this day the Hebrew University is a reality. Our university, formed by Jewish learning and Jewish energy, will mold itself into an integral part of our national structure which is in process of erection. It will have a centripetal force attracting all that is noblest in Jewry throughout the world; a unifying center for our scattered elements. There will go forth, too, inspiration and strength, that shall revivify the powers now latent in our scattered communities. Here the wandering soul of Israel shall reach its haven, its strength no longer consumed in restless and vain wanderings. Israel shall at last remain at peace within itself and with the world. There is a Talmudic legend that tells of the Jewish soul deprived of its body, hovering between heaven and earth. Such is our soul today; tomorrow it shall come to rest, in this our sanctuary. That is our faith.

—Chaim Weizmann from Eisenberg

50. The immediate prelude to the outbreak of disorder in August, 1929, was a provocative demonstration and counter demonstration of Jewish and Arab nationalism respectively. On the 15 August the Jews marched in procession to the Wailing Wall. On the next day the Arabs did likewise. A week later the fire which had so long been kindling burst into flame. From the 23rd to the 29th August murderous attacks were made on the Jews in various parts of the country. The most violent were directed not against the new settlements but against the old-established Jewish communities in the Arab hill-country at Hebron and Safad. At Hebron over 60 Jews were killed, including women and children, and more than 50 injured. Much Jewish property was destroyed, synagogues were desecrated, and a Jewish hospital looted. Only the courage of the one British police officer in the town prevented the outbreak from developing into a general massacre. At Safad 45 Jews were killed or wounded, and there was similar looting and destruction in the Jewish quarter. Less sanguinary outbreaks occurred at Jerusalem and Jaffa. In the rural areas several Jewish colonies were attacked and six of them virtually destroyed. There was little retaliation by the Jews. The worst cases were at Jaffa, where an Arab Imam and some six others were killed, and at Jerusalem, where a mosque of great antiquity was damaged and desecrated.

51. When peace had been restored, with the help of troops rushed up from Egypt, it was reckoned that 133 Jews had been killed and 339 wounded. Of the Arabs, as far as could be ascertained, 116 had been killed and 232 wounded. As in 1921, the majority of Arab casualties were inflicted by the troops or police. In the subsequent judicial proceedings 27 death-sentences for murder were finally confirmed, one of them on a Jew. Three Arabs were hanged; the rest of the sentences were commuted by the High Commissoner to terms of imprisonment.

52. In the report of the Commission of Enquiry, under Sir Walter Shaw, which visited Palestine from October to December, 1929, the causes of the outbreak were clearly stated. "There can, in our view, be no doubt that racial animosity on the part of the Arabs, consequent upon the disappointment of their political and national aspirations and fear for their economic future, was the fundamental cause of the outbreak of August last." On the political side, the commissioners pointed out that the schism between the races was a development of postwar days and was mainly due to the conflict between the interpretations placed by Arab and Jewish nationalists respectively on the war-time pledges given by the British Government. The following sentence deserves special attention: "A National Home for the Jews, in the sense in which it was widely understood, was inconsistent with the demands of Arab nationalists which the claims of Arab nationalism, if admitted, would have rendered impossible the fulfillment of the pledge to the Jew."

53. These political and economic fears, the Report explained, had been intensified on the one hand by

the number of Jewish immigrants, who, despite the set-back of 1926–8, had already settled in the country, and on the other had by the amount of land they had already acquired.

"In other words, those consequences of Jewish enterprise which have most closely affected the Arab people have been such that the Arab leaders could use them as the means of impressing upon their followers that a continuance of Jewish immigration and land purchases could have no other result than that the Arabs would in time be deprived of their livelihood and that they, and their country, might ultimately come under the political domination of the Jews. Racial antipathy needed no other stimulus, but it was further encouraged by a spirit of mutual intolerance which has unfortunately been a marked feature of the past decade in Palestine. From the beginning the two races had no common interest. They differed in language, in religion, and in outlook. Only by mutual toleration and by compromise could the views of the leaders of the two peoples have been reconciled and a joint endeavor for the common good have been brought about. Instead, neither side had made any sustained attempt to improve racial relationships. The Jews, prompted by eager desire to see their hopes fulfilled, have pressed on with a policy at least as comprehensive as the White Paper of 1922 can warrant. The Arabs, with unrelenting opposition, have refused to accept that document and have prosecuted a political campaign designed to counter Jewish activities and to realize their own political ambitions."

54. Subsequent events, in our opinion, have confirmed the truth of these observations. which again revealed the real gravity of the problem. The hopes on which the optimism of 1925 had rested had been shown to be illusory. The sense of peace and security which had inspired the reduction of the garrison had proved false and dangerous. So far from drawing together during the last four years, the races had drifted further apart. And the breach had been widened far beyond its breadth in 1925 by the events of 1928–9.

—Palestine Royal Commission
Reports, 1937

During World War II the southern wing of the King David Hotel in Jerusalem was taken over to house the central institutions of the British regime: Military G.H.Q., and the Secretariat, the civil Government. As the revolt against British rule intensified, the great hotel was developed into a veritable fortress in the heart of the city. In a neighboring building, the British Military Police and the famous Special Investigation Bureau established their headquarters. In the open space between the two buildings a strong military unit was encamped. Machine-gun nests were constructed at a number of points. Soldiers, police and detectives maintained a close and constant watch on the building which housed the supreme British rulers in Eretz Israel.

The authorities no longer depended on miracles. They had learnt from experience. Before our attack on police headquarters, Catling had boasted: "They won't come, but if they do, they'll get such a welcome. . . . "

We came; and Catling's welcome evaporated. When the building went up into the air, he and his chief, Giles, narrowly escaped with their lives.

The host of watching eyes surrounding the King David Hotel saw nothing of our reconnaissance— the messengers of the underground remained unseen, but saw what they had to see, and found out what they sought. The plan for an attack on the King David Hotel began to take shape. In the Spring of 1946 we submitted our plan for the first time to the Command of the Resistance Movement. I informed Sneh and Galili that we would undertake to penetrate the Government wing of the King David Hotel and to carry out an extensive sabotage operation. Without going into details, I emphasized that the employment of explosives would be distinguished by a new device, invented by Giddy. On the one hand our "mines" could not be moved or dismantled as they would blow up on contact. On the other hand we would be able to fix the moment for the explosion of these "mines" by a time mechanism, half an hour or even an hour after their introduction into the building. This would allow for evacuation by hotel guests, workers, and officials. The rules we had laid down for ourselves made the evacuation of the hotel essential. There were many civilians in the hotel who we wanted, at all costs, to avoid injuring. We were anxious to ensure that they should leave the danger zone in plenty of time for their safety . . . .

On the 29th of June 1946 the British occupied the Offices of the Jewish Agency. The Jewish Agency was regarded as "Jewish Headquarters." So, according to the doctrinaire argument we must repay them in kind and attack their headquarters, in the King David Hotel.

The Haganah's request that we attack the Hotel reached us several weeks after they had at first rejected the same plan. In the meantime a number of circumstances had changed. As a result, we had to carry out anew all the reconnaissance operations and reconsider the whole of the operational details. We were well aware that this was the largest of our operations to date and that it might turn out to be unique in the history of partisan wars of liberation. It is no simple matter to penetrate the very heart of the military government, to deliver a blow within the fortified headquarters of a heavily armed regime. I doubt if this operation had any precedent in history.

A prime consideration was the timing of the attack. Two proposals were made: one for eleven a.m., the other for between four and five o'clock in the afternoon. Both plans were based on the same reasoning. The milk-cans could be brought into the Government wing of the building only by way of the "Regence Cafe" situated in the basement of the wing occupied by Barker and Shaw. In these morning and afternoon hours the Cafe was usually empty. At lunch-time it was filled with customers, among them civilian men and women as well as Army officers. It was essential that the attack be delivered at an hour when there were no customers in the Cafe.

Of the proposed hours, which both met this condition, we chose the earlier—11 a.m.—because it was easier than to coordinate our attack with that planned by the F.F.I. on the David Brothers Building—"Operation Slave and Redeemer." It was clear that these operations must be simultaneous: otherwise the one would interfere with the other.

Next we considered how to give the warnings so as to eliminate casualties. First, to keep passers-by away from the building, we decided to let off a small cracker-bomb, noisy but harmless. Then we chose three offices to receive a telephoned warn-

ing, which would be given as soon as our men had got away from the basement of the hotel. These three were: the King David Hotel management; the *Palestine Post*, and the French Consulate-General which is close to the Hotel. Finally, warning placards would be placed next to the milk-cans: "Mines. Do not Touch"—in case British experts should attempt to dismantle the explosives after our telephoned warning had been sent out.

At ten minutes past twelve, Gideon reached the spot at which our "telephonist" was waiting. She immediately telephoned the King David Hotel and warned them that explosives had been placed under the hotel and would go off within a short time. "Evacuate the whole building!"—she cried to the hotel telephone operator. She then telephoned the office of the *Palestine Post* and announced—as was later testified by the *Palestine Post* telephonist, that "bombs have been placed in the King David Hotel and the people there have been told to evacuate the building." The third and final warning was given to the French Consulate, accompanied by the advice to open the consulate windows so as to prevent the effects of the blast.

But while our Assault Unit in the lion's den had done everything possible to ensure the timely evacuation of the hotel, others had taken a different line. For some reason the hotel was not evacuated even though from the moment when the warnings had been received there was plenty of time for every living soul to saunter out. Instead, the toll of lives was terrible. More than two hundred people were killed or injured. Among the victims were high British officers. We particularly mourned the alien civilians whom we had had no wish to hurt, and the fifteen Jewish civilians, among them good friends, who had so tragically fallen. Our satisfaction at the success of the great operation was bitterly marred. Again we went through days of pain and nights of sorrow for the blood that need not have been shed.

With the gathering of evidence and the revelations of the Haganah Information Service, it was widely suggested that a high official had deliberately prevented the evacuation of the King David Hotel in order, for some reason best know to himself, that a major disaster should occur.

After weighing the matter during the years that have passed I am convinced that *this* theory is contrary to the facts known to us, and is not true. The question of the ancient Roman jurists *Qui prodest?* (whom did it profit?) does not provide the key to the mystery. The question remains open.

At any rate it is clear that we did all we could to ensure the early and complete evacuation of the hotel; that the warnings were given and received in time by the authorities; they had time enough to evacuate the hotel twice over, and that somebody, for some dark purpose, or because he lost his head, or to protect a spurious prestige, ordered that hotel should not be evacuated.

—Menachem Begin,
The King David Hotel, 1972

Supplying the hospital and the university to which Dr. Ben-David was bound has been a problem for the Jewish Agency since partition. The only road to the hilltop passed through the Arab stronghold of Sheikh Jarrah. As early as December, Arab ambushes had forced the Jewish Agency to resort to a weekly armed convoy to keep the two institutions on Mount Scopus supplied. For the past month a tacit truth had ruled along the road, and the passage of the convoys had been relatively free of incidents. There seem no reason to doubt that the convoy of Tuesday, April 13, would have an equally easy trip.

At the foremost Haganah guard post at the end of the Street of the Prophet Samuel, Moshe Hillman, a Jewish officer, held up the convoy while he made a routine check with a British police inspector named Webb.

"Send the convoy up" Webb told the Haganah liaison officer. "The road's clear. We just patrolled it."

Hillman waved the line of vehicles off on the two-and-a-half mile trip to Mount Scopus. An armored car led the way. Behind it came an ambulance bearing the red star of the Magen David Adom, the Jewish Red Cross, then two buses, another ambulance, four trucks, and a second armored car to protect the rear. Driving one of the trucks was a stubby little man named Benjamin Adin. For five hundred pounds he had purchased in December the dubious right to run a truckload of goods up the hill once a day. Scooting out of back streets at odd times, banging across open fields and dirt tracks, he had succeeded so well he had won

the nickname Mishugana, the Crazy Man. Today, for the first time, the Haganah had forced him to make his run in the convoy. He also had a passenger, a man who had begged him for a ride because his wife had just had a baby at Hadassah Hospital.

Packed into the buses and ambulances ahead of his truck was an astonishing assembly of professors, doctors, researchers and scholars, the most precious cargo a Haganah convoy could carry through the dangerous curves of Sheikh Jarrah to Mount Scopus. Distinguished products of the most famous faculties of Europe, they had fled the persecutions of the Continent to come here and found a prestigious array of hospitals, laboratories and research centers. From Berlin, Vienna and Krakow they had come, bringing an intellectual capital of inestimable value to the fledgling Jewish state. Today they were members of the Faculty of Medicine of Hebrew University or the Hadassah Medical Organization, a philanthropic body founded by an American Jewish woman in 1912 to apply in Palestine the byword of Jeremiah, "Cure my people." Sustained by the contributions of American Jewry, Hadassah had built medical institutions all across Palestine. The most important among them, the temple of Jewish medical science, was the ultramodern hospital on Mount Scopus.

Crouched in a ditch alongside the road, his fingers fixed on the plunger of an electric mine, a tailor named Mohammed Neggar watched the convoy's approach, calculating the instant at which to fire his explosives. Forty-eight hours before, in a bar he frequented, Neggar had been given the date and the hour of the convoy's passage by a British officer. Moreover, the Britisher had told Neggar that if his men attacked the convoy, they would not be molested as long as they did not fire on British patrols.

His words were an invitation to attack it. To the Arabs, Mount Scopus also represented a Haganah strongpoint from which their foes sometimes launched assaults on their rear. All the next day in the back room of his tailor shop, while Neggar shuttled in and out to give his customers fittings, his aides had planned the ambush. Counting on British indifference, they had decided to strike from the roadside ditch near a clump of cypress trees beyond the Orient House Hotel. The road began to flatten out there and the Jews might be expected to relax their vigilance.

The din of the convoy's motors rose, and finally the lead armored car appeared around a bend on the road. Tensely, Neggar watched it crawl toward him. It seemed to the tailor like "an enormous black beetle." He tightened his fingers until he hear the click of the plunger. An explosion shook his ditch, and a cloud of smoke enveloped the armored car. When it cleared, Neggar blinked. He had pushed his plunger too soon. Instead of destroying the vehicle, he had blown an enormous crater in the road. Unable to stop in time, the heavy vehicle had lumbered forward and tumbled into the hole.

Behind the car, the rest of the convoy ground to a halt. So abrupt was the stop in Esther Passman's ambulance that the nurse dropped her thermos of tea. For a moment, the concerned passengers sat in their darkened vehicles, wondering what was happening outside. A signal from Neggar to the score of men with him in his ditch gave them the answer. A rain of gunfire swept into the stalled convoy.

The explosion, the gunfire, attracted the attention of all Jerusalem. By the scores, then by the hundreds, Arab irregulars poured toward the ambush site from the villages neaby and the walls of the Old City. In the suffocating darkness of the metal prisons, the passengers began to hear a new sound mingling with the din of the gunfire. It was guttural clamor, a furious call for vengeance, the name of the Arab village the two wounded men in Esther Passmans ambulance had help assault three days earlier: "Deir Yassin!"

By the time Colonel Churchill arrived, the lead armored car, the Yassky's ambulance and the two buses were caught in Neggar's trap. Armed Arabs were arriving from all sides. The Jews in the armored car were holding them off, firing through the slits of their vehicles. Churchill cupped his hands and yelled for a cease-fire. His words were lost in the clatter of gunfire. He quickly understood the gravity of the situation. The Arabs had occupied the houses all along the road, and, at the rate at which they were arriving, the Jews would soon be hopelessly trapped.

At ten-thirty he radioed Jerusalem headquarters requesting half a troop of Life Guard armored cars, an observation officer to arrange for shelling the houses in which the Arabs had taken position, and permission to use his three-inch mortars. He was denied his last two requests, and it would be almost an hour before the Life Guards would receive orders to move. That baffling indifference to the convoy's plight characterized the British headquarters reaction to the tragedy all day long. Whether from a bureaucratic and inept application of procedures, a subliminal desire to punish the Jewish community for Deir Yassin, or the active complicity at some level in the command of the officer who had given Neggar the green light for the operation, the British would be responsible for an unconscionable delay in coming to the convoy's rescue.

Furious at the answer to his requests, Churchill fumed, "They don't realize we're going to have a tragedy here. If they don't hurry, nobody's going to get out alive." Determined to do what he could to save the trapped Jews himself, Churchill rushed back to St. Paul's Hospice for a truck and a half-track to mount a rescue operation of his own.

His determination to do something was all the more remarkable since the Haganah had not yet realized the urgency of the situation. Another convoy on the opposite edge of Jerusalem had the attention of the organization's leadership that day. It was the second to arrive from Tel Aviv since Operation Nachshon had reopened the road to Jerusalem. Informed of the ambush as he watched the convoy's one hundred and seventy-eight vehicles roll down Jaffa Road, David Shaltiel immediately asked the convoy commander for the loan of the armored cars in his escort. The commander refused. He had strict orders to return to Tel Aviv as fast as possible. All Shaltiel had available was three cars of his own, commanded by a young officer named Zvi Sinai.

The operation turned into a nightmare. The first car was hit by heavy fire, took several wounded and bolted past the trapped convoy to deliver its injured to Hadassah Hospital. The car in the rear turned back to Jerusalem after taking several killed and wounded. Sinai's car, driven by a soldier from Tel Aviv who did not know the road, stumbled onto the mine crater that had trapped the convoy's lead armored car. Only one man remained alive in that car, Sinai discovered, and he was wounded. Then his own car stalled. His driver, paralyzed by fear, refused to start it again.

Calmly Sinai put his pistol to the boy's head. "You have two possibilities," he said. "Either you're going to be killed by the Arabs or you'll be killed by me if you don't start this car." As the stunned youth turned the engine over, however, there was an explosion outside. An Arab mine had torn off a front wheel. Another metal hulk was caught in Neggar's trap. To the prisoners of the Haganah convoy were added the fourteen Palmachniks in Sinai's car.

Meanwhile, Colonel Churchill had returned with a G.M.C. and a half-track. To his immense chagrin, he learned that Dr. and Mrs. Yassky were among the trapped passengers. Barely a week earlier, Churchill had dined with the doctor and his wife on their flower-covered Mount Scopus terrace. His Dingo armored car in the lead, Churchill moved out to the trapped vehicles.

"If the Arabs shoot at me, blow their bloody heads off," he told Cassidy, the half-track gunner. Then he leaned out of his car and banged on the door of the last bus with his swagger stick. He told the nurse who came to the grill to open the doors and run for his half-track.

"Can you guarantee us safety?" asked the nurse.

"No, I can't," replied Churchill. "Open the door and run for it."

But we'll all be killed!" screamed the nurse.

"If you stay there, you'll all damn well be killed," Churchill told her. Again he urged her to run the few feet between their bus and his half-track, promising that his gunner would cover them.

"But we're all right here," pleaded the nurse.

"You won't be all right very long," Churchill shouted.

Then another voice inside the bus yelled, "Why don't your soldiers chase the Arabs away?"

By now Churchill was furious. At the risk of his life he had come out to save these people, and all he was getting was an argument. Someone else added, "We'll wait here until the Haganah rescues us."

At that instant, Churchill heard a shout behind him. Cassidy, the gunner of the half-track, had been hit in the neck. Churchill gave the trapped passengers a last chance to flee. They refused. Staggered, Churchill backed off to take his dying gunner to Antonio's House. The only serious British effort to save the imperiled Jews had failed.

From rooftops, from balconies, from windows, from Government House and Mount Scopus, half of Jerusalem would now witness the dying agony of the convoy. The British remained impassive despite the dozens of beseeching calls pouring down on them. At eleven-thiry, two hours after the first word of the incident, the first Life Guard armored cars reached the scene. The lead car fired one round and its gun jammed. It was two more hours before additional cars arrived. Colonel Churchill did not receive permission to use his mortars until noon. Permission to use anything heavier would never be forthcoming. The Haganah was bluntly informed that its men would be fired on if they intervened.

Almost six hours after the explosion of Mohammed Neggar's mine, shortly after half past three, the British command finally authorized the men on the spot to intervene vigorously in the ambush. While Churchill and his soldiers of the Highland provided cover fire, Captain Michael Naylor Leyland led his Life Guard armored cars to the besieged vehicles. When he got in close, he radioed back for smoke to cover their movement. To his fury, there "was some interminable chitchat about what kind of smoke." Finally he fired all his own car's smoke himself.

He and his men then took their car covers and, using them to screen a passage between the trapped vehicles and their cars, got the survivors out. There were barely half a dozen left alive.

By nightfall it was over. A ghastly silence reigned at last on the bend in the road to Mount Scopus where Mohammed Neggar had detonated his mine. A few ribbons of smoke, the putrid stench of burned flesh, and the carbonized remains of the convoy's trapped vehicles remained to greet the falling dusk. Dr. Moshe Ben-David had been faithful to his appointment in Samarra. The bus after which he had so frantically run had been his coffin. At least seventy-five others, most of them men and women who had come to Palestine to heal, not kill, had died with him. So completely had the flames devoured their victims that twenty-four of their bodies would never be identified.

The following morning, Moshe Hillman, the Haganah man who had cleared the convoy's departure, picked through the ruins, removing a skull, an arm, a hat, a stethoscope, a pair of glasses. When he had finished, he turned the wreckage over to a team of British demolition experts.

"The remaining vehicles were blown up to clear the road," laconically noted the daily log of the Highland Light Infantry, "and the road mended, and reopened to traffic."

—Collins and Lapierre, *O Jerusalem!*

Deepening the Sources

Each of the readings represents something that could have been witnessed or heard from Mount Scopus. Assign each of the five documents to a small group. Allow time to read the material and prepare a presentation from the perspective of someone standing on Mount Scopus. Summarize the event and reactions to it. This will require the use of both the sources and the imagination.

ADDITIONAL LEARNING POSSIBILILTIES

1. Movie: *Hill 24 Doesn't Answer*
2. Books: *The Will to Survive; O Jerusalem!; Exodus*

Pertinent Sites to Visit in Israel

- Mount Scopus: Hebrew University, Hadassah Hospital
- King David Hotel
- Jewish Quarter—what was destroyed and what rebuilt
- Burma Road and Road from New City to Mount Scopus; monuments to the destroyed convoys
- Turjeman Post, Mandelbaum Gate
- Mount of Olives Cemetery

JERUSALEM
OF THE NATIONS

CHAPTER 8

RELIGION AND STATE

BACKGROUND

Israel has been a parliamentary democracy since its establishment by the Declaration of Independence on May 14, 1948. Election by universal suffrage of the Knesset which, in turn, passed the Transition Law (1949), created a government with a strong democratic base. The Transition Law is the foundation of the government and regulates the work and relationships of the president, parliament, and cabinet. Israel does not have a constitution; it has, instead, a series of Basic Laws that govern how the country is run.

The Knesset, which gets it name and membership of 120 from the Great Assembly convened by Ezra, comprises representatives of the country's political parties. The Knesset is elected every four years. Voters vote for parties that have issued lists of candidates for office. A certain number of votes entitles the party to appoint the top name, or names, on its priority list to the Knesset. The next election year is 1996.

Israel has always been ruled by a coalition government because no party has ever had a majority in the Knesset. The two major parties, Labor and Likud, must create coalitions through the give and take of negotiations in order to gain a majority control of the government (61 seats). This often gives a great deal of power to small parties, and 1996 will be no exception.

This negotiation for votes creates one volatile area in the Israeli government system. A second is the role of religion and state. When the state was established, David Ben-Gurion wanted the unified support of all elements of the Jewish population.

He therefore entered into an agreement with the religious parties setting out the guidelines that still enable the religious parties to remain within the government. Recent efforts to improve the quality of the Israeli government have centered on the need for a constitution, a revision of the voting procedure, and the role of religious law in government. This latter is of great concern to the Progressive Movement in Israel. The most recent innovation is the direct election of the Prime Minister. Needless to say, change takes place slowly and change in governments takes place even more slowly. Nevertheless, there has been some progress.

1996, AN ELECTION YEAR IN ISRAEL

It is possible to divide the complex Israeli political scene into six blocs, ranging from the Radical Left to the Radical Right. The following review will attempt to analyze the functioning of these blocs after the June 1992 elections and to suggest possible future trends.

The Left-of-Center: Labor Party

The Labor Party received 44 seats in 1992, four more than in 1988. The additional support came from new immigrants, Arab voters, and some disenchanted Likud supporters. Rabin's main goal has been to try and move the peace process forward. His focus has been the Palestinian problem, which he hoped would be solved by the process initiated by the September 1993 Declaration of Principles, whereby Israelis and Palestinians would "recognize their mutual legitimate and political rights, [to] strive to live in peaceful coexistence and mutual dignity and security and achieve a just, lasting and comprehensive peace settlement and historic reconciliation through the agreed political process." This approach has not been easy to implement and the level of violence has increased. Rabin realizes that unless there are improved relations with the Palestinian Entity and a sharp decline in attacks on Israelis, his political chances in the 1996 elections will be dismal. His status has improved with the Jordanian peace agreement and relations with several Arab countries. Economic agreements in the Middle East, with Israel playing a central role, will certainly influence the Israeli voter.

The Radical Left (Arabs)

In 1992, this bloc consisted of two parties, the *Democratic Front* (three MKs) and the Arab *Democratic Party* (two MKs) supported mainly by Israeli Arabs. The *Progressive List for Peace* failed to pass the 1.5% threshold. Israeli Arabs have traditionally split their votes between the radical left, left, and left-of-center. There was a move toward the center in 1992, perhaps as these voters realize that their political power in the radical left camp was limited. Their expectations of playing a more central role as Rabin supporters have been disappointed and hopes of receiving a ministerial position were not fulfilled. There will be increased support for radical viewpoints in the future largely within Islamic frameworks, which have been influenced by wider trends in the Middle East.

The Left: Meretz

After the three leftist parties (Mapam, Ratz, and Shinui) combined to form Meretz, just prior to the last elections, there was skepticism about their abilities to remain united. It has succeeded in this. There are tensions between the two central figures, party leader Shulamit Aloni and minister of environment Yossi Sarid. He is favored by Labor Party leaders and is hoping to be a dominant political figure in the future. Meretz has enthusiastically supported the peace process and has used its

12 seats to encourage Middle Eastern initiatives. In the long run, it has probably gained by being identified as an "establishment" party, although there are some who believe that this role has brought about unsatisfactory compromises. Meretz's future is hampered by its appeal to a relatively small clientele—well-educated Ashkenazi voters.

The Right-of-Center: Likud

The Likud's status was severely damaged by its receiving only 32 seats in 1992, after its electoral success in 1988 with 39 seats. During the Shamir era, the party had experienced major internal tensions, with conflicts between the Shamir, Levy, and Sharon camps. The new leader Bibi Netanyahu was expected to revive the party and to initiate an ideological debate. Opinions divided on his success in these two realms. He has certainly gained from the problems facing the Labor Party's peace process and from ongoing attacks on Israeli citizens, but it is unclear if he has managed to forward a clear alternative in terms of the Middle East. He has failed to unify the party and a David Levy split is always possible. He has a more pleasing political style than Rabin and his success may just depend on Labor's failures. There are demands being made on the Likud by Jewish settlers in the Territories and its inability to assist these settlers may result in electoral losses in 1996.

The Right and Religious Right

This bloc is not easy to define. It is basically supported by people who do not want any territorial changes, though some of them may favor a Likud-type autonomy plan. The largest member of the bloc is *Tsomet*, which won an impressive eight seats in the 1992 elections, from only two in 1988. Its right-wing stand included a call for more honest government and the induction of ultra-Orthodox men into the army. However, Tsomet has experienced severe internal tensions and a breakaway three-person faction is in the coalition government. Eitan's five-member party gains from ongoing security problems and its demand for an active policy in the Territories is widely supported.

The second member of this bloc is the *National*

Religious Party (six MKs). This modern Orthodox party has declined in power since the 1950s and 1960s and is still trying to find its unique niche. In most situations, its political voice is often similar to Likud or Tsomet, although it also emphasizes religious issues. While it sees itself as the supporter of modern Orthodox settlers in Judea/Samaria and Gaza (many of whom are Gush Emunim people), it is wary of being identified with the radical right. As an opposition party, it has lost much of its power after decades in the government.

The religious right wing *Tehiyah* lost all its three seats in 1992, receiving some 7,000 votes under the 39,227 threshold.

The Ultra-Orthodox (Haredim)

In 1988, the three Haredi parties received an impressive 13 seats, while in 1992 the number fell to 10. This bloc is divided on ethnic lines. The six person SHAS party is mainly supported by Asian-Africans (Sephardim) and found itself in a powerful position after the last elections, joining Rabins coalition government. With time, it declined as a result of internal tensions and a serious corruption scandal involving party leader Arye Deri. Shas is dominated by Rabbi Ovadia Yosef and does not comfortably fit into the left-right spectrum, functioning on narrow pragmatic interests. Its political future is unclear.

The Ashkenazi ultra-Orthodox are represented by an uneasy combination of Hassidic-Mitnagdim factions in the four-member *United Torah Jewry* party (Agudat Yisrael and Degel Hatorah, who in 1988 received seven seats). Like Shas, they experienced internal tensions and corruption scandals. Their tendency is to isolate themselves from mainstream Israeli society where possible, although sociological realities tend to involve them in Israeli life. It is unclear if they will experience any major changes in the coming years, although they may even lose votes to certain right-wing parties that are more involved in national politics.

New Parties

Rumors of new immigrant and ethnic parties abound in Israel. Russian immigrants are still finding their political feet and although their DA party received only 11,681 votes in 1992 (out of a required 39,227), some still hope to reach the 1.5% threshold in 1996. Labor received 47% of immigrants' votes, Likud 18%, and Meretz 11%. The founding of an Asian-African party is also mentioned, although ethnically based parties have not had much success, except Shas.

Conclusion

Politics in Israel remains dominated by issues of peace and land. The major challenge is the Palestinian-Israeli relationship and the final nature of the Palestinian Entity. In addition, will Israel become an integral part of the wider Middle East? Religion and economics do on certain occasions become important and can influence crucial political decisions and voting patterns.

Paul Liptz,
Israeli Politics: 1992–1995

Against all odds: Knesset votes for direct election of PM

The Knesset on Wednesday approved a sweeping electoral reform under which the prime minister will be chosen directly by the voters.

The success of the controversial law, which drastically changes the system of government, was sealed when the Likud executive lifted faction discipline and allowed its MKs to vote according to their conscience . . . .

The final draft of the law contains three major changes from the original proposal:

It calls for a majority of 61 instead of 70 MKs to bring down the government and force new elections.

The Knesset will have the power to approve or reject the prime ministers cabinet proposal. The original law did not include that prerogative to enhance the prime ministers independence.

The law will go into effect for the elections for the Fourteenth Knesset, scheduled for 1996, instead of the upcoming elections on June 23.

Likud representative Uriel Lynn said this Knesset had passed a series of democracy-strengthening laws which no previous Knesset or government had been able to do because the law committee had succeeded in establishing a dialog with the haredim. "I proved we could do it by persuasion," said Lynn. "After all, we are one people."

Lynn said the amendments to the original draft would cause "no harm." There was no difference between a 70-member or a 61-member majority to bring down the government, he asserted. Any Knesset would hesitate to do so because they would themselves have to stand for reelection.

As for the requirement that the Knesset approve the cabinet, this would assure a nonconfrontational parliament. "I think we are taking the best of the two systems—the parliamentary and the presidential," said Lynn. He predicted that European countries would eventually copy the Israeli system.

The remaining mystery is why the Likud changed its mind and allowed a free vote when Shamir had been so adamantly against the bill and the Likud Central Committee had voted overwhelmingly against it.

According to one source, Likud-ordered polls have shown that the party would have lost at least three mandates (120,000 votes) in the upcoming elections because of its opposition to the bill. Or, as another source put it: "Out of exaggerated fear that they might lose the race for government (if the law had been enacted), they would have lost the race for government [through their opposition to the law]."

—*Jerusalem Post*, March 19, 1992

Deepening the Sources

Describe the nature of Israeli government, specifically, the election process. The Encyclopaedia Judaica *and* Facts About Israel, *produced by the Israel Ministry of Foreign Affairs, provide easily accessible information. Paul Liptz describes the political parties in Israel. Why are political parties so significant? How does this system give disproportional power to minority parties?*

Read the Jerusalem Post *article. Why was this seen as "a victory for democracy?" Why did most people think this could never happen? How did party politics influence the outcome even though the action had been characterized as "putting the interests of the country above party interests?"*

RELIGION AND STATE: WORK OF THE REFORM MOVEMENT
The Challenge of Freedom of Religion in Israel

The Background and the Current Crisis

Everyone has the right to freedom of thought, conscience, and religion. Men and women of full age, without any limitation due to race, nationality or religion, have the right to marry and to found a family. They are entitled to equal rights as to marriage, during marriage, and at its dissolution.

> From "The Universal Declaration of Human Rights," United Nations General Assembly, 10 December 1948

The State of Israel . . . .
Will be based on the principles of freedom, justice, and peace as envisaged by the Prophets of Israel.
Will ensure complete equality of social and political rights to all its inhabitants, irrespective of religion, race, or sex.
Will guarantee freedom of religion, conscience, language, education, and culture.

> From "The Declaration of Independence of the State of Israel," 14 May 1948

In the United States and Canada, human and civil rights are better protected than in most places around the world. Everyone is allowed to practice his/her religion freely, and religious freedom is entrenched in the legal code.

However, that is not the case in Israel. Despite the guarantees proclaimed in its Declaration of Independence, the Jewish state is the only democracy in the world where Jews do not have full religious freedom. For Israeli Jews, all life cycle events—marriage, divorce, circumcision, and burial—come under the authority of the Orthodox religious establishment. This establishment consists of the Chief Rabbinate, local religious councils, Rabbinic courts, the Ministry of Religious Affairs (historically controlled by one of the Orthodox parties), and various interlocking Orthodox institutions.

Israel does not have a written constitution or bill of rights, and all legislative power is invested in the Knesset. Unlike in the United States, where the Supreme Court can strike down laws which violate or restrict religious freedom, the Israeli High Court does not have the same power. The current law of the State of Israel, which can be changed only by Knesset legislation, grants Orthodox Judaism a monopoly over all Jewish religious matters. The principal piece of legislation which establishes this monopoly is the Rabbinical Courts Jurisdiction (Marriage and Divorce) Law 5713-1953 which provides that "matters of marriage and divorce of Jews in Israel, being nationals or residents of the State, shall be under the exclusive jurisdiction of rabbinical courts" and continues, "marriages and divorces of Jews shall be performed in Israel in accordance with Jewish religious law [interpreted by the courts to mean Orthodox *halakha*]." The Chief Rabbinate, which appoints local rabbis, and the rabbinical courts themselves are exclusively Orthodox.

This status quo continues to be maintained because the Orthodox political parties play a key role in the formation of government coalitions. Even if the three Orthodox parties, Shas (ultra-Orthodox Sephardi), United Torah Judaism (ultra-Orthodox Ashkenazi), and the National Religious Party (modern Orthodox) together receive only fifteen percent of the Knesset seats, they still hold the crucial votes which either the Labor or the Likud party (neither of which has ever won an outright majority) needs in order to form a ruling coalition. As a result, not only are the Orthodox parties able to prevent any changes in the status quo, they also gain control of crucial government Ministries including Religious Affairs and the Interior (responsible, among other things, for the Population Registry and the status of new immigrants).

The political importance of the Orthodox parties explains why there have been no legislative initiatives to grant religious equality to non-Orthodox Judaism. This, despite a recent survey which indicated that close to 80% of the Israeli public supports equality for Reform and Conservative Judaism.

As a result of its political power, Israeli Orthodox institutions are heavily funded by the state. Reform and Conservative Judaism have only recently begun to receive some small allocations for their programs and institutions, and this occurred only after fighting hard-won court battles (initiated by the Reform Movement's Israel Religious Action Center). Not only are non-Orthodox streams of Judaism discriminated against in terms of state funding, but Reform and Conservative rabbis are not even recognized by the state as rabbis.

In the absence of a constitution which guarantees freedom of religion, Knesset legislation and coalition agreements have created and preserved the "status quo":

Only Jews who meet the criteria of the Orthodox rabbinate may marry in Israel.

A woman who has been refused a *get* by her husband cannot remarry and any subsequent children she has (including from a new marriage in a legal, civil ceremony abroad) are considered *mamzerim* and cannot marry in Israel. There are an estimated 10,000 such women in Israel who are denied the right to remarry and establish new families.

The Ministry of Health and the Rabbinate refuse to certify non-Orthodox *mohalim*.

New immigrants who are not considered Jewish according to the Chief Rabbinate may not be buried in Jewish cemeteries; at best they may find a spot next to the fence of the cemetery.

There is no public transportation in most of the country on *Shabbat*, thus forcing a de facto observance on nonreligious Israelis who cannot afford private transportation.

Orthodox organizations receive government funding for their private education systems, while the state authorities fight against the establishment of liberal Jewish educational alternatives.

These are only a few examples of religious coercion and discrimination that exist in Israel. The Israel Religious Action Center has made some headway in the areas of state funding and allocation of public land for cemeteries through ongoing litigation. But where it hurts the most, in terms of the right to marry and establish a family and the right to be recognized as a Jew, there is still no freedom of conscience and religion in Israel.

The Problem of Marriage

The issue of marriage in Israel is but one of many that must be addressed before the promises made in the Declaration of Independence are realized. However, this issue is probably the most acute in terms of its current impact and the impact it will have over the coming years.

The problems faced by new immigrants are bringing the existing crisis surrounding marriage and divorce to a head. Currently, veteran Israelis who either prefer not to be married in an Orthodox ceremony or who are simply refused by the Orthodox authorities based on halakhic reasons (such as the marriage of a *cohen* to a divorcee or the marriage of a *mamzer* to a *non-mamzer*), are forced to travel abroad in order to be married. Since there is no civil divorce in Israel, thousands of Israeli women are *agunot*—literally "chained women." They cannot remarry or establish a new family because their husbands refuse to grant them a *get*, a religious divorce. The Orthodox establishment has thus far been incapable of solving this problem.

Now, in addition, tens of thousands of *olim* are being denied their right to marry and establish a family. This is a fundamental right promulgated by international laws and covenants on human rights. The situation in Israel is of increasing urgency. American and Canadian Jews are needed to help Jews everywhere achieve the same freedom of choice they enjoy.

The issue in essence is the denial, for a large number of *olim*, of the basic human right to marry. These *olim* are considered to be Jewish according to the definition used by the Law of Return, so they enter the country and become Israeli citizens. They are not, however, considered Jewish according to the criteria utilized by the Rabbinate who then refuse these *olim* the right to marry.

These *olim* fall into three categories:

1. children of mixed marriages whose mothers are not Jewish
2. those who cannot prove their Jewish identity to the satisfaction of the Orthodox Rabbinate
3. Jews-by-choice converted by non-Orthodox rabbis

These *olim* are caught in a "Catch-22" situation. On the one hand, the Orthodox Rabbinate will not marry them, and on the other hand, there exists no civil marriage or any legally recognized non-Orthodox alternative.

Thus, the only way these *olim* can marry is to leave the country or undergo an Orthodox conversion. As the situation now stands, these *olim* are second-class citizens, a situation which cannot be allowed to continue. All citizens of Israel must have equal rights and freedoms as guaranteed by the Israeli Declaration of Independence and as are accepted by all enlightened, democratic nations. This requires the provision of legal, recognized alternatives.

Jews from diaspora communities who are guided by the ideals of pluralism and free choice must lend their support to help *olim* and other Israelis overcome this obstacle. American and Canadian Jews have been in the forefront of the struggle to bring these *olim* to Israel. They should continue to be involved by spearheading the efforts to deal with issues which deny the *olim* religious freedom and basic human rights. Aren't these people entitled to enjoy the same basic right—the right to marry— that Jews in the West, without exception, enjoy?

—Report from the ARZA-sponsored
Israel Religious Action Center

Deepening the Sources

The "status quo" agreement between David Ben-Gurion and the Orthodox establishment at the creation of the state provided the guidelines that still describe the government's religious policy. What are its components? Why was this necessary? Ben-Gurion felt that this agreement allowed Jews to live together within a minimal religious framework without coercing each other or violating each other's principles. It united the Jewish population in support of the state and laid the foundation for the role of the religious parties in government. In exchange for Orthodox support, Ben-Gurion agreed to maintain the religious practices that had become customary during the Mandate: Shabbat would be the official day of rest, all public institutions would observe the laws of kashrut, the religious school system would be maintained and funded by the state, marriage and divorce would be controlled by religious law.

The premise is being challenged today by the Progressive Movement in Israel. Look at the report from the Israel Religious Action Center. What issues are being addressed? What progress is being

*made? The Progressive Movement is well repre-
sented in Jerusalem by Har El, Kol HaNeshama,
and the new Mevasseret Yerushalayim synagogues, Hebrew Union College, the Progressive
Movement's Center for Continuing Education,
and Beit Shmuel. Ask someone who may have
used these facilities or visited them to report on
the experience.*

Deepening the Sources

*ARZA, an organization of the Reform Movement,
serves as the link between the United States and
Israel. A separate membership organization that
can be joined through each Reform Congregation
or directly through the ARZA office, ARZA provides programs and materials that educate and
encourage support of the Progressive Movement in
Israel. Provide students with materials that will
inform them about ARZA programs and services.*

IN SUMMATION

- Israel is a parliamentary democracy.
- Elections are universal, countrywide, secret,
  proportional.
- The control of the Knesset, and thereby the
  government, is determined by which party is
  able to create a coalition government.
- There are both secular and religious aspects of
  the Israeli government. For most, "religious"
  means Orthodox.
- The Progressive Movement has a growing presence in Israel and a growing influence on government policy-making. It remains, however,
  very slight in the context of Israeli life.
- ARZA links us with Israel.

ADDITIONAL LEARNING POSSIBILITIES

1. An interactive video hook-up between study
   groups in North America and representatives
   of the Progressive Movement in Israel is being
   explored as this is being written. Information
   will be forwarded.
2. Efforts are under way to create e-mail connections with Reform Jews in Jerusalem. The goal
   is to be able to communicate during the study
   period and then meet with computer comrades in Jerusalem.
3. Can/should the American Jew have a role in
   determining religious policy in Israel, specifically those issues that deal with liberal Judaism? Discuss pros and cons.

PERTINENT SITES TO VISIT IN ISRAEL

- Knesset
- ARZA-sponsored Israel Religious Action Cen-
  ter
- World Union for Progressive Judaism
- Beit Shmuel
- Hebrew Union College
- Israel Movement for Progressive Judaism
- Reform Congregations: Har El, Kol
  HaNeshama, Mevasseret Yerushalayim
- Archaeological Museum and Library
- Meeting with leaders of the Progressive Move-
  ment
- Meeting with computer comrades

CHAPTER 9

THE MAKING OF MODERN JERUSALEM

BACKGROUND

In all of Jerusalem's history after the First Commonwealth there were only two periods of greatness and these were separated by two thousand years. Both occurred when Jerusalem was under Jewish rule. The first was during the time of the Hasmoneans just before the destruction of the Second Temple. The second period is today.

Since 1967, when Jerusalem was reunited, the city has been rebuilt and built, its gardens have been planted with sculptures and vegetation, its parks filled with art, artifacts, and playgrounds, its unequaled archaeological riches have been made accessible to its citizens and visitors.

The Old City of Jerusalem remains a city within walls, remnants from history that today reflect divisions among its citizens. The city is not without its serious problems like any modern city. But, in addition, the diversity of the people in Jerusalem may be a cause for tension. That same diversity is also a source of Jerusalem's richness, color, and excitement.

Governing, planning, and growing Jerusalem have been primarily under the guidance of Teddy Kollek, who became mayor in 1964 and served as Jerusalem's mayor for over thirty years. His idealism coupled with deep knowledge of the people he governed made modern Jerusalem into the city it is today.

This lesson will explore the people, culture, and art of a unique city suspended between the holy and the secular.

TEDDY KOLLEK AND THE MAKING OF MODERN JERUSALEM
What It Means To Be Mayor of the City of Peace

The first British governor of Jerusalem, Sir Ronald Storrs, used to say that "there is no promotion after Jerusalem," that governing Jerusalem offers challenges unlike any other task and that the satisfaction gained in meeting them is uniquely rewarding—and I heartily agree.

According to one definition the name Jerusalem itself means "City of Peace." But while the first vision of universal peace came from Jerusalem and from the Prophets who preached here, the city has known little fruit of the message it gave to the world. In ancient times it saw a succession of conquerors, for whom Jerusalem held the key to the Hold Land. In modern times, the City has seen war in 1917, 1948, and 1967, as well as riots in 1921, 1929, 1936–39, 1946–48, 1963, and 1966. Nineteen years of truncated existence, from 1948–1967, brought hardships to the citizens on both sides of the armistice lines, incidents of shooting were not unusual.

I would be the last person to maintain that we have brought heaven on earth to Jerusalem. The threat of violence is still with us. The gap between the rich and poor still exists, as do the differences between Jews and Jews, Muslims and Muslims, Christians and Christians—and among these groups. Yet we have avoided any major clash, interracial or interfaith strife. I believe that this is not a small achievement. It could be an omen for the future and an example not only for our own area of the world.

Governing Jerusalem, however, means more than keeping the peace. Before reunification, Israel's capital was at a dead end, geographically, at the edge of a frontier with hostile neighbors. Its lack of industry and capital investments place severe restrictions and a heavy strain on the Municipality's ability to provide adequate services for its citizens. Since 1967 Jerusalem has regained its proper place at the center of the country. It has been a magnet for both Israelis and new immigrants, and has begun to suffer many of the blights of modern urban life. Even before reunification more than half of Jerusalem's population consisted of immigrants. Most of these new settlers came from the Arab countries, Asia, and North Africa. Their standard of education and economic status was lower than the Israeli or Western-born Jerusalemites and their families larger. Jerusalem had the largest number of families in the country with five or more children. It had the highest rate of natural increase—twice that of Tel Aviv. It had the greatest proportion of elderly and the highest rate of exodus of young people in search of better economic conditions.

In 1967 the problems were compounded. Seventy thousand Muslim and Christian Arabs were added to the city's population. The birth rate among these new residents was one of the highest in the world—almost double that of the Jews—and their social, economic, and educational conditions far below the standards of west Jerusalem. The Old City, with its unique religious and historical heritage, became a part of the Municipality's responsibility, along with the overcrowded slums it contained.

And Jerusalem became the true capital of the State of Israel. Thousands clamored to live within its borders, all seeking proper housing and municipal services.

I felt that the challenge of my first task was to make the City's services available equally to all residents, to overcome fear and suspicion and, with time, to develop a sense of civic unity and pride. Within a comparatively short time the standards of living in East Jerusalem were elevated, educational facilities were improved, there was full employment, and cooperation in the daily life and functioning of the City became commonplace. Today, as I mentioned earlier, peaceful coexistence is a fact, and no one thinks any longer in terms of partition and the redivision of the City.

The second challenge was to give practical expression to the Government's declaration regarding the complete freedom of worship to the various religious denominations, as well as unimpaired access to their holy shrines and places of worship. This was implemented immediately, and good relations and cooperation exist between the various Christian and Muslim institutions and the Municipality.

The third challenge is one which is still with us—it is the challenge of making Jerusalem a vibrant and viable city, of protecting its unique and rich past without turning the city into a museum or sacrificing progress in the late twentieth century idiom. But even more it is the challenge of providing equal opportunity, equal services, and equal status to all segments of the city's population. Jerusalem must not become a melting pot, a city with a mono-culture. Its ethnic and cultural diversity is a major factor in the city's charm and attractiveness. We have made every effort to ensure that Christian and Muslim cultures should flourish, alongside the traditions of the various Jewish communities, and we will continue to do so. The practical application of the principle is to ensure that the wealth of evidence of a rich past should be made the basis of vital and creative activities.

Moreover, we are trying to close the gap between the have and have nots. Where it is impossible to increase the size of a family's dwelling, we increase its living space by providing a park in the neighborhood, a community center, a youth club.

We are attempting to bridge the educational differences by establishing libraries in the poorer areas, building better-equipped schools and providing supplementary lessons. We have established joint activities between Arab and Jewish youth.

Above all, we seek to plan for the future. With an ever-present eye on the universal interests in Jerusalem, we are attempting to create a city which will meet the human, social, and economic needs of a modern urban population. I believe, along with leading figures in the fields of art and history, theology, town planning and architecture, that what people do and how they live is as organically vital to the character of Jerusalem as are its ancient buildings and landscapes.

Our sages have taught us that before reaching the heavenly Jerusalem of the spirit it is necessary to inhabit the earthly Jerusalem. It is in the latter that we live and work—but always with our eye toward the former.

This then is the challenge and the satisfaction—frustrating and elating, disappointing and rewarding, infuriating and satisfying, but always, always, alive and exciting.

> —Teddy Kollek, "What It Means to Be Mayor of the City of Peace" in John M. Oesierroichor, *Jeruslaem*

Rebuilding the Eternal City

The last shots had been fired in Jerusalem; the tanks had withdrawn from the Mt. of Olives. The Six-Day War was over. Jerusalem had a few quiet days in which to breath easily. And then it started. The rumble of heavy motors and the sounds of explosions were heard again throughout the city. But it was not the sound of war which disturbed the peace of the Holy City this time.

This time the vehicles were tractors bulldozing their way through the concrete barriers separating the two halves of the city, and the explosions marked the progress of the army engineers blasting their way through minefields planted in the former no mans land.

These were clearing operations, opening the way for the realization of a city planners dream—nothing less than the building of a New Jerusalem. For centuries, development of the city had been ignored or deliberately frozen. Under the Turks, Jerusalem had been a provincial backwater squeezed into an area of one square kilometer behind the walls erected by Suleiman the Magnificent in the 16th century. The British, who conquered Jerusalem in 1917, carefully controlled its subsequent growth to preserve the city's quiet, stone-clad beauty. With the departure of the British in 1948, another freeze occurred as thousands of acres in the heart of Jerusalem—some of the

most cherished real estate in the world—fell into the no man's land between the Israeli and Jordanian sectors of the city. This vacuum was punctured by the Six-Day War and Israeli authorities rushed headlong into it in the summer of 1967 . . . .

The Ministry of Religions asserted its authority over the Western Wall area and other sacred landmarks. The Department of Antiquities drew up plans for a massive archaeological dig around the Temple Mount. The Hebrew University and Hadassah Medical Organization reclaimed their buildings atop Mt. Scopus and jealously guarded against infringements by a proposed national park. At least half a dozen different planning groups, several of them with overlapping jurisdiction, were charged with drawing up proposals for the development of the area . . . .

In northern Jerusalem . . . families moved into Ramat Eshkol, a new 1,800-unit housing development built on a former minefield girdling the Jordanian fortifications on Ammunition Hill, site of the fiercest battle of the Six-Day War in Jerusalem. Designed and executed by the Housing Ministry at extraordinary speed, the completely preplanned community is the first to be built across the former "green line" which split the city. The development is as much a strategic settlement as any kibbutz on the border. It is designed to provide a permanent land bridge between Jewish Jerusalem and Mt. Scopus—which for nineteen years had been an enclave a mile inside Jordanian Jerusalem—and to assert in a concrete manner Israeli sovereignty in both halves of the City . . . .

Within the Old City itself, a new Jewish Quarter is slowly rising out of the ruins of the old. Until 1948, the quarter was a closed world where pious men made their way to the synagogues through winding alleys and women lowered jars of gefilte fish into the wells on Friday evening to pull them up ice-cold for the Sabbath meal. This world was blown apart in 1948 when the Arab Legion overcame the quarters defenders.

When the Israelis returned to the Old City on the third day of the Six-Day War they found half the Jewish Quarter buried in rubble, some of it created by the Jordanians, some of it the result of earthquakes earlier in the century. After considering the more extreme alternatives open to them—a complete restoration of the old Jewish quarter or the demolition of those buildings still standing and the construction of an entirely new community—the Israelis chose an in between course.

Of the 200 buildings found, two-thirds will be preserved after being given face liftings. But the renovated Jewish Quarter will be composed of new buildings designed along modern lines while retaining the traditional use of stone and adhering to the quarter's modest scale. The religious life of the quarter will be revived with the construction of several yeshivas and two large student dormitories to be built on a promontory overlooking the Western Wall. A number of Sephardic synagogues, used by the Jordanians as stables, are being rehabilitated with loving care.

Despite the reintroduction of these religious elements, the old Jewish Quarter will no longer be a secluded cloister. There will be coffee houses, tourist shops, small hotels, and residents who are not necessarily religious. Deputy Premier Yigal Allon moved into his swank official residence in the quarter this summer.

The Israelis are determined to see to it that the cramped and crowded conditions which once characterized the Old City are eliminated for good. The pre-1948 figure of four persons to a room in the quarter will be reduced to one and a quarter persons per room.

The most far-reaching proposal made to date for Jerusalem is a plan for a 750-acre national park around the Old City. Despite its name, the proposed park will be more than a recreation area covered with trees and flowers. It is designed to cope with the mass tourism which began to reach the Old City only after the Six-Day War. "The area is unprepared to cope with mass visits," declared Yosef Yanai, chairman of the National Parks Authority. He warned that the flood of tourists would make some makeshift development of the area unavoidable. It could "stimulate piecemeal activity with harmful long-term results. Whatever is done should be done right—from the start—and in accordance with a well-conceived master plan.

Aware of the keen worldwide interest in Jerusalem's development, the city council has invited the participation of internationally famous experts in the discussions over Jerusalem's future shape. Mayor Kollek invited over sixty distinguished architects, educators, and churchmen from every continent to participate in the first meeting of the Jerusalem Committee, an international advisory body which was to discuss proposals for the development of the Old City. It was a lively session.

During the coming four years, Kollek plans to continue his considerable efforts to beautify the united city. Small parks will be opened in crowded neighborhoods, and the harsh lines of modernistic housing developments will be softened by newly planted trees. Kollek's enthusiastic salesmanship has already brought more than a million Israeli pounds from foreign contributors for development of the National Park around the walls of the Old City. The first neighborhood park the Arab section of the city has ever known was opened last month in the Silwan Quarter and has already proved immensely popular with the local residents. More parks will be opened in East Jerusalem in the near future, Kollek has promised.

The next four years will see a dramatic expansion of tourist facilities. Three major hotel chains—Hilton, Sheraton, and Holiday Inn—have already announced plans for the construction of major facilities. A charming outdoor restaurant-cafe complex has just been opened in the Hinnom Valley outside the Old City walls below David's Tower, and a similar venture is planned for an old Turkish inn near the railroad station. David's Tower itself will be turned into a museum . . . .

—A.Z. Rabinovich, "Rebuilding the
Eternal City" in A. Eisenberg,
Jerusalem Eternal

Deepening the Sources

In 1967, for the first time in two thousand years, a unified Jerusalem became the Jewish capital. In 1964, Teddy Kollek had been elected mayor of Jerusalem. Born in 1911 near Budapest and named after Theodor Herzl, Teddy, as he is universally known, came to Palestine in the mid-thirties and helped found Ein Gev Kibbutz. He considered Ben-Gurion his mentor and served as the director of his office when Ben-Gurion was prime minister. He was involved behind the scenes in a myriad of cultural and political activities until Ben-Gurion's career ended. It was then that he ran successfully for mayor of Jerusalem.

At the end of the Six-Day War, Teddy found

himself the mayor of an expanded, united Jerusalem with two city governments, a suspicious Arab population, and an Old City filled with rubble and memories.

With unrelenting energy and creativity, Teddy confronted one problem after another and shaped a city where people are learning to share the same ground and to live side by side with mutual respect. He worked tirelessly to restore Jerusalem to its former beauty and grandeur and to balance the new with the old. Key questions are, Will the new Jerusalem damage the old? Will the new be worthy of the old?

With this introduction, the students will act as members of the Jerusalem Committee responsible for restoration and for building a united Jerusalem after 1967. The Committee is to consider:

A. What will happen to the holy places in Jerusalem, the Western Wall, the Church of the Holy Sepulchre, the Temple Mount on which the Dome of the Rock stands? Note that although international law insists that the ruling party allow access to all holy sites, Jews were unable to pray at the Western Wall during Jordanian occupation, 1948–1967. Keep in mind, too, that there are those who say that the Dome of the Rock is built on the site of the Holy of Holies of Solomon's Temple.

B. What should be done to what remains of the Jewish Quarter? Should its synagogues, homes, and streets be totally restored to the state they were in prior to 1948? Should remaining old buildings be demolished and an entirely new community be constructed? Should there be guidelines, or restrictions, for builders?

C. What should be done to the area around the Western Wall? Consider religious, aesthetic, and security issues.

D. How should it be determined who can reside in the Jewish Quarter? Should it be a home for the ultra-Orthodox? Should anyone be able to settle there? How should the decisions be made?

E. Should only synagogues and Yeshivot occupy the public areas of the Old City, or should there be allowances for tourist shops, art galleries, coffee houses, restaurants, and hotels?

F. How should we integrate the rebuilding of the Old City with the plans for a massive archaeological project by the Department of Antiquities?

G. What do we do with the former minefields

and no-man's-lands surrounding the areas formerly occupied by the Jordanians?

H. What do we do with the walls of the Old City? David Ben-Gurion recommended that the walls be ripped down; no ghettos should be allowed in a Jewish city.

I. Now that Mount Scopus is accessible, do we need two Hebrew University campuses and two Hadassah Hospitals?

To see how the discussion and conclusions compare with what really has occurred since 1967, students should read the selection by A.Z. Rabinovich. End this section by reading aloud "What It Means To Be Mayor of the City of Peace."

THE FLAVOR OF JERUSALEM
Sephardic Sabbath Morning Specialties

If anything in Jerusalem is holy it is Saturday morning. No buses operate; store shutters are closed: the usually noisy and crowded streets are hushed and peaceful as people dressed in the Shabbat best take advantage of this day of rest. A pleasant quiet reigns throughout the city. Some people sleep late, others go to the seashore, others hike in the nearby hills and still others walk to their synagogues to pray.

Rachel Molho was born in the Jewish Quarter of the Old City of Jerusalem. Today Rachel reminisces about life in the Jewish Quarter. "On Shabbat everything was clean and shining in the Jewish Quarter. All day Friday was spent scrubbing and whitewashing. Special foods were prepared for the holy day. There was a communal oven, and it was a grand event when the bread and Burekas were pulled out crisp and golden. As a child I was frightened by the man in the room with the oven who roared loudly when the door was opened.

"Very early on Saturday morning, about six a.m., my father went to the synagogue. When he returned, about nine-thirty or ten a.m., we children were dressed and ready for his arrival and would then have our Shabbat breakfast, which you might call brunch. In the winter we ate *hamin*, which means 'hot' and is similar to the Ashkenazic Cholent, a robust stew, while in the summer we ate *hamindavo*, eggs cooked for so long they turn brown; *soutliash*, a rice porridge; and Burekas, cheese, spinach or eggplant pastries.

"The Saturday morning meals were such a treat—especially the homemade Burekas. Cooking is not permitted on the Sabbath, so the meal had been kept hot over a low flame all night long since its preparation the day before. In fact, the long cooking gave an extra flavor to the foods as well as to the coffee," said Rachel nostalgically.

Today the Molho family frequently takes walks to the Old City on Saturday mornings; Rachel is eager for her grandchildren to be old enough for her to show them the places where she played as a child.

The Bathtub Would Be Best— The Ingenuity of an American Immigrant

The notice tacked up in the hallway announced that Giveret (Mrs.) Shosh's challah, with or without raisins, was for sale in Apt. 21. Orders were to be given no later than Thursday evening. Penciled in the end of the notice was the stipulation: "Because of the egg shortage, please bring one egg for each challah ordered." (This was one of the shortages that occurred during the Yom Kippur War.)

Shoshanna (Hebrew for "Rose") officially changed her first name when she and her husband Sid, a high school teacher, arrived in Israel three years ago with their two young children. Unlike a move from one city to another in the United States, it has not been easy for them. There is no comparison between their four-bedroom home near Boston and their four-room apartment in Jerusalem, to say nothing of the unheated, overcrowded absorption center where they studied Hebrew for six months. Adjustment was not easy.

"I lived in Israel for one year and then I went back to the States to visit. After having devoured as many hot fudge sundaes and pancakes as I could, I began to miss Israel. Something seemed wrong with my friends' lives in Boston—no definition, no goals. I realized what an honor it is for a Jew living in the twentieth century to be in Jerusalem. It's worth staying here even with all the hardships; worrying about wars; paying the highest taxes in the world. Here I have a Jewish identity which is far more than my once-a-week Sunday school visit gave me in the States. Moses and Abraham are alive for my children. Israel represents a continuity in our lives."

"I am baking my way to Switzerland," laughed Shoshanna, who began catering friends' parties to help out financially and then decided to begin a business selling home-made challah (braided bread eaten with the Shabbat meal). On Rosh Hashanah, the Jewish New Year, the challah is round—to pray for a good year "all year round."

On Friday morning Shoshanna gets up at 3 a.m. to prepare the large batches of dough. Her friends have donated their largest cooking pots for the operation—Shoshanna still says the bathtub would be best but might scare off her customers! By 7:30 the neighbors' children are knocking at her door to pick up their orders, encouraged by the delicious aroma of homemade bread wafting through the corridor. As we left Shoshanna's apartment smelling the bread, we wondered how many challahs actually last until the Sabbath blessing is made of the bread.

Marry Her If She Can Cook Kubbeh . . . .

One day we visited Katamon, a neighborhood in Jerusalem that is home to the immigrants from Kurdistan; Kurdistan was at one time a rural area that included parts of present-day Turkey, Persia, and Iraq. When we entered the home of Hannah Nehemia, we noticed that she seemed somewhat embarrassed by our presence. She quickly put aside her notebook and blushingly explained that she had been doing her "homework," which was learning to read and write Hebrew.

We would have thought that Hannah probably had enough "homework" with her ten children, but she told us that she was pleased now to be able to spend some time studying. She explained that she had married at the age of fourteen, according to the custom in Zacho, their village in Kurdistan, which they left in 1952. She is now in her late thirties and can let her older children take care of the younger ones. "Reading and writing were always secondary to a woman's role as wife and mother where I come from," she explained. And she asked Joan, "Why aren't you married? I'll find you someone. It just isn't right for a woman not to get married and have children."

During our chat with Hannah, her husband came home after a tiring day of construction work. The Kurds are well known in Jerusalem as the builders of roads and buildings—always working together in groups. We had previously learned that Kurds were in fact so clannish that even today in Jerusalem people from the same village of Kurdistan tend to marry one another. Over a glass of tea we asked Ovadia if he would mind if his son chose to marry a non-Kurdish woman. His reply was rapid: "As long as she can make Kubbeh, I don't care who my son marries."

The main ingredient in Kubbeh is bulghur (cracked wheat), originating thousands of years ago in Kurdistan. Kubbeh consists of a meat or rice filling inside a dough made with bulghur and is formed in the palm of ones hand into torpedolike shapes before being cooked. Hannah insisted upon giving us a lesson in the many ways of making this delicacy. Even Ovadia was relatively pleased with the results, although he still thinks that no one can make Kubbeh as well as a woman from Kurdistan.

A Yemenite's Recipe for a Long and Good Life

According to some theories the "real" Jews of the Diaspora lived in Yemen, a country in southwest Arabia bordering on the Red Sea. These Yemenite Jews spoke Arabic with their Moslem neighbors but Hebrew among themselves and always yearned to return to the Holy Land. Since they have rarely married outside their group, their chiseled dark features are considered by some to be the purest Jewish features. Yemenite families began immigrating to the Holy Land as long ago as the sixteenth century. With the birth of the State of Israel in 1948, the Zadok family and thousands of their fellow countrymen finally realized their age-old dream: they were carried to Israel by a "great bird," which landed in the midst of a field near Aden, a large port on the Red Sea, and swept them, as if by magic, to what is now the David Ben-Gurion Airport. This feat was appropriately dubbed "Operation Magic Carpet."

To learn more about the Yemenites, we visited in Jerusalem with members of the Zadok family—a name that has become synonymous with Yemenite leadership and fine jewelry and silverwork. In their immaculately clean homes—every Yemenite home is spotless—we met Yosef Zadok, the patriarch of the family and rabbi of the local commu-

nity. Young craftsmen were deeply engrossed in designing silver in one room and Yosef was guiding them with a steadiness of hand remarkable for a seventy-seven-year-old man. To our question about the secret of his obvious contentment and healthful countenance he responded, "Baruch Hashem—blessed be His Name. Everything is fine. The air is better in Jerusalem than anywhere else. What more do I need?" We later learned that ever since Yosef Zadok arrived in Jerusalem in 1948, he has never once left the city.

As it was only 8:30 in the morning when we arrived, we asked if it was too early to talk to him. "No, I have been up since 4:30, when I went to pray at my synagogue. After that I walked to Mahane Yehuda to buy my wife's groceries. I came home to study the Talmud, drank *zhum* and now I'll work until 12:30, when I'll eat a little bread and a small piece of meat"—Yemenites eat most parts of an animal, including genitals, tail, leg, belly, and udder. "Sometimes I take a nap for a quarter or half hour—not more—then back to work until 5:30, when I go to synagogue for two more hours of prayer. The rest of the evening I spend studying."

When we asked about the delicious aromas coming from the kitchen, Yosef replied that his wife, Yona, was cooking, not so much for him as for the craftsmen. "My secret is to work hard, keep clean, and eat just enough. *Baruch Hashem*, my sons are following me in the same tradition." In fact, we later discovered that not only do his two sons, Avram and Haim, make jewelry, but also his grandson is beginning to learn and next year, after his bar mitzvah, is looking forward to praying each morning and evening with his father, uncle, and grandfather.

A Recipe Arrives in Jerusalem Before Columbus Discovers America

Seven years before Columbus discovered America, even before the time of the Spanish Inquisition, when all Jews were expelled from Spain, the first members of the Eliachar family immigrated from Spain to Jerusalem. Although they could have sought refuge in Holland, Turkey, Morocco, France, or Italy, they chose instead the place dictated by their hearts, the "Holy City."

As we described in "Sephardic Sabbath Morning

Specialties," Sephardim—Jews of Spanish or Oriental origin—formed the majority of Jerusalems population until the nineteenth century. Their lives were centered around their synagogue, located in the Jewish Quarter of the Old City, and their cultural identity was retained in all aspects of life, including their use of Ladino, a medieval Spanish dialect containing Hebrew, Turkish, and other elements, written with Hebrew script.

Many of Jerusalems old families can claim one or two community leaders of stature, but the Eliachar family is unique in that every generation, for hundreds of years, has consistently contributed a prominent citizen—a chief rabbi, a mayor, a historian, or a leading businessman. Today, within that tradition, Eli Eliachar is president of the Jerusalem Sephardic Community Council.

At home his wife, Rachel maintains the traditional Spanish cuisine. She often compares recipes that were handed down to her from her first Jerusalem ancestors with those of the new immigrants from other Sephardic countries—and there is surprisingly little difference! Medias, vegetable halves stuffed with meat, are a family specialty that has been handed down from generation to generation since the first Eliachars arrived in Jerusalem.

The Bukharans—
Jerusalem's First "City Planners"

In 1891 Jerusalem's first town planners and city engineers arrived to construct an entire quarter for Jewish immigrants from Bokhara in Central Asia, just north of Iran and Afghanistan, now part of the Soviet Union. This was the Bukharan Quarter, adjacent to Mea Shearim outside the Old City, and the first and only area composed of straight, wide streets and lavish stone houses. Until the Bukharans came to Jerusalem, many of the city's immigrants had been observant Jews of very little means who came to Jerusalem to fulfill their lifelong dream—to die and be buried on the Mount of Olives Cemetery in the Holy City. But the Bukharans, most of them wealthy merchants, were different; they came to visit Jerusalem on pilgrimages and then decided to establish a foothold for their families by building homes here. With their ornate jewelry and richly embroidered

clothing they bore a certain inborn dignity in the then rather poor city of Jerusalem. Their pink and green robes, round embroidered caps, and splendid jewels provided a rich contrast to their much duller surroundings. With the passing of time and fortunes after the Russian Revolution in 1917, the Bukharan Quarter lost much of its wealth, but even though the large houses have now been divided into small apartments and family riches are no longer what they were, the word "Bukharan" still carries an aura of respect, stateliness, and largesse.

When we visited Haim Simchayoff, head of the Bukharan community in Jerusalem, he and his wife Sara showed us the beautifully made traditional garments and old family jewelry, which the Simchayoffs still wear for holidays and the Sabbath. Rather a large man himself, Haim was eating an enormous portion of meat when we first came into their home in one of the original buildings. "Milk products are not filling enough for Bukharan men," said he. "We need lots of meat to keep us going. Why do you think streets in the quarter are so wide? If three Bukharans are walking side by side, no one else can get by. Our engineers knew how to build for us!"

Pilaf for a Persian Policeman

A Jew living in New York is a Jew. A Jew living in Iran is a Jew. It is only in Israel that a Persian Jew becomes a Persian. Although police officer Joseph Gabai left Persia illegally as a draft evader thirty-eight years ago to work for the Haganah and has been a ranking member of the Israel police force since its inception in 1948, he is still considered "the Persian." When his chief of police was recently invited to visit Iran, the by now Major Gabai, accompanied by his sabra wife, spent two weeks being officially wined and dined throughout Iran with the official delegation of the Israel police force. "The trip was like a dream," exclaimed Esther Gabai with a happy sparkle in her eyes, "but the fruit wasn't as good as it is in Jerusalem."

First, during the British Mandate as a patrolman in the Jewish Quarter of the Old City and then from 1948 to 1967 as a guard at the Mandelbaum Gate—the only entrance between the two parts of the divided city at that time—Joseph was one of the few Israelis to come in constant contact with East Jerusalemites. At his post at the gate he escorted official visitors and clerics to the Jordanian policeman awaiting on the other side—usually a former colleague or an old friend.

Joseph, like more than 80 percent of Jerusalem's eight-hundred-member police force consisting of Jews and Arabs (including women), speaks perfect Hebrew and Arabic. Until 1948 the Gabais lived in a mixed community near the Mandelbaum Gate, in the American Colony, where Esther, the most renowned cook of all the policemens wives in the city, shared recipes with her Jewish and Arab neighbors. Now living nearby in the Bukharan Quarter, she also exchanges cooking ideas through the constantly open windows with new immigrants from Persia who have come to live near their old friend Joseph Gabai. Until today, however, no one can rival Esther's Pilaf recipe.

Indians in Jerusalem— The "Real Thing" in Curry

Jews have lived in India for nearly two thousand years. The two ancient cultures flourished simultaneously and in perfect harmony. Indian Jews have always called themselves "Benai Israel" (the Sons of Israel), and like Jews all over the world, many of them felt drawn to live in the city of Jerusalem.

Dvora and Isaac Joseph came to Israel from Bombay in 1950, two years after the State of Israel was born. They were the only married couple in a group of seventy-five young Indian immigrants, and they needed all the idealism they could summon up to overcome the problems they encountered in the new, undeveloped, desert country. In Beersheva, where they settled, the only available homes were tents. Jobs were difficult to find, food was scarce, and there was only one place to bathe in the entire settlement. The shy and modest Indian women would all go to the one public bath together while the men "kept guard" outside—safety in numbers! Most painful to Isaac and Dvora, who had come to live in Israel for the sake of their children, was the complete lack of facilities for Jewish education. After two years of struggling without success, they felt forced to return to India.

"But we just couldn't stay away," Isaac remembers. "We felt an irresistible desire to live in the land of Israel and a few years later with three more children and my parents, we came back to try again."

Life was also hard the second time around, but they say, "the love of Israel somehow pulled us through. The education of our children was our single-minded aim and while we often had only bread and tea for dinner, we did in fact accomplish our goal, and I say this with pride."

Today the Josephs live in Jerusalem, the city that symbolizes their lifelong love of Israel. They are a close-knit family of gentle, soft-spoken people. When we visited them we were truly impressed with the respect the three generations showed for each other in this household.

Isaac's and Dvora's mothers sat together in the living room discussing recipes to give us. They spoke in their native Indian dialect, Marathi. Both wore saris and golden hoop earrings, and had their hair knotted in silvery gray buns.

The old saying goes that too many cooks spoil the broth. In the Joseph family, however, two cooks (and two mothers-in-law at that!) cook together and spoil their family—but certainly not the broth!

The Simcha (Joy) of an Orthodox Woman

"A woman of valor who can find? For her price is far above rubies. The heart of her husband doth safely trust in her. And he has no lack of gain. She doeth him good and not evil all the days of her life." This is part of the Proverb recited at the Friday night services in Jewish households.

Many feminists today question the woman's role in Jewish tradition, as did Barbra Streisand when she first visited the Western Wall, where a partition separates the praying men and women. However, many religious women wear modest, long dresses, and hair-covering wigs (sheitels), and the pride in the special role they play in maintaining religious homes. While their husbands spend their days praying and studying the Talmud, wives, mothers, and daughters—these proverbial "women of valor"—attend to the practical side of Orthodox Judaism. Sometimes this might also mean maintaining shops to support the family financially while the men study, but no matter what else they do, they must always prepare meals and clean the home.

Throughout the week, except on the Sabbath, the day of rest, Rachel Shapira devotes her energies to purchasing, cooking, and cleaning foods according to *kashrut*, ancient Jewish dietary laws that treat food and the Sabbath in a very special way. Since food is an integral part of life, there are prayers recited for everything—over the wine, the first fruits of the year and the daily bread, and thanks at the end of the meal.

Because cooking is prohibited on the Sabbath, three meals for that day must be prepared in advance. And so from Thursday night until Friday at midday, Rachel is busy in the kitchen preparing gefullte fish, matzoh balls Cholent, and the inevitable Kugel or noodle pudding, which has become her trademark. From Friday at noon until *havdallah,* the ceremony signaling the end of the Sabbath and ushering in the new week, the house is filled with relatives who come to enjoy the day of rest. Even before Rachel lights the candles to begin the Sabbath, her husband and children sing praise for the good woman who is the center of the family. For Rachel, seeing her children, grandchildren, and visitors enjoying her cooking and hospitality is her pride and joy—described by the Yiddish word *naches*. Rachel explained to us that she creates *simcha* (joy) for her family at the table—indeed the center of the home. Here the Shapiras eat and they pray. She feels she has a greater purpose in life than she would as a housewife who simply went to the grocery store and sought ready-made food. For food is not just physical sustenance, as Rachel puts it, it is also God's providence, and so each food is blessed accordingly.

Every Saturday morning after prayer in the "Presidential" synagogue, where Rachel's husband Eliahu works as a *shamas* (caretaker or deacon) and former Israeli president Zalman Shazar prayed, the participants attend a *kiddush,* a blessing said over wine. They also eat portions of Rachel's Jerusalem Kugel, which over the years became such a favorite of President Shazar's that he received a special one each week for his many guests.

Maimouna—
A Moroccan Community Picnic

Folklore customs often change when ethnic groups leave one country for another, and ever since the Jews became dispersed through the world their holidays have taken on different customs and traditions, all variations on the original significance of each occasion. A unique end-of-Passover tradition, called Maimouna, is celebrated in Israel by a group of the country's most ebullient and colorful immigrants, the Moroccan Jews. In Morocco, Maimouna was celebrated on the evening of the last day of Passover. It was followed by a trip to the countryside or seashore. On that evening Moslem friends visited their Jewish neighbors to wish them happiness and prosperity, bearing trays of fresh yeast (leavened bread is prohibited during the eight days of Passover), fresh bread, honey, flour, and butter among flowers, greens, and lettuce. Often a fresh fish, symbolizing fertility, was placed in the center of the tray, to be cooked the following day with lots of almonds, a springtime delicacy in Morocco. With the emigration of Jews from Morocco after 1948 the locale changed, but not the festivities.

Nowadays in Israel, on the day after the end of Passover thousands of Moroccans flock to Jerusalem from all the country to congregate in a large park reserved for the celebration. Moroccans are excused from work on this special day, and in fact the Histadrut (the national labor union) closes the entire port of Ashdod and charters buses so that the employees are free to visit the Holy City. They celebrate the arrival of spring in a spirit of fraternity with their neighbors, friends, and relatives. For many of the participants who live far apart in Haifa, Tel Aviv, Asdod, or Jerusalem it is a rare opportunity to visit each other, since many are religious Jews to whom it is forbidden to travel on the Sabbath, the one day of rest in our one-day-weekend country.

The overall scene is one of bright color and noise. Women wearing headdresses decorated with coins flash their long skirts as they dance to Moroccan music and the hearty singing of their friends. Men in embroidered caps stamp their feet in accompaniment and everyone expresses their feelings of joy by sending forth what can only be described as a "war whoop"—a special cry emitted to show pleasure. (The same cry is also heard at Moroccan bar mitzvahs, weddings, and other special occasions.) The aromatic smells of frying fish, garlic, Turkish coffee, and honeyed sweets are in the air, and delicacies are sold throughout the celebration. All around, many different traditions are being carried out: in one group, the elderly grandfather gives his family a blessing accompanied by a piece of lettuce dipped in honey for a happy and "sweet" year; in another, someone is placing a coin in a sack of flour—"a lucky dip"—to ensure a prosperous year.

One explanation for the exotic-sounding name of the holiday is that "Maimouna" means "bring happiness" in Arabic. Another is that the day is celebrated to commemorate the death of Rabbi Maimon, father of Moses Maimonides, the philosopher, theologian, and physician who lived in Morocco for a long period of time in the twelfth century. Whatever the original meaning of the word, these salad recipes are colorfully placed in dishes on blankets during Maimouna.

—Joan Nathan, *The Flavor of Jerusalem*

Deepening the Sources

The title comes from a book by Joan Nathan and Judy Stacey Goldman that captures the rich diversity of people in contemporary Jerusalem. It is also a cook book! Assign the descriptive readings to individuals and ask each to create a list of ethnic groups and the qualities characterizing each group. Space limitations preclude reproducing the recipes. Get the book and taste the flavors of Jerusalem. Consider these for a final banquet. Examples of characteristics of the groups might be:

- *Giveret Shosh: American immigrant, seeking Jewish identity, hard adjustment, hard work*
- *Hannah Nehemia: Kurdistan immigrant, married at 14, 10 children, construction workers, clannish—marry one another*

MALLS AND MIKVEHS
The Ultra-Orthodox Takeover of Jerusalem

Within a decade, Jerusalem could well have an ultra-Orthodox mayor, heading a coalition of ultra-Orthodox and Arab politicians, with secular and modern Orthodox Jews left out in the cold.

An investigation by The Jerusalem Report has established that in the year since the election of Mayor Ehud Olmert, ultra-Orthodox politicians newly appointed to head key departments at City Hall have systematically used their power, influence, and budgetary clout to attract thousands of new ultra-Orthodox families in the city, and smooth the way for the expansion of existing ultra-Orthodox neighborhoods, while relegating secular needs and the creation of industrial and manufacturing infrastructure to the margins.

With secular and modern-Orthodox Jews fleeing for the suburbs in growing numbers, a majority—52 percent—of Jewish Jerusalem children under 10 are now ultra-Orthodox. If the trend continues, experts predict, ultra-Orthodox Jews will comprise half of the city's Jewish population within a generation, and will thus hold an unshakable grip on the running of the capital.

The Report has learned that five of the seven most senior staffers at the city Engineer's Department have resigned in the past year, despairing at their ultra-Orthodox political master's insistence on redirecting resources to meet ultra-Orthodox needs, at the expense of the rest of the city's population.

The city's demographic map is being rapidly redrawn, as ultra-Orthodox Jews move to take over the entire northwest region of Jerusalem and close it completely to traffic on the Sabbath and holidays.

As a consequence, say many disillusioned former city employees, Jerusalem is gradually becoming a city of three semi-independent boroughs—ultra-Orthodox, other Jewish, and Palestinian—a divided capital in which ultra-Orthodox leaders are pulling more and more of the strings. Having come to power with the support of ultra-Orthodox voters, Olmert forged a coalition in which their parties hold nine seats and his Likud-linked party only five. The secular Olmert could quickly be thrown aside by his partners.

Three factors combine to explain the growing ultra-Orthodox domination of the capital: Ultra-Orthodox families tend to have many more children than other Jewish families; new ultra-Orthodox families are being attracted to the city because they know their needs are being addressed by the City Council; and disillusioned secular and modern Orthodox Jews are moving away.

Over 30 percent of Jewish households in Jerusalem have six or more members—in Tel Aviv or

Haifa the figure is barely five percent—and for the most part these are ultra-Orthodox homes. For the most part, too, these families live in badly overcrowded conditions—hence the expansion to new neighborhoods.

In the ultra-Orthodox neighborhood of Meah Sharim, for example, most families have seven to ten children, and live with an average of three persons to a room. In the most secular Rasco neighborhood, by comparison, the average family has the proverbial "1.5 children," and lives with 0.9 persons per room.

Today ultra-Orthodox Jews comprise a little under 30 percent of the city's Jewish population of 410,000. And given that the authoritative Jerusalem Institute for Israel Studies has projected their share increasing only to 40 percent by 2010, Mayor Olmert asserts blithely that they are "far from gaining control of the city."

But Prof. Yosseph Shilhav, of Tel Aviv's modern-Orthodox Bar-Ilan University, notes acerbically that these projections were made more than a year ago, before Olmert defeated Teddy Kollek in the November 1993 city elections, "triggering the political change now fueling the rapid growth of the ultra-Orthodox community."

The secular and modern-Orthodox exodus is speeding up the shift. In 1993, 10,000 Israelis moved into the city from other parts of the country, while 16,000 moved away. About half of the arrivals were ultra-Orthodox Jews, says Israel Kimchi, of The Jerusalem Institute, a former city planner. About 80 percent of the departees were secular and modern-Orthodox, most of whom cited the lack of jobs and affordable housing as factors in their departure. "We expect to see this trend continuing in the 1994 figures," Kimchi adds.

The ultra-Orthodox community has been seeking some kind of limited autonomy ever since the days of the British Mandate. In the early 1920s, prestate Haganah fighters assassinated an extreme ultra-Orthodox activist, Jacob de Haan, who had secured Jordanian king Abdullah's support for separate status.

Today, the ultra-Orthodox are in a position to implement their goal: establishing a discrete and homogeneous community across a wide swath of the city's northwest. A heated takeover battle is currently being fought in the mixed Ramot neighborhood there, The city has given high priority to the construction of an ultra-Orthodox neighborhood on the Shuafat ridge a little further north. Plans are being considered for an ultra-Orthodox extension to Ramot, on a hill called Allonah. And the incongruous presence of a large army base, Schneller, in the heart of ultra-Orthodox territory, will also be a thing of the past. The complex is to be bulldozed, and homes for five thousand people erected.

Olmert vehemently denies that what amounts to a third of the city is rapidly becoming an ultra-Orthodox-only area, and reels off a list of still-mixed neighborhoods in the north to prove his point. Besides sections of Ramot, he mentions Pisgat Zeev, French Hill, Ramat Eskol, and adjacent Givat Hamivtar.

But the first two of these are outside the ultra-Orthodox target zone. And, official denials notwithstanding, the other two are high on the agenda for ultra-Orthodox expansion. Rabbi Haim Miller, who heads the city's newly created Torah Culture Department—and is best known for spending 50,000 shekels of city funds to erect public sukkot last fall—tacitly acknowledged to The Report that Ramat Eshkol is in his sights. With a touch of wishful thinking, he asserted that Bar-Ilan Street, which he and his colleagues would like to close on the Sabbath, "runs through 100 percent ultra-Orthodox neighborhoods—you know, Ramat Eshkol and other nearby areas."

Housing is the top priority for the ultra-Orthodox population. Proof of this came during the city coalition negotiations a year ago, when ultra-Orthodox councilors insisted on control of the Planning and Building Committee.

The radical change in political directives—from an emphasis on industry and manufacturing infrastructure in Kollek's day—prompted an exodus of city planning professionals, leaving several key positions still unfilled months later.

The shift in focus is clearly being felt. Hundreds of manufacturing jobs have been lost in the past year, says a spokeswomen for the Jerusalem branch of the Israel Manufacturers Association.

Unperturbed by the environmental implications of densely packed neighborhoods, consuming precious open space, Deputy Mayor Lupolianski is nevertheless quick to invoke environmental arguments to block industrial projects that might adversely affect his community. Since taking office, he has been stalling approval of a proposed $1 billion expansion of the capital's Intel Electronics computer-chip plant. "How can I approve plans for a plant that could destroy nearby neighborhoods?" he asks indignantly, citing unnamed experts who he says have told him that, were the city to be hit by a serious earthquake, the new plant might release hazardous gases.

That's all very well, notes a former city planner dryly. "But if a major earthquake hit the capital, the destruction would be widespread. One could block every planning move, and tear down half the existing factories, on those grounds.

Insisting on anonymity, this ex-official wonders whether Lupolianski's objections to Intel stem more from the fact that the proposed expansion would have been adjacent to northwest Jerusalem's ultra-Orthodox Sanhedriah Murkhevet neighborhood, limiting its potential for growth.

—*The Jerusalem Report*,
December 29, 1994

Israel 2010

"There will be lots of lanes, hamburger joints, gas stations. It'll be just like the United States." That's how one Housing Ministry employee wryly describes Highway 6, a new toll road slated to slice through the middle of Israel, from Beersheba in the south to Yokneam in the north.

Highway 6 could open to traffic as early as 2001. If it does, it will be one more sign of the Americanization of the Israeli landscape. Top government planners estimate that over the next 20 years, the country's population will skyrocket to 7 million, from the present 5 million. That includes Soviet aliyah; it doesn't include the territories. Plans by officials and developers to meet the needs of the next generation include shopping malls, industrial parks, and highways, with the four major urban centers—Tel Aviv, Jerusalem, Haifa, and Beersheba—playing critical roles. As big cities get bigger, and closer together, Israel 2010 will probably look a lot like Los Angeles 1992.

Israel's pioneers envisaged a balance of big cities and small towns, interspersed with rural settlements. But today, says Bezalel Art Institute architect Michael Turner, former director of Jerusalem's urban planning unit, "We all lack vision. There are no Ben-Gurions or Herzls, and we don't respond to fantastic people who are visionaries."

If there's no vision, it's not for want of planners. At the national level, the Housing, Interior, and Environment ministries and the Israel Lands Authorities are working together to craft a national master plan. But their multivolume blueprint for Israel's development, completed in March, focuses on the larger issues: energy needs, water resources, transportation networks, demographic patterns, and so on. Each individual city is left to plan its own development. Business interests may then alter the city's plans. The result is urban sprawl.

"In the future you will drive from one place to another without knowing where one city starts and another ends," says Israel Kimchi, a researcher at the Jerusalem Institute for Israel Studies. And as Israel's cities expand, today's problems will only worsen. Sewage, water purity, traffic snarls, and disappearing green spaces will become even more pressing concerns. One of the most crucial issues, says Valerie Brachya, head of the Environment Ministry's planning department, will be the lack of land. Everybody wants a house with a garden, but that clogs up land that could be used for parks or nature reserves.

A possible solution for saving land: building underground. "It must happen," Brachya insists. "When you have space pressure, one way to go is up. The other is down. There are big environmental advantages: You save on heating and cooling and you save space. If it's noisy, smelly, ugly, if it does not need natural lighting—stick it underground."

Going underground doesn't erase the specter of mass, faceless urbanization. Yet the countrys planners don't seem fazed by the notion of Israel as a megalopolis. At the Housing Ministry, the director of the department of urban planning briskly sums up the government's master plan: "It's important to expand to three centers—Haifa, Beersheba and a great unified metropolis of Tel Aviv and Jerusalem together. Tel Aviv will continue to suburbanize. We want to direct it toward Jerusalem, with the new city of Mod'in in between."

But architect Turner is horrified by this vision

of Israel's future and hopes that next generation will have the chance to change it. Otherwise, he says, "we risk turning Israel into a banal, homogeneous country."

Jerusalem:
Is Aimless Sprawl
Substituting for a Grand Vision?

Building Jerusalem has always been more a matter of politics than of rational urban planning. Through the centuries, rule over the city switched hands countless times, and each new regime put its own distinctive mark on the physical development of the city.

The latest spurt of development has proceeded in a city reunified in the wake of Israel's victory in the Six-Day War, and has involved the construction of a ring of new neighborhoods on the perimeter of a city with enlarged boundaries. The political point: to establish facts on the ground by reinforcing the city's Jewish majority and assuring that Jerusalem could not again become a divided city.

As the city expanded over the ensuing 25 years, strategic considerations remained primary, says architect David Kroyanker, author of several books on Jerusalem. "There has been no real planning. What we have ended up with is urban sprawl."

Jerusalem in the year 2010 is likely to still be facing a similar fate, expanding rather than fundamentally changing. City engineer Elinoar Barzacchi, who implements plans crafted by a combination of the City Council and urban planning professionals, says, "We want more tourism, more hotels, more commerce, and we need to make the city center more attractive."

"Things are happening too fast," charges Tzipi Ron, spokeswoman for the Society for the Protection of Nature. "All the open spaces are being closed off and all the green hills ruined." What's more, she claims, the city jumps from one project to the next, without bothering to step back and assess the impact. The answers, she says, aren't "another shopping mall, another road."

But the mall seems to be a fad that's caught on. Three major shopping centers are already under construction in different parts of the city: the mall at the Manhat project, which also includes hous-

ing, a zoo, and a fifteen-acre, $50 million industrial park, will be completed next year. Next to the Old City's Jaffa Gate, the Mamilla project, with its 120 shops, cinemas, restaurants, and hotel, should be finished in two or three years. And the Talpiot Industrial Zone, expanding month by month, has taken off as a consumer mecca. On the top floor of yet another mall, still under construction in Talpiot, patrons are already flocking to a state-of-the-art complex of seven movie theaters.

Other major development projects are under way. Binyanei Ha'umah, the convention center near the entrance to the city, is being vastly expanded—although construction has been temporarily halted while a Roman military camp, discovered during excavation, is studied. A trio of towers—one of which, at nineteen stories, is claimed to be the city's tallest building—is currently going up downtown.

Construction has begun on a revamped government complex alongside the Knesset, to include a new Prime Minister's Office and the Foreign Ministry. The first building in the complex, the new Supreme Court, is due to be completed soon.

Work on the $100 million City Hall complex, concentrating all municipal offices in one square at the corner of Jaffa Road and Rehov Shivtei Yisrael, is in progress, refinanced after the city's loan from Canada's financially ailing Reichmann brothers fell through.

And the Russian Compound, today's local police headquarters, and the site of a dismal detention center and several court buildings are also to be revamped.

For the malls to succeed, notes Israel Kimchi, a Hebrew University professor of geography and a researcher at the Jerusalem Institute for Israel Studies, "the economic base in the city has to change, to raise the level of purchasing power."

The current trend, however, is toward an even poorer population, as the well-off, the young and professional, and the secular leave the city.

One way of attracting young professionals and raising living standards is to "go high-tech," says Erel Margalit, one of the principal players at the Jerusalem Development Authority, a corporation responsible to the Finance Ministry that was set up in 1989 for strategic planning in Jerusalem. Margalit hopes to create 30,000 high-tech positions by the year 2000 in several industrial parks, including Manhat and the already-existing Har Hotzvim, which will double its size from thirty-five to seventy acres in the coming few years.

To get to these new jobs and malls, City Hall, the Jerusalem Development Authority, and the Ministry of Transportation recommend adding 172 kilometers to the city's road system by 2010, including major byways transecting residential neighborhoods in order to unsnarl traffic.

But residents near these proposed roads are far from thrilled. "They're bringing more cars into the city instead of creating good public transportation," says Lottie Schweig, a member of a citizens' committee objecting to two four-lane roads slated for open space in the German colony. Fellow committee member Ehud Halevy fears a city cut apart by highways: "If that's what I want," he says wearily, "I'll move to Los Angeles."

—*The Jerusalem Report,*
September 10, 1992

Deepening the Sources

Read and summarize parts of "The Ultra-Orthodox Takeover of Jerusalem" and "Israel 2010." What will happen to the modern Orthodox and liberal Jews living in Jerusalem? On the other hand, the city is following the rest of Israel in becoming more "Westernized," epitomized by suburban sprawl and large, upscale shopping malls. Can Jerusalem maintain its unique qualities while encompassing both the ultra-Orthodox and the Westernized dimensions of Israeli life?

IN SUMMATION

- Teddy Kollek has done more to shape the modern city of Jerusalem than any other individual in modern history.
- After 1967, there were a series of decisions to make about the future of the Old City, decisions that would shape Jerusalem forever.
- The ultra-Orthodox are becoming a strong force in determining the nature of Jerusalem.
- Westernization of Jerusalem is becoming a reality.
- Jerusalem, as Israel itself, reflects the diversity of the people who live there.

PERTINENT SITES TO VISIT IN ISRAEL

- Synagogues in the Old City
- Architecture tour of the Old City
- Interview with mayor of Jerusalem or with Teddy Kollek
- Park tour of Jerusalem: Billy Rose Sculpture Garden, National Park outside of Old City Walls, Yemin Moshe, Sultan's Pool, Rothschild Square in the Old City
- Siebenberg Archaeological Museum in the Old City and, if possible, hear his story
- An evening at the new Jerusalem Mall

JERUSALEM OF LIGHT

CHAPTER 10

JERUSALEM AND ITS HOLY PLACES: Links Between Humanity and God

BACKGROUND

Jews have claimed Jerusalem as their center of religious life for three thousand years. Christians and Moslems also claim Jerusalem as one of the centers of their religious life. The three faiths consider Jerusalem to be a holy city, believe in one God, observe a day of rest, possess holy writings to support their beliefs and behavior, communicate to God through prayer, and have feasts and life cycle observances. Yet war has destroyed lives and razed the city of Jerusalem no fewer than seventeen times.

What is it about this piece of land that galvanizes the kingdoms of heaven and earth?

Jerusalem is the Eternally Holy City of the Jews. Since the time of David until today, and looking into the future, Jerusalem is the heart and soul of the Jewish people. Jews have been slaughtered and driven out of the city only to return to rebuild and defend what is theirs.

Byzantine Christians rebuilt the city; the Crusaders left it a pile of rubble. Christian pilgrims sought out and continue to visit sites marking events in the life of Jesus. The holiest city of Christianity is the heavenly city of Jerusalem. At the same time, the center of Christian life moved to places other than Jerusalem, like Antioch and Rome.

The Dome of the Rock was built by the Moslems in 685 on the site where tradition says Abraham bound Isaac and where nearly three thousand years ago, Solomon built the temple. Islamic tradition identified this spot as the place from which Mohammed ascended to heaven to receive Allah's revelation. Moslem pilgrims who are unable to make a hajj to Mecca journey to Jerusalem to visit the Dome of the Rock. For Islam, Mecca and Medina are religiously superior to Jerusalem.

Each of the three monotheistic faiths perceives Jerusalem's holiness in different ways. All changed the face of Jerusalem in the process of embodying their beliefs in monuments, works of art, and places of worship. Jews constructed many synagogues, but the Western Wall remains the most powerful religious symbol. There are many churches in Jerusalem, but the Church of the Holy Sepulchre is the most significant. Tops of mosques fill Jerusalem's skyline, but The Dome of the Rock, with Al Aksa, is the primary Moslem structure.

Later in this chapter, we shall read about these three Jerusalem sites, attempting to acquire some sense of the religious passions the city engenders. For a fuller view of Christianity's and Islam's ties to Jerusalem, please consult outside sources.

HOLINESS OF JERUSALEM TO JEWS: ORIGINS

Thus says Adonai, who gives the sun for a light by day, and the fixed order of the moon and of the stars for a light by night, which divides the sea when its waves roar; Adonai of hosts is God's name. If those ordinances depart from before me, says Adonai, then the seed of Israel also shall cease from being a nation before me for ever. Thus says Adonai; If heaven above can be measured, and the foundations of the earth explored below, then I will also cast off all the seed of Israel for all that they have done, says Adonai. Behold, the days come, says Adonai, when the city shall be built to Adonai from the Tower of Hananeel to the Corners Gate. And the measuring line shall go further straight to the hill Gareb, and shall turn around to go to Goath. And the whole valley of the dead bodies, and of the ashes, and all the fields as far as the brook of Kidron, to the corner of the Horse Gate toward the east, shall be holy to Adonai; it shall not be plucked up, nor pulled down any more for ever.

—Jeremiah 31:34–39

The word that Isaiah the son of Amoz saw concerning Judah and Jerusalem. And it shall come to pass in the last days, that the mountain of God's house shall be established on the top of the mountains, and shall be exalted above the hills; and all nations shall flow to it. And many people shall go and say, Come, and let us go up to the mountain of Adonai, to the house of the God of Jacob; and God will teach us of Divine ways, and we will walk in God's paths; for from Zion shall go forth Torah, and the word of Adonai from Jerusalem. And God shall judge among the nations, and shall decide for many people; and they shall beat their swords into plowshares, and their spears into pruning hooks; nation shall not lift up sword against nation, nor shall they learn war any more.

—Isaiah 2:1–4

It shall be eighteen thousand measures around; and the name of the city from that day shall be, Adonai is there.

—Ezekiel 48:35

Thus says Adonai of hosts: It shall yet come to pass, that there shall come people, and the inhabitants of many cities; And the inhabitants of one city shall go to another, saying, Let us go speedily to entreat the favor of Adonai, and to seek Adonai. I will go also. And many peoples and strong nations shall come to seek Adonai in Jerusalem, and to pray before Adonai. Thus says Adonai: In those days it shall come to pass, that ten people from the nations of every language, shall take hold of the robe of a Jew, saying, We will go with you; for we have heard that God is with you.

Zechariah 8:20–23

HOLINESS OF JERUSALEM TO JEWS: HISTORY

By the rivers of Babylon, there we sat down, we also wept, when we remembered Zion. We hung our lyres on the willows in its midst. For there those who carried us away captive required of us a song; and those who tormented us required of us mirth, saying, Sing us one of the songs of Zion. How shall we sing God's song in a foreign land? If I forget you, O Jerusalem, let my right hand forget its cunning. If I do not remember you, let my tongue cleave to the roof of my mouth; if I do not set Jerusalem above my highest joy. Remember, O Eternal, against the Edomites, the day of Jerusalem; who said, Raze it, raze it, to its foundation. O daughter of Babylon, you are to be destroyed! Happy shall one be, who repays you for what you have done to us! Happy shall one be, who takes your little ones and dashes them against the rock!

—Psalm 137

The Passover service has now been concluded according to its rules, ordinances and customs

As we have been deemed worthy to perform it now, so may we be worthy to observe it in the Temple.

You, who dwell on high, raise up the Innumerable people [Israel]

Hasten to lead us, the plants of Your vineyard, again redeemed to Zion with joyous song.

"Next year in Jerusalem!"

—Haggadah

If at any time the rite of hallowing did not include all of the above provisions and in the order stated, the hallowing (of the Temple site) was not complete. And when Ezra prepared two thank-offerings, he did so merely as a memorial (of the rite). The (Temple) site was not hallowed by his ceremony, since neither a king was present nor did the Urim and the Thummim function. How then was the site hallowed? By the first sanctification which Solomon had made, for he had hallowed the Court (of the Temple) and Jerusalem for both his own time and for all time to come.

Therefore, it is permissible to offer all manner of sacrifice (upon the hallowed site), even though there was as yet no Temple erected, and to eat most holy offerings in any part of the Court even though it has been destroyed and was no longer surrounded by an enclosure; also to eat less holy offerings and the Second Tithe in Jerusalem, even though there were no walls enclosing the city—because the first sanctification (under Solomon) had hallowed these sites for his own time and for all time to come.

Now why is it my contention that as far as the Sanctuary and Jerusalem were concerned, the first sanctification hallowed them for all time to come, whereas the sanctification of the rest of the Land of Israel, which involved the laws of the Sabbatical year and tithes and like matters, did not hallow the land for all time to come? **Because the sanctity of the Sanctuary and of Jerusalem derives from the Divine Presence, which could not be banished.** Does it not say "and I will bring your sanctuaries unto desolation" [Lev. 26:31], wherefrom the Sages have averred: even though they are desolate, the sanctuaries retain their pristine holiness.

Even though the Sanctuary is today in ruins because of our iniquities, we are obligated to reverence it in the same manner as when it was standing. One should not enter save where it was permissible; nor should anyone sit down in the Court or act irreverently while facing the East Gate; for it is said: "You shall keep My sabbaths and reverence My sanctuary" [Lev. 19:30]. Now just as we are obligated to keep the Sabbath for all time to come, so must we reverence the Sanctuary for all time to come; for even though it is in ruins, its sanctity endures.

Maimonides, *Mishneh Torah*, quoted in Peters, *Jerusalem*

Ha-Tikva

As long as deep in the heart
The soul of a Jew yearns
And toward the East
An Eye looks to Zion.

Our hope is not yet lost
The hope of two thousand years
To be a free people in our land
The Land of Zion and Jerusalem

—Naftali Hertz Imber in N. R. Lichtenberg '95, Rumania 1978

HOLINESS OF JERUSALEM TO JEWS: TODAY
Retaking the Old City

Let me be perfectly candid. The thing I dread the most is that this city, so beautiful, so meaningful, so holy to millions of people, should ever be divided again; that barbed-wire fences, mine fields and concrete barriers should again sever its streets; that armed men again patrol a frontier through its heart. I fear the redivision of Jerusalem not only as the mayor of the city, as a Jew and as an Israeli, but as a human being who is deeply sensitive to its history and who cares profoundly about the well-being of its inhabitants.

Israeli paratrooper who helped conquer Jerusalem's old city in the Six Days War of 1967: In 1967, when attacked by the Jordanians, the Jews were willing to sacrifice their lives for Jerusalem. They would again. Some would give up. . . the Golan, the Sinai, the West Bank. But I do not think you will find any Israelis who are willing to give up Jerusalem. This beautiful golden city is the heart and soul of the Jewish people. You cannot live without a heart and soul. If you want one simple word to symbolize all of Jewish history, that word would be Jerusalem.

The words of one of the young soldiers who fought in the battle for Jerusalem: I think you have to make a distinction between the problem of Jerusalem and the rest of the territories we're talking about. As long as security problems dictate that we stay in the territories beyond our previous borders, then we have to say there. But the minute these problems are solved, then in my opinion we've no more right to stay there, at least as long as our only right is that of military success. And it's got nothing to do with who started the war, or the background against which it all began. But I wouldn't say the same about Jerusalem, because Jerusalem's got some far deeper meaning. It's something in our hearts, something to do with the way we feel. It was the source, the cornerstone of the whole Jewish people. Jerusalem really symbolizes our whole history, its a thread that goes right through the story of our people. It was always the focus. Jerusalem's not just an idea; it's a whole world that embraces everything . . . .

—Teddy Kollek, "Retaking the Old
City," in Idinopulos, *Jerusalem
Blessed, Jerusalem Cursed*

Ethical Will

Dvora Waysman is a distinguished writer in Israel who contributes articles and studies to the English-language Jewish press in many countries. She and her family were olim, *settlers in modern Israel. The problems of migrating to a new land are many and, with young children, intensified. In her ethical will, she speaks eloquently and poetically of her deep love for Israel and of her everlasting joy at her family's becoming part of the Land and its people.*

As I write this, I am sitting on my Jerusalem balcony, looking through a tracery of pine trees at the view along Rehov Ruppin. I can see the Knesset, the Israel Museum, and the Shrine of the Book—that architectural marvel resembling a woman's tilted breast, that houses the Dead Sea Scrolls.

I am at an age where I should write a will, but the disposition of my material possessions would take just a few lines. They do not amount to much. . . had we stayed in Australia where you—my four children—were born, they would be much more. I hope you won't blame me for this.

For now you are Israelis, and I have different things to leave you. I hope you will understand that they are more valuable than money in the bank, stocks and bonds, and plots of land, for no one can ever take them away from you.

I am leaving you the fragrance of a Jerusalem morning . . . unforgettable perfume of thyme, sage, and rosemary that wafts down from the Judean hills. The heartbreaking sunsets that give way to Jerusalem at night . . . splashes of gold on black velvet darkness. The feel of Jerusalem stone, ancient and mellow, in the buildings that surround you. The piquant taste of humas, tehina, felafel—foods we never knew about before we came here to live.

I am leaving you an extended family—the whole house of Israel. They are your people. They will celebrate with you in joy, grieve with you in sorrow. You will argue with them, criticize them, and sometimes reject them (that's the way it is with families!). But underneath you will be proud of them and love them. More important, when you need them—they will be there!

I am leaving you the faith of your forefathers. Here, no one will ever laugh at your beliefs, call you "Jew" as an insult. You, my sons, can wear *kippot* and *tzitzit* if you wish; you, my daughters, can modestly cover your hair after marriage if that is what you decide. No one will ridicule you. You can be as religious or as secular as you wish, knowing it is based on your own convictions, and not because of what the "goyim" might say. You have your heritage . . . written with the blood of your people through countless generations. Guard it well and cherish it—it is priceless!

I am leaving you pride. Hold your head high. This is your country, your birthright. Try to do your share to enhance its image. It may call for sacrifice, but it will be worth it. Your children, their children, and all who come after, will thank you for it.

I am leaving you memories. Some are sad . . . the early struggles to adapt to a new country, a new language, a new culture. But remember, too, the triumphs, the feeling of achievement when you were accepted, the "they" became "us." That is worth more than silver trophies and gold medals. You did it alone—you "made" it.

And so, my children, I have only one last bequest. I leave you my love and my blessing. I hope you will never again need to say: "Next year in Jerusalem." You are already there—how rich you are.

—Reiner & Stampfer, '94,
Wills from the Land of Israel

Riot Erupts in Old City

The peace of Christian Holy Week was shattered yesterday as police battled Palestinian youths near the Greek Orthodox Patriarchate in the Christian Quarter of Jerusalem's Old City. The clash followed Wednesday's occupation by 150 Jews of a building belonging to the patriarchate.

The settlers, who call themselves *Ne'ot David*, are affiliated with the Ateret Cohanim Yeshiva in the Moslem Quarter of the Old City. Greek Orthodox officials had described the entry as a violation of the status quo concerning church property.

In a frenzied spate of court appeals and counterappeals, the Jerusalem District Court ordered the settlers to leave the building, near the Church of the Holy Sepulchre, today. The settlers had originally been given four days' grace in order to appeal the decision, at the request of the patriarch, the delay was retracted and the settlers ordered out today. They are still certain to appeal, and the police have said they will not become involved until the appeal is heard.

Yesterday, which was Holy Thursday, Greek Orthodox Patriarch Diodoros I began the day by conducting the annual foot-washing ceremony, one of the focal rites in the Orthodox observances preceding the Easter on Sunday. He followed the ceremony, however, by leading a demonstration to the disputed building, in which Faisal Husseni, the leading PLO-affiliated personality in East Jerusalem, participated.

As police fought to separate demonstrators and settlers, some of the protesters lifted up a young monk, who removed a Star of David that had been affixed to the facade of the building. In the ensuing uproar, the police sprayed the crowd with tear gas, the patriarch fell, and the cross which tops his symbol of office was broken.

In the afternoon, as Christian and Moslem leaders called upon the patriarch to express their sympathy and support, dozens of Palestinian youths filled the anteroom, chanting slogans. Their enthusiasm reached a fever pitch when Sheikh Jamal of the Islamic High Council emerged with the patriarch.

As masked youths began waving PLO flags and the crowd began to chant anti-Jewish slogans, the patriarch quickly left the room and returned to his office. But he later emerged to tell the crowd: "The Jews have desecrated our holy day."

Soon youths began taking up positions on the roof, where they started hurling down rocks, tiles, and debris. Their action coincided with the arrival of Jerusalem Mayor Teddy Kollek, who had come to call upon the patriarch to express his sympathy.

Before he was able to call upon the patriarch, Kollek was forced to wait in the road for almost an hour while rocks rained down only metres from where he stood. Police and Border Police eventually gained control of the street, moving along rooftops and firing tear gas grenades.

When he entered the Patriarchate, the mayor was accompanied by scores of police and Border Police, who found some 40–50 youths barricaded in the patriarchs reception hall. Eventually, through Kolleks intervention, the patriarch prevailed upon the police to leave without confronting the youths.

Meanwhile, the settlers—25 couples and 100 children—seemed oblivious to the furor caused by their presence. They were setting furniture in place while the children scampered through the long hallways, stopping for spins on the occasionally available tricycles.

Ateret Cohanim spokesman Jonathan Blass, who was prepared with glossy literature on the settlement, was not concerned that the patriarchate might have a legal case against *Ne'ot David*. "A lot of money was invested in this project by careful investors. They checked things closely." Blass said the rumoured $5 million paid to Partyos Matossian, the former lessee, was as correct as "a ball-park figure."

"Matossian had to be compensated for his troubles," Blass said. "I'm not surprised he disappeared. In any case, the property is massive."

The settlers were visited by MKs Ariel Sharon and Tzahi Hanegbi (Likud), Geula Cohen (Tehiya), and Hanan Porat (National Religious Party.)

Sharon, who leases an apartment in the Moslem Quarter from Ateret Cohanim, said that settling in the Christian Quarter was no different from settling in the Moslem Quarter. "They're all Arabs," he said. Popular Front for the Liberation of Palestine head George Habash is a Christian.

"All the areas leased by Ateret Cohanim were owned by Jews," Sharon said. "MK Yehoshua Matza's grandfather lived in this very building." Settlers at the building claimed to have found a mezuza set in the wall in the 1920s.

Sharon added that he saw no problem with scheduling the move just before Easter. "Are Jews in this country part of an underground that they need permission to do things? The previous tenant left on Tuesday, and there was no point in leaving the building empty."

Porat agreed that the Easter holiday was not a consideration in making the move. "These [Greek Orthodox Christians] have not been averse to spreading the blood libel against Jews around this time of year," he said.

Citizens Rights Movement MK Yossi Sarid called on the government to evict the settlers immediately. He said the settlers intended upsetting Jerusalem's delicate balance.

A spokesman for Peace Now condemned the government for allowing the settlement. "It threatens Jerusalem's status, its standing and its unity," the spokesman said.

The Hadash Knesset faction has called for a special session of the Knesset to discuss the matter.

Oz Veshalom, the religious peace movement, said the settlement during Christian Holy Week showed a lack of sensitivity, and the need for neighbourly relations to maintain the peace of Jerusalem.

Police Chief Superintendent Ya'akov Tener implicitly criticized the settlement, saying that "the next four days are likely to be very tense in Jerusalem." He said this was to be expected "when 150 Jews settle among Christians" after purchasing property from someone "probably not authorized to sell. Things were quiet before, now problems have arisen."

Ateret Cohanim, which is primarily devoted to study and preparation for the Third Temple, has long been active in settling Jews in the Moslem Quarter.

Jerusalem police spokesman Uzi Sandori defended the police action in the Old City, saying the police had tried to contain the Palestinian rioters without using tear gas for an hour. "When they started throwing stones from rooftops, the force commander saw a need for tear gas."

He said that the patriarch "was not hurt" during the clashes and added that "the police are there to protect everyone, Christian and Jew alike."

—*Jerusalem Post*, April 11, 1990

The Voyage of the Children of Ethiopia to the Land of Israel and Jerusalem

This poem symbolizes the inspiration and hope Jerusalem represents for Jews in the diaspora.

From above the moon stands guard
He watches as we try so hard
To cross the endless desert. My mother's
Promise to my little brothers

Go! Let's go! It's not too late
We'll soon see Jerusalem
And pass through its gate!

The moon remains steadfast in the sky
The food is gone, the canteen dry
The desert with its frightening sounds . . .
My mother calms the little ones down:

Soon, very soon we will be redeemed
In the Land of Israel
Just as we dreamed.

With knives and with swords they attacked us at
  night
The moon was our witness, and saw the whole
  sight
So not it is I who calms the others
As did mom, I promise my brothers:

Come on! Let's go and in no time at all
We'll be in Jerusalem
We'll pray at the wall

In the moon the face of my mother is clear
Do not leave me now that the end is so near
I need you with me! It is only you
Who can make them believe that I am a Jew

In the moon the face of my mother is clear
Do not leave me now that the end is so near
I need you with me! It is only you
Who can make them believe that I am a Jew

Just a while longer, redemption is near
In the Land of Israel
We hold so dear

Soon, very soon

Look up: I see the light
There is Jerusalem! O what a sight!

—S. Grunich in Rachel Nr
Lichtenberg, ed. *Jerusalem*, New
York: JAJZE, 1995

THREE HOLY SITES:

The Western Wall

With the fall of Jerusalem in 70 C.E., the Temple was destroyed by fire and subsequently a pagan shrine was built there. For a certain period Jews were denied access to the area around the Temple and even to the city of Jerusalem. The Jews, mourning for their national loss and praying for the restoration of former times, were wont to gather on the Mount of Olives from which they could look down on the holy site. From about the beginning of the 16th century, the Western Wall became the focal point for Jewish prayer. According to one tradition, the wall had been buried under mountains of dung and garbage until the reign of the Sultan Selim I or his son, Suleiman the Magnificent, who built the walls of Jerusalem in the 16th century. Selim (or Suleiman), so the legend goes, did not know the site of the Temple and set his servants the task of discovering it. When nearly at the point of despair the overseer of the search met a woman carrying a container of dung. He asked her where she was taking it and she answered "to a certain place."

"Where are you from?"

"From Bethlehem."

"Are there no dung heaps there that you come all this way?"

"We have a tradition that it is very meritorious act to bring dung to this place."

The sultan ordered that site excavated and discovered the Western Wall. He had it washed with rose water and also gave the Jews permission to pray there.

Towards the end of the 12th century, the area in which the Wall is located became the property of the Waqf, the Moslem religious charitable organization and at the beginning of the 14th century the Mograbi Quarter, occupied by Arabs from North Africa (the Magreb), was erected facing the Wall. In the 19th century many unsuccessful efforts were made by Jews to buy the Wall and the surrounding area. Perhaps the most interesting was that of Baron Edmond de Rothschild who, in 1887, offered to buy the whole Mograbi Quarter from the Waqf who would build another quarter for its inhabitants. The negotiations reached a very advanced stage but broke down for reasons which are still unclear. It seems that the rabbinical authorities of Jerusalem in addition to various Moslem elements, objected to the project.

Sir Moses Montefiore, the Anglo-Jewish philanthropist who did so much for Jerusalem, tried to get permission from the Moslem authorities to put furniture at the wall to help people who came to pray and erect a canopy to protect them from the rain. He finally succeeded and also got permission to pave the narrow area in front of the Wall and to build the Wall a little higher to prevent garbage from being thrown over it from the other side. In the 20th century the Anglo-Palestine Bank also tried to buy the Wall but negotiations came to nothing because of the outbreak of World War I.

Throughout the ages, the Moslem religion had shown no interest in the Wall, which was devoid of any religious significance as far as they were concerned. However, after the Balfour Declaration, which encouraged Jewish hopes of a national homeland, the Wall became a focus of nationalist aspirations, in addition to its religious function. The Moslem religious authorities then claimed that it had religious significance in Islam since it was by the place where the prophet Muhammed tethered his horse, Al Buraq, when he made his miraculous journey to Jerusalem. The area in front of the Wall was therefore called Al Buraq Street and a plaque fixed onto the Wall with that name on it.

The question of Jewish prayer at the Wall then became one of great importance. The Arabs did all they could to prevent it and even opened up the area to through traffic so that the camels and donkeys would disturb the Jews. An international committee of inquiry was set up by the British Mandate authorities and its conclusions were that the Wall belonged to the Moslems but that the Jews had the right to worship there and to place chairs for that purpose in the street. The committee forbade Jews to sound the *shofar* at the Wall. This last clause was the cause of many disturbances because the Jews refused to accept it and every year, at the close of the Yom Kippur services a *shofar* would be smuggled into the area and sounded accompanied by frantic searches on the part of the British police.

In 1947, when relations between the Jews and Arabs of Jerusalem deteriorated, the former were unable to approach the Wall for fear of their lives. The Armistice Agreement between Jordan and Israel guaranteed the right of access to the Wall but the Jordanians never honored their commitment and until Jerusalem was liberated in 1967, no Jews could visit the Wall. Immediately after the 1967 Six Day War, the whole Mograbi Quarter, which consisted of ruined hovels, was demolished and a huge square was created in front of the Wall. The military authorities of Israel opened the area to the public and on Shavuot, 1967, it is estimated that 250,000 Jews came there to pray.

The Wall itself is an interesting structure. It is basically a wall supporting the western side of the Temple Mount and as such it was approximately 500 meters long. However, most of the Wall's length is hidden by buildings which have been erected against it and only some 28 meters were visible and constituted the Western Wall until 1967. The Wall was 18 meters high on the western side and six meters high on the east side, i.e., on the Temple Mount. the lowest five rows of stone date from the Second Temple times are dressed in the typical Herodian style; a depressed border runs along all four edges, that of the upper side being slightly wider than the other three. Some of these stones are immense, as much as 12 meters long and one meter high, and weigh over 100 tons. On top of these five rows are four rows of smaller stones dating from the Roman period and on top of these, rows of still smaller stones from the Arab period (after the 7th century). The top rows of the stones were added by the efforts of Sir Moses Montefiore in the 19th century. The rows of the large stones are set each a little further back than the one below so that the Wall actually leans to the east; this, together with the accurate cutting, gave it amazing stability and it survived the many earthquakes that have struck Jerusalem in the two thousand years since the Wall was constructed. Until 1967, a narrow alley approximately three meters wide ran along the length of the Wall and there the Jews conducted their prayers.

The Wall and its immediate adjacent area was examined from an archaeological point of view several times in the 19th century. In 1867 a British archaeologist sunk a shaft and discovered that below the ground there were another 19 layers of huge stones and it can be assumed that the lower of these date from the time of Solomon's Temple. What is today a flat area, was originally a valley which has been filled with rubble from collapsed buildings throughout the ages. When Israel cleared the area in front of the Wall, it also excavated two of these covered rows of stone and so the visible Wall is now two meters higher than it was. The whole Wall—covered and uncovered—is some 37 meters high; it must have been an awe inspiring sight.

The large paved open area in front of the Wall is divided into two sections: a lower level adjacent to the actual Wall for prayer and a raised level for tourists and sight-seers. A further section of the Wall, to the north, has also been uncovered behind the buildings and prayer services take place there too. That area provides protection against the inclemencies of the weather. To the south, the entire south-western corner has been excavated together with a section of the southern Wall and a road from Herodian times. The excavations were conducted by an Israeli team of archaeologists helped by volunteers from abroad. These excavations have added a great deal to our knowledge of the area and the plan of ancient Jerusalem.

In 1838, very distinct stones were discovered high up on the Western Wall towards its southern end. It was assumed that these stones were the anchor stones of an arch or bridge which spanned the valley and led from the upper city, where the king's palace was, directly into the Temple courtyard. It was named Robinson's Arch after its discoverer. The Israeli excavations revealed that there was no arch or bridge at all and that these special stones were the anchor stones of a gigantic monumental staircase leading up from the valley into the Temple. The remains of the foot of the staircase where discovered together with the remains of shops that operated there.

The Western Wall occupies an exceedingly important place in Jewish religious folklore. According to the *midrash*, the Western Wall survived the destruction of the Temple because it was built by the poor people who really sacrificed to make their contribution. The rabbis taught that the *Shekhinah*, the Divine Presence, is in the west and thus the belief developed that God's presence hovers over the Wall. In folk consciousness this further developed into a belief that at night a white dove, symbolizing the Congregation of Israel, appears at the Wall and sadly weeps for the destruction of the Temple and the exile of Israel. In the cracks between the stones, high up on the Wall, there is a certain amount of foliage and small white birds nest there.

It is a very common custom to insert scraps of paper in the cracks with prayers or requests written on them. Some of the very pious, however, refrain from touching the actual stones because of their sanctity and content themselves with standing before them. There was an old custom for people to drive nails into the cracks; it was believed that the nail would protect the one who knocked it in and particularly that a Jerusalemite who had to make a journey out of the city would be assured of a safe return if he drove a nail into the Wall. Happily, that custom has ceased. Another custom was for supplicants to impress their hand-prints in blue dye on the stones. The idea seems to have been to leave a "part of themselves" so that the Wall would not forget them.

Thousands visit the Wall for private prayer and there are also prayer services in process for most of the hours of the day. On Tish Be-Av, the fast day commemorating the destruction of the Temple, the Wall is naturally the center of prayer in Jerusalem as it is on the happier day, the 28th day of Iyar, the anniversary of the liberation of Jerusalem. The Wall also performs the function of a national gathering place and many official events take place there such as the main service on the memorial day for those who have fallen in Israel's wars. The Old City of Jerusalem was liberated by the Paratroop Division and the swearing-in ceremony of recruits to that unit is often held at the Wall.

There can be no doubt that the Western Wall, or the *Kotel*, as it is fondly known in Hebrew, is the most powerful symbol in the State of Israel. It symbolizes religious yearning and national aspirations; it is the last vestige of the ancient Temple of a people that has suffered so much, pointing to a better and more holy future. For Jews, the Wall seems to be alive and indeed it is hard to find a better description than that of Rabbi Abraham Isaac Kook, the late Chief Rabbi of the Holy Land, who wrote: "There are men with hearts of stone and stones with hearts of flesh." He was referring to the Western Wall, the Kotel Ha-Ma'aravi.

—Haliv, Ben Avraham, *A Modern Guide to the Jewish Holy Places*

Plan of the Temple Mount During the Second Temple Period

Plan of the Temple Mount during the Second Temple period in which an attempt has been made to assemble all existing data about the Temple

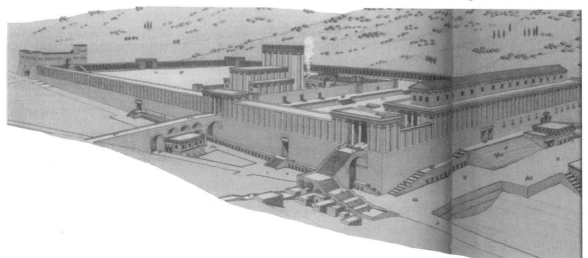

Figure G. Plan of the Temple Mount During the Second Temple Period

Mount from historical sources, from archaeological remains, and through comparison of buildings on the Temple Mount with similar structures in countries in the region.

In the center is the Temple, with its courtyards and buildings. The Temple is divided into two parts—in the eastern part is the women's section with its four chambers, and in the middle of the western part is the sanctuary (Hekhal), in front of which was the altar. The area around the Temple Mount is apparently the Hasmonean boundary, to which the laws of uncleanliness and purity related. For this reason, it was separated by a low wall upon which were stone inscriptions warning that this was the entrance to a holy place. Herod extended the Temple Mount area beyond the Hasmonean structure, and built four porticoes around the new courtyard, thereby creating a structure of three porticoes and the southern portico which was of particular interest. It was here that Herod built the Royal Portico, a structure of the type that existed in other temples of that period. It is thought that it was in these three porticoes and the Royal Portico that visitors to the city during the pilgrimage festivals passed their time. The illustration reveals the reason that the eastern portico, called Solomons Portico, was the earliest to be built. It was not constructed on the area added by Herod, but was erected earlier on the Hasmonean Temple Mount and later adapted to the Herodian structure.

Below the Royal Portico, underground passages can be seen, leading from the street south of the portico to the Temple Mount. To the west of the mount were two similar underground passages connecting the Temple Mount with the Upper City. There, too, two more passageways ran above the bridges between these two areas. One was the bridge above Wilson's Arch, over which ran the aqueducts bringing water from Solomon's Pools to the Temple. The second passageway ran above Robinson's Arch, and from there to the imposing steps that descended from the Royal Portico to the street. Further on was a stairway which led to the Upper City itself. In addition there was a passage to the east, in the vicinity of the southeastern corner of the mount, evidence of whose existence is provided by the stones of the archway within the eastern wall, near the "seam." A further passageway existed in the north, leading to the Antonia

fortress. Between the Antonia and the Temple Mount was a gate, but no remains of it have been found in the Temple Mount area.

The plan shows the network of streets outside the Temple Mount, whose existence has been proven by archaeological excavations. A beautiful paved street has been uncovered, running along the length of the western Temple Mount wall, and recently sections of it were found in the northwestern section of the mount. Its breadth was not uniform throughout, since a square was built (for architectural purposes) in front of each underground gate. A street ran along the Tyropoeon Valley to the present-day Damascus Gate in the north and to the Siloam Pool area in the south. From this network of streets, other streets ran to the west. One street branched off from the main street in an easterly direction, ran along the southern wall of the Temple Mount, and at certain places steps were built, as dictated by the topography of that particular section of the hill. Two sets of stairs led to this street from the City of David in the south and then to the Temple Mount through the Double and Triple Gates.

In the vicinity of the western street, a Hasmonean period structure was discovered by Charles Warren, who called it the Hall of the Freemasons. It would seem that this was an important public building. Another building was found north of Robinson's Arch facing the paved road adjacent to the western wall of the Temple Mount.

In the tractate of Middot of the Mishnah, it is stated that the early Temple Mount (from the Hasmonean period) had five gates: the two Huldah Gates in the south, Kiponus' Gate in the west, the Tadi Gate in the north, and the Shushan Gate in the east. In the course of extending the Temple Mount, Herod erected two gates in the south, four in the west, and an unknown number in the north. In the eastern side, in the area where Herod did not make any changes, apparently only one gate was left. The diagram points up the relationship between the proportions of the Temple and the entire Temple Mount, and for this reason the Temple has not accurate in detail.

The term **"seam"** is used to describe a point in the eastern Temple Mount wall, 1,205 feet (32 m) north of the southwest corner of the city wall, where two styles of dressed stones are evident.

These are clearly visible in the photograph. To the north (right) of this line is the Temple Mount wall, built from coarse, marginally dressed stones, and to the south (left) are finely hewn stones, with raised smooth faces, and delicate margins along the edges.

Scholars are of the opinion that the northern part of this section of the wall is the eastern side of the southeastern corner of the Temple Mount wall from the Hasmonean period. Another assumption is that these are the remains of the Acra fortress from the Hellenistic period. The style in which the stones were cut on the section south of the "seam," and the style of building in this section, are characteristic of the Herodian period. It is now generally accepted that this section of the wall is an extension of the Temple Mount wall built by Herod when he extended the area of the Hasmonean Temple Mount toward the north, west, and south. This has strengthened the conclusion that the section north of the "seam" is part of the Hasmonean Temple Mount wall. This assumption is based on the fact that the stone (blank) and the construction at this part were done in a style similar to that of third- and second-century buildings found on other sites in Mediterranean countries. In the area south of the "seam," projections (about 40 square cm) remaining in the wall can be discerned. These stones were used to carry the large stones to their destination, but once the building operation was completed, these stones were not cut as was customarily done. Also visible is part of a large archway, which is evidence of the existence of a bridge which served as a passageway for persons leaving through the two gates situated above the archway. On the lower courses of this section of the wall, lying on bedrock, remains of inscriptions in ancient Hebrew were found by Warren, who sunk one of his shafts at this point. In these inscriptions, the letter *kof* recurs. This may indicate the use of the word *kodesh* (holy) by the builders of this colossal wall.

Scholars are convinced that the existence of the Second Temple tombs in the Church of the Holy Sepulchre upholds the theory that in the first century CE the church area lay outside the city walls and served as a burial ground. Thus it cannot be presumed that it came within the area of the Second Wall, which served as the city wall in the time of Jesus.

The Third Wall is described in detail by Josephus (*Wars 5,4,2*). According to his account, it was Agrippa I who planned it and began its construction, but was forced to cease building at the order of the Romans. It was completed by the Zealots in 41–44 and again in 67–69, prior to the siege of Jerusalem.

The wall ran from the Hippicus Tower to Psephinus' Tower in the west of the city, passed opposite the Tomb of Queen Helene and the Royal Cave, bypassed the Fuller's Monument, touched the Old Wall of the Temple Mount and descended to the Kidron Valley. We still do not know how and where it linked up with the ancient walls, since its eastern and western sections have still not been found, despite the numerous excavations carried out along the course it was presumed to have followed. Perhaps the great dam built by Herod to block up the Beth Zetha Valley, thus creating the Pool of Israel just north of the Temple Mount, served as the base for the Third Wall at the connecting point with the Temple Mount wall.

Remnants of the northern section of the Third Wall have been preserved to this day. Already in the nineteenth century remains have been found in the north of the city (to the east and the west of the American Consulate in the eastern city). The sections found were about 2,950 feet (900 meters) long, and ran in an east-west direction. From the numerous archaeological finds made along the length of the wall between 1925 and 1974 (especially by E.L. Sukenik and L.A. Mayer), it has become apparent that these are sections of the wall demolished at the time of the destruction of Jerusalem in 70 CE.

In the area between the present-day Old City wall and the Third Wall, hardly any remains of Second Temple period buildings have been found. This fact shows that little construction work was carried out in the new section of the city (the Bezetha quarter, or the New City as Josephus called it), about the time of the destruction of Jerusalem.

The Temple and the Temple Mount were the focal point of religious, spiritual, and political life during the Second Temple period. The archaeological data reveal a most impressive picture of the development of the Temple Mount in this period, which reached its climax during Herod.

Jerusalem of Light

The topography of the Temple Mount was changed radically by Herod. He quarried into and leveled the hill northwest of the mount, and thus expanded the Temple compound and its sanctified area. He built a broad platform encompassing the mount—to the north, south, and west—upon which the portico was later erected. It would seem that from the outset of the Temple Mount was built more or less in the form of a square, and according to the Mishnah its dimensions were 500 x 500 cubits (approximately 820 x 820 feet [250 x 250 meters]). The traditionally accepted description of the shape and size of the Temple Mount is quite ancient, possibly from the Persian period, and the Book of Ezekiel describes it as being square (45:2). The key to understanding the changes that were brought about lies in the "seam" in the eastern wall (105 feet [32 meters] north of the southeastern corner of the Temple Mount). As mentioned earlier, the two styles of construction merged at this juncture. The northern section was typical of the style found in other Hellenistic sites; the style of the southern section was typically Herodian. It may well be that the "seam" was the pint where the Hasmonean structure merged with Herods expansion. However, this explanation is not accepted by many scholars, and there are those who believe that the seam was the meeting point between the Acra—the fortress built by the Seleucids in Jerusalem—and the expansion carried out during Herods rule.

—Bahat, Dan, *The Illustrated Atlas of Jerusalem*

Wedge Me Into the Fissure

Wedge me into the fissure with each fallen stone
Hammer me till I grow strong.
Perhaps I shall appease my land and atone
For the peoples sin: the ruins unmended so long.
To be one of the stones of my city is all my desire.
Were my bones knitted in the wall, how glad I would be.
Is my body less than my soul, that through water and fire
Stayed by the people, who shrieked or went silently?
With the stones of Jerusalem wedge me into the wall.

Clothe me in mortar, and from
The very depths of the stones my bones shall call
Till the Messiah come.

—Yehuda Karni in Jagodnik '85

A Visit to the Western Wall

I had entered the Old City of Jerusalem through the Jaffa gate. Immediately, I was confronted by a noisy, bustling market place. Ahead of me was David Street, which I knew led somewhere toward The Wall, my ultimate goal. It is called simply The Wall, Ha-Kotel, no longer The Wailing Wall, perhaps reflecting a change in the outlook of the Jewish people to whom it has been a holy site for over a thousand years. It is the western supporting wall, the only structure remaining that indicates the location of Solomon's Temple and the Second Temple destroyed by the Romans in 70 C.E.

All along the narrow, crowded street leading toward the Wall were a multitude of niches containing wares of all varieties. There were old men sitting on stone steps along the shaded passageway, which was actually the walls of homes and shops. Dark-eyed children played in the street, darting agilely in and out of the crowds. As I walked down the street it became narrower and darker. Where there had been sky above me there were now arched ceilings covering the passage almost completely. A small sign instructed me to turn to the right to reach the Wall.

I was aware of a sense of light and openness as I emerged from the dim passage. For an unexplained reason, I did not want to look at the Wall before I passed through a security checkpoint where my purse and camera were inspected carefully. Having moved beyond the guards I walked to the side out of the way of others filing in. I raised my eyes and found before me a high golden rough stone wall at the far edge of a still plaza. A sharp contrast to what I would witness a few hours later, when people gathered at the wall to welcome the Shabbat, my first encounter with the Wall was a silent one. There were a handful of people walking quietly to and fro. Two men in traditional Hasidic garb were davening.

Before me was a tall mass of very old stones. Jews don't believe stones are holy, I told myself: "Things" are not holy. Besides, this was not even a part of the Temple. It was just a wall built around it. And it wasn't even built by Solomon. It was built much later. I am not any closer to God here than I am anywhere else in the world. He can be experienced everywhere, so what's so special about this spot? I've seen bigger walls, more beautiful walls, walls in more aesthetic settings. I've visited sites that were ostensibly more religious.

Still, I can remember the statement from some philosopher I studied in college, "The heart has reasons the mind cannot know."

I walked slowly across the plaza and sat down on an embankment. I was filled with gratitude and joy at being near the Wall. I remembered the feeling of frustration ten years before in 1964, standing on a hillside outside of Jerusalem, gazing at the Old City Jews could not enter. Someone pointed to the location where the Wall was supposed to be, and I wasn't even sure if I was looking at the right spot. I remembered the generations of my ancestors who prayed facing East, toward the Wall, and asked God each day to permit them to come to Jerusalem to stand where I was. I remember Jews through the ages who intoned the desire at every Pesah seder, L'shana ha-ba'a b'Yirushalayim, and whose last request before their death was to be buried in the soil of the land they could not reach in their lifetime.

I thought too of those Jews today who want to come to this site and who cannot; but even more, my thoughts dwelled on those who do not want to come, who will not allow themselves the opportunity to feel the identity, the affinity, the joy I was experiencing.

I left reluctantly, having forgotten to take a photograph but knowing I would never forget this meeting. I left the Old City by way of a gate other than the one by which I had entered.

The Jewish Sentinel, "Joys of Judaism," Betsy Dolgin Katz

The Paratroopers' Cry

This Wall has heard many prayers
This Wall has seen the fall of many other Walls
This Wall has felt the touch of mourning women
This Wall has felt petitions lodged between its stones
This Wall saw Rabbi Yehuda Halevi trampled before it

This Wall has seen Caesars rise and fall
But this Wall has never seen paratroopers cry.
This Wall saw them tired and wrung out
This Wall saw them wounded , infiltrated
Running to it with excitement, cried and silence
And creeping as torn creatures in the alleys of the Old City
As they are covered with dust and with parched lips
They whisper "If I forget thee, if I forget thee Jerusalem"
They are swift as eagles and strong as lions.
And their tanks—the fiery chariots of Elijah the Prophet
They pass by with noise
They pass by as a stream
They remember the two thousand awful years
In which we had not even a Wall to place our tears before
And here they stand before it and breathe in dust
Here they look at it with sweet pain
And tears run down and they look at one another perplexed.
How does it happen that paratroopers cry?
How does it happen that they touch this wall with great emotion?
How does it happen that their weeping changes to song?
Perhaps because these boys of nineteen born at the same time as the state
Perhaps because these boys of nineteen carry on their shoulders two thousand years.

—Haim Hefer, translated by Michael Graetz

Prayers to Be Said at the Wall

During the eleventh century a prayer was composed to be recited when visiting the Western Wall:

We thank You, Adonai our God and God of our ancestors who has kept us alive and granted us the privilege of coming to Your chosen sanctuary which You selected above all of Jacob's settlements for Your abiding affection, both while it was standing and now that it is in ruins. As we have been allowed to see it in ruins, so may we be deemed worthy to admire it after its restitution, when all of Israel's exiles will be gathered therein . . . . May it be Your will, Adonai our God and God of our ancestors, to take pity on its ruins, having compassion on its woe, clear away its dust, purify it from defilement, restore and rebuild its desolate breeches, and return us to this glorious sacred site so that we may dwell there as in ancient days according to the verse, "Therefore thus says Adonai: I return to Jerusalem with compassion: My house shall be built in it, says Adonai . . . " (Zechariah 1:16).

Another section from the same prayer of thanksgiving to be offered at the Western Wall reads as follows:

I thank You, my God, for having sustained me and granted me life and strength to arrive here and behold the site of Your holy Temple for whose restoration all the people of Israel pray, that they may rest in its shade and lie in its dust. I, a servant son of your maidservant, have been privileged to see what I yearned for, and adore the object of my prayers, namely, to stand in front of your holy Temple. Although it lies in ruins, Your holiness pervades it. The nations may have defiled it, but it remains chaste by virtue of Your presence and Your promise: although You deny it to us now, You have sworn to return us to it and rebuild it.

May it be our will, Adonai, our God, and God of our ancestors, that You select me among those chosen to behold the fulfillment of your promises.

—Avraham Holtz, *The Holy City*

DOME OF THE ROCK AND AL AKSA

To the Muslims Jerusalem is known as 'Al Quds, "the Holy." Quite apart from its associations with the Old Testament figures, Abraham, David, Solomon and others whom they venerate, the Muslims cherish a strong traditional connection between Jerusalem and the Prophet Muhammad. The tradition of the Prophets Night Journey is alluded to in the Quran thus: 'I declare the glory of Him who transported His servant by night from the Masjid al-Haram (the mosque at Mecca) to the Masjid al-Aqsa (the further mosque) at Jerusalem.' Here is meant the whole area of 'the Noble Sanctuary,' not just the main building of the Aqsa, which, in the Prophet's days, did not exist.

According to the received account, Muhammad was on this occasion mounted on the winged steed called Al-Burak—'the Lightning'—and, with the Angel Gabriel for escort, was carried from Mecca, first to Sinai and then to Bethlehem, after which they came to Jerusalem. 'And when we reached Bait al-Makdis, the Holy City,' so runs the tradition mentioned in the Chronicle of Ibu Al-Attir, 'we came to the gate of the mosque and here Jibrail caused me to dismount. And he tied up Al-Burak to a ring, to which the prophets of old had also tied their steeds.'

Entering the Haram Area by the gateway, afterwards known as the Gate of the Prophet, Muhammad and Gabriel went up to the Sacred Rock, which from ancient times had stood in the center of Solomon's Temple; meeting there a group of prophets, Muhammad proceeded to perform his prayer-prostrations before this assembly of his predecessors—Abraham, Moses, Jesus, and other of God's apostles. From the Sacred Rock, Muhammad, accompanied by Gabriel, next ascended by a ladder of light up into heaven; here, in anticipation, he was vouchsafed a vision of the delights of Paradise. Passing through the seven heavens, Muhammad at last stood in the presence of Allah, from whom he received injunctions on the prayers his followers were to perform. Thence, after a while, he descended again to earth; and alighting from the ladder of light stood again on the Sacred Rock at Jerusalem. The return homeward was made after the same fashion—on the back of the steed Al-Burak—and the Prophet reached Mecca again before the night had waned. Such is the tradition which sanctifies Jerusalem, the Rock and the Haram, or Sanctuary area, in the sight of all Muslims. After the capitulation of Jerusalem to Omar in 635, that khalif caused a mosque to be built on what was considered to be the ancient site of the Temple of David.

In the early days of Islam—that is, under Omar and his successors—mosques were constructed of wood and sun-dried bricks and other such perishable materials, so that of the building erected on Omars days, probably very little remained even half a century later to be incorporated into the magnificent stone mosque erected by the orders of the Omayyad khalif, 'Abd al-Malik, in about the year 690. It seems probable, also, that this latter khalif, when he began to rebuild the Aqsa, made use of the materials which lay to hand in the ruins of the great St. Mary's Church of Justinian, which must originally have stood on approximately the same site on which the Aqsa Mosque was raised.

The Chronicles make no mention of the date or fact of 'Abd al-Maliks rebuilding of the Aqsa Mosque, and the earliest detailed description of this mosque is that given by Muqaddasi in 985, some three centuries after 'Abd al-Malik's days. Of the Dome of the Rock, on the other hand, we possess detailed accounts in the older authorities, describing both the foundation in 691 and its general appearance. It would appear that the Arab chroniclers and the travelers who visited the Haram Area during this period were more impressed by the magnificence of the Dome of the Rock than by the main buildings of the Aqsa Mosque, of which the Dome of the Rock was in fact but an adjunct.

When referring to the Arab descriptions of the Haram Area at Jerusalem, an important point to remember is that the term *Masjid* applies not to the Aqsa alone but to the whole of the Haram Area, with the Dome of the Rock in the middle and all the other minor domes, chapels, and colonnades. The Dome of the Rock (misnamed by the Franks the 'Mosque of Omar'), is not itself a mosque or place for public prayer, but merely the largest of the many cupolas in the Court of the Mosque, in this instance built to cover and do honor to the Holy Rock which lies beneath it.

The main building of the Aqsa Mosque has six doors. The door opposite to the Mihrab is called the Great Brazen Gate; it is plated with brass gilt, and is so heavy that only a man strong of shoulders and of arm can turn it on its hinges. To the right of this [Great Gate] are seven large doors, the midmost covered with gilt plates; and after the same manner there are seven doors to the left. And further, on the eastern side [of the Aqsa] are eleven doors unornamented. Over the first-mentioned doors, fifteen in number, is a colonnade supported on marble pillars, lately erected by 'Abd Allah ibn Tahir.

On the right-hand side of the court [that is, along the west wall of the Haram Area] are colonnades supported by marble pillars and pilasters; and on the back [or north wall of the Haram Area] are colonnades vaulted in stone. The center part of the main building [of the Aqsa] is covered by a mighty roof, high-pitched and gable-wise, over which rises a magnificent dome.

On 14 July 1099, the Crusaders, under Godfrey de Bouillon, captured the Holy City. The Haram Area was given over to the Knights of the recently established Order of the Temple, who derived their name from the Dome of the Rock, which the Crusaders imagined to be the Temple of the days of Christ and named *Templum Domini*. The Aqsa Mosque, on the other hand, was known as the *Palatium* or *Templum Solomonis*. The Templars made considerable alterations to the Aqsa Mosque and the adjoining portions of the Haram Area, but left the Dome of the Rock untouched. On the west of the Aqsa, along the south wall of the Haram Area, they built their armory. In the substructures of the south-east angle of the Haram Area, to the west of the Cradle of Jesus, they stabled their horses, using probably either the ancient 'Triple Gate' or the 'Single Gate' as an exit from these vaults. The Latins considered the Aqsa Mosque to hold a very secondary place (while the Dome of the Rock was in their eyes the true *Templum Domini*); hence the Knights Templars felt no compunction in remodeling probably the whole building, when they turned part of the Aqsa into a church for the Order and established their main guard and armory in the outlying quarters of this great Mosque.

After Saladin's reconquest of the Holy City in 1187, the whole of the Haram Area and its various buildings underwent a complete restoration.

Over the Great Mihrah, in the Aqsa Mosque, may still be read the inscription set here by Saladin after this restoration was completed:

In the name of Allah the Compassionate, the Merciful! Hath ordered the repair of this holy Mihrab, and the restoration of the Aqsa Mosque—which was founded in piety—the servant of Allah, and His regent, Yusuf ibn

Ayyub Abu-1 Mudhaffer, the victorious king, Salah ad-Dunya wa'ad-Din [Saladin], after that Allah had conquered [the City] by his hand during the month of the year 583. And he asked of Allah to inspire him with thankfulness for this favour, and to make him a partaker of the remission [of sins], through His mercy and forgiveness.

The Mosque we see today was entirely renovated between 1938 and 1943. During this period all the long walls and arcades were demolished to the foundations, with the exception of the two western aisles and the arcades flanking the dome. The nave and eastern aisles were reconstructed on arches carried by monolithic marble columns. The upper part of the north wall was also reconstructed and the whole refaced. The central doors and porch were also repaired. The work was supervised by the Director of the Department for the Preservation of Arab Monuments, in the Egyptian Government, which presented the magnificent gilded ceiling. At the southern end of the Mosque are the only surviving Fatimid mosaics and construction in Jerusalem; here is also a fine rose-window and mihrab in the place of the Forty Martyrs, and a very beautiful pulpit and mihrab installed by order of Saladin. Perhaps the most impressive sight of all, however, that of some four thousand men, line after line in perfect order and action, covering every square meter of carpet in this vast mosque—the brotherhood of Islam at worship.

In remarkable contrast with the little that is known of the early architectural history of the Aqsa Mosque, is the very full account of the date and the historical incidents connected with the foundation of the Dome of the Sacred Rock. From the earliest times, also, there are extant such detailed descriptions of this beautiful building that it may be affirmed with almost complete certainty that the edifice as it now stands is (with regard to ground-plan and elevation) substantially identical with that which the Khalif 'Abd al-Malik erected in the year 691. The cupola, it is true, has on many occasions been shattered by earthquakes, and the walls have been damaged and repaired, but the octagonal ground-plan and the system or concentric colonnades have remained unaltered through all the restorations; even down to the number of windows, the Dome of the Rock, as described in 903 by Ibn al-Fakih, is almost exactly similar to the Dome of the Rock of the present day.

The Dome of the Rock for Muslims ranks in sanctity only after the Ka'ba in Mecca, according to Muslim tradition erected by Abraham and Ishmael, and the Tomb of the Prophet in Medina. This Rock on Mount Moriah was already held sacred, even before the Dome was built upon it, as the site of Abrahams offering of Isaac, and also as the ancient 'Qibla' of Moses, for Muslims hold that the Ark of the Covenant was placed on this Rock. As the direction of prayer of Moses, it was adopted as the first 'Qibla' of Islam. It was also the very spot from which Muhammad made his famous Night-Journey to heaven. It was, however, a political situation nearly a century later that resulted in the erection of a sanctuary on this site and in its becoming a place of pilgrimage.

Professor E. H. Palmer gives us the condition of the Omayyad khalifate at the period when the Dome of the Rock was built:

In AD 684, in the reign of 'Abd al-Malik, the ninth successor of Muhammad, and the fifth khalif of the house of Omayyad, events happened which once more turned peoples attention to the City of David. For eight years the Muslim Empire had been distracted by factions and party quarrels. The inhabitants of the two Holy Citys, Mecca and Medina, had risen against the authority of the legitimate khalifs, and had proclaimed 'Abd Allah ibn Zubayr their spiritual and temporal head. The Khalif Yazid abd M'awiyah had in vain attempted to suppress the insurrection; the usurper had contrived to make his authority acknowledged throughout Arabia and the African provinces, and had established the seat of his government at Mecca itself. 'Abd al-Malik trembled for his own rule; year after year crowds of pilgrims would visit the Ka'ba, and Ibn Zubair's religious and political influence would thus become disseminated throughout the whole of Islam. In order to avoid these consequences, and at the same time to weaken his rival's prestige, 'Abd al-Malik conceived the plan of diverting mens minds from the pilgrimage to Mecca, and inducing them to make the pilgrimage to Jerusalem instead.

The history of this political move, which was doomed to failure, is told by Ya'qubi, one of the earliest (AD 874) Arabic historians:

Then 'Abd al-Malik forbade the people of Syria to make the pilgrimage [to Mecca]; and this by reason that 'Abd Allah ibn azZubayr was wont to seize on them during the time of the pilgrimage, and force them to pay him allegiance—which, 'Abd al-Malik having knowledge of, forbade the people to journey forth to Mecca. But the people murmured thereat, saying, "How dost thou forbid us to make the pilgrimage to Allahs house, seeing that the same is a commandment of Allah upon us?" but the khalif answered them, "Hath not Ibn Shihab az-Zuhri told you how the Apostle of Allah did say: *Men shall journey to but three Masjids, Al-Masjid Haram [at Mecca], my Masjid [at Medina], and the Masjid of the Holy City [which is Jerusalem]?* So this last is now appointed for you in lieu of the Masjid as-Haram. And this Rock, of which it is reported that upon it the Apostle of Allah set his foot when he ascended into Heaven, shall be unto you in the place of the Ka'ba." Then 'Abd al-Malik built above the Sakhra a Dome, and hung it around with curtains of brocade, and he instituted door-keepers for the same, and the people took the custom of circumambulating the Rock, even as they had paced round the Ka'ba, and the usage continued thus all the days of the dynasty of the Omayyads.

Had 'Abd al-Malik's attempt succeeded, it is a question whether Jerusalem might not then have become the capital of the Omayyads, in place of Damascus. As events turned out, the khalif failed to divert the Muslim pilgrimage to the Holy City of Palestine, and Mecca did not lose its preeminence as the religious center of Islam.

That the Khalif 'Abd al-Malik was the builder of the Dome of the Rock is further confirmed by the well-known inscription which may still be read above the cornice of the octagonal colonnade supporting the cupola. Running round this is a magnificent Cufic script, in yellow on blue tiles, which

must have been placed here by 'Abd al-Malik when the building was finally completed. It is dated 691.

One of the early accounts shows the setting of the Dome of the Rock within the Haram or Sanctuary Area. In the 978 Ibn Haukal abd Istakhti writes:

The Holy City is nearly as large as Ar Ramlah [the capital of the province of Filastin]. It is a city perched high on the hills, and you have to go up to it from all sides. There is here a mosque, a greater than which does not exist in all of Islam. The Main-building [which is the Aqsa Mosque] occupies the south-eastern angle of the mosque [Area, or Noble Sanctuary], and covers about half the breadth of the same. The remainder of the Haram Area is left free, and is nowhere built over, except in the part around the Rock. At this place there has been raised a stone [terrace] like a platform, of great unhewn blocks, in the centre of which, covering the Rock, is a magnificent Dome. The Rock itself is about breast-high above the ground, its length and breadth being almost equal, that is to say, some ten ells and odd, by the same across. You may descend below it by steps, as though going down to a cellar, passing through a door measuring some five ells by ten. The chamber below the Rock is neither square nor round, and is above a mans stature in height.

The city suffered several severe earthquake shocks between the time of Muqaddasi and the arrival of the Crusaders. In the year 1016, the Dome fell in and restorations were undertaken in 1022 and 1027. The last account before the Crusaders is that of Nasir-i-Khusran, in which occurs a description of the Rock itself together with its place in Muslim tradition.

The Rock itself rises out of the floor to the height of a man, and a balustrade of marble goes round about it, in order that none may lay his hand thereon. The Rock inclines on the side that is towards the Quiblah [or south], and there is an appearance as though a person had walked heavily on the stone when it was soft like clay, whereby the imprint of his toes had remained thereon. There are on the Rock seven such footmarks, and I heard it stated that Abraham—peace be upon him!—was once here with Isaac—upon him be peace!—when he was a boy, and that he walked over this place, and that the footmarks were his.

In the house of the Dome of the Rock men are always congregated—pilgrims and worshippers. The place is laid with fine carpets of silk and other stuffs. In the middle of the Dome, and over the Rock, there hangs from a silver chain a silver lamp; and there are in other parts of the building great numbers of silver lamps.

In 1099 the Crusaders took Jerusalem, and the Dome of the Rock, considered by them to be the *Templum Domini*, passed to the Knights Templar. Holding this building to be the veritable Temple of the Lord, its outline was emblazoned by the knights on their armorial bearings, and in both plan and elevation the edifice came to be reproduced by the Templars in the various Temple churches which the order caused to be built in London, Cambridge, Laon, Metz, and other cities throughout Europe. Godfrey de Bouillon established a house of Augustinian Canons to which he entrusted the care of the building. An altar was erected on the Rock and a golden cross upon the Dome.

In 1187 Jerusalem was, as we have already mentioned, retaken by Saladin, who effected a complete restoration of the Haram Area to its pristine condition. The state into which the Rock had come through the zeal of the Franks for the acquisition of relics, is described in the Chronicle of Ibn al-Athir. Saladin removed the marble pavement with which the Christians had covered the Rock in order to prevent pilgrims from chipping off pieces of it.

After Saladin had completed his restoration, he set up inside the cupola of the Dome, above the Rock, a beautiful inscription in tile-work on a series of bands and medallions, which may still be seen *in situ*.

Up until 1855, non-Muslims were not allowed to enter the Dome. Under the mandate, the British government handed over responsibility for Muslim buildings to the Supreme Muslim Council, and after the earthquake of 1927 this Council set about their task with refreshing vigor. In the fighting of 1948 the Dome was slightly damaged and one worshiper was killed. Partition left the Mosque in Jordanian hands and it was a matter of great pride to King Hussein that, as a Muslim, he should prove himself worthy of the high privilege with which he found himself possessed. The last of these restorations was carried out by Egyptian engineers between 1958 and 1962. The old foundations were exposed and reinforced with concrete. Certain columns were replaced within the drum of the Dome, and the old lead sheeting on the Dome was replaced with a special aluminum bronze alloy that shines like gold in the sun.

—Christopher Hollis and Ronald Brownrag

Made in Heaven

The aura of church sanctity hovering over Jerusalem impressed the early Muslim leaders, but it also challenged them. After Muawiya was installed as caliph in the city he went to pray at Golgotha, at Gethsemane, and at the Tomb of Mary in the Kidron Valley. This was more than a show of respect for the Christian shrines; it demonstrated the triumph of the Prophet's faith in the Holy Land of both Christians and Jews whose religious wisdom Islam had raised to a higher level of truth. What could emphatically, visibly show all peoples of the empire simultaneously this inheritance, this transcendence, this triumph? The caliph answered with plans for the construction of a monument commensurate with his pride, power, and wealth. The result was the Dome built over Abraham's Moriah rock, the symbolic foundation of monotheism.

The construction of the Dome was left to Caliph al-Malik, who in 685 employed Greek architects, Armenian artisans, and Syrian laborers to erect a spectacular, eight-story, octagonal structure in the Byzantine style, a more sumptuous imitation of Constantine's original Church of the Resurrection two hundred yards west.

As the Dome's form was inspired by Constantine's Golgotha church, so it in turn gave birth to Christian imitations, such as the Temple

Church in London and the sanctuary in Aix la Chapelle. The rounded shell that is the dome itself was made of lead and gold, and in the winter a hood of animal skin was placed over the structure to protect it against ice and Jerusalem's fierce winter winds. When the spring came the hood was removed and the dome sparkled in the sun, moving the famous Jerusalem Muslim geographer al-Mukaddasi to record this impression in the tenth century:

> At the dawn, when the light of the sun first strikes on the Cupola, and the Drum catches the rays; then is this edifice a marvelous sight to behold, and one such that in all Islam I have never seen its equal; neither have I heard tell of aught built in pagan times that could rival in grace this Dome of the Rock.

The dome protects Abraham's Moriah, *Even Shetiyah*, the Hebraic "Foundation Stone" at which Islamic tradition places Muhammad's Heavenly Ascension. The massive outcropping of rough-faced limestone appears in sharp contrast to the splendid artistry surrounding it. Yet there is nothing brute or ugly in the stone; quite the opposite. Because it is attached to the earth in only one place, the giant object seems suspended in air—an effect which gave rise to a charming legend. When Muhammad began his Heavenly Ascent, the stone in reverence tried to follow him. But the angel Gabriel, who was the Prophet's guide, pressed the stone back with his own hands, shouting to it, "Your place, O Stone, is on earth. You have no part in the Prophet's Garden of Eden." Today Muslim guides are pleased to point out the imprint which one of Gabriel's hands made on the holy stone, not far from the place where Muhammad's footprint can be found.

The legend about the stone's hovering in the air persisted, and the belief spread that if the stone should fall to earth it would signal the coming of the Messiah, bringing the redemption of Israel. The Ottoman Turks believed the legend. They sought to prevent the entry of the Messiah Jesus by walling up the Golden Gate, and they also hoped to prevent the appearance of Israel's Messiah by constructing a firm support to prevent the stone's fall.

On the underside of the mysterious stone lies a cavern which is especially precious to Muslims as the place where Muhammad prayed before his journey to heaven; a depression in the ceiling marks the spot where his head inclined during his prayers. In the recesses lining the walls of the cave are tiny chapels dedicated to the Prophet's predecessors—Abraham, David, Solomon, and Elijah. It seems that the layers of sanctity in this shrine have no end: the dome covers the rock, and the rock sits over the cave, and the cave hides a well beneath it. It is the terrible fathomless well where the souls of all the departed lie, anxiously awaiting the Judgment Day in Jerusalem when the righteous and wicked will receive their just rewards. Muslims and Jews share the belief that the center of the world—the point at which earth is separated from heaven above and hell below—is located not at the foot of Christ's Tomb, as Christians hold, but at the mouth of the well below the Foundation Stone. And here in the well, too, is "the source of all the springs and fountains from which the world drinks its water"—a description which touches on truth, for we know that beneath the stone floor or the Haram are numerous vast cisterns for catching rainwater.

Encircling the stone are two wide ambulatories to be used in the sacred walk (*tawaf*) performed by pilgrims who cannot travel to Mecca to perform the obligatory encircling of the Kaba. The Persian traveler Nasir-i-Khosrau tells us that, unable to make the *hajj* to Mecca, as many as twenty thousand would gather in Jerusalem at Ramadan to pray at the Dome.

In the courtyard facing the Dome in all directions are tall decorative, open-air stone arches, like slender hands clasping the shrine with fingers pointing skyward. Arabs call the arches *mawazeen* (scales), because they believe that on Judgment Day moral scales will be hung from the arches to weigh the good and evil deeds of every human being.

Caliph al-Malik spared no expense in constructing this shrine. It cost him the fortune of seven years' revenue from Egypt. But he must have treasured his creation, for he himself performed a ceremonial cleaning of the shrine, "sweeping and washing it with his own hands," establishing a ritual custom for all the caliphs who would follow him. For daily cleaning, however, he employed over fifty cleaners who washed the rock with a mixture of saffron, musk, and rose water. Most of the jobs were taken by Jews, who also made lanterns to light the shrine at night and looked on their work as a *mitzvah*; for they "viewed the renewed use of the Temple site as the beginning of the Redemption." The lamps in the Dome held a further meaning for the Jews. Legend says that on the ninth night of the Hebrew month of Av, which commemorates the destruction of the Temple, the lamps will go out and nothing can light them until the next day.

Why was such a large and expensive structure built in Jerusalem and not in the Umayyad capital of Damascus or in the religiously more important cities of Mecca and Medina? The old theory that Caliph al-Malik wished to divert pilgrims from Mecca to Jerusalem in order to undermine a rival, Caliph Abdallah Ibn al-Zubayr of Mecca, was refuted by S. D. Goitein on the ground that had al-Malik acted so foolishly, he would have been branded a *kafir* (infidel) against whom the Imams would have been right to preach *jihad* (holy war). The political struggle between the two leaders was another stage in the long drawn-out conflict of succession between the descendants of Muawiya and their opponents, including the Shite followers of Ali. If this struggle influenced al-Malik's decision to build his monument in Jerusalem, it was to demonstrate that he, not his rival, was the true champion of the Prophet's faith.

Al-Malik's wish was not to displace Mecca with Jerusalem but to foster the sacral significance of Jerusalem for Muslim worshipers so that they would accept the city on the same level of veneration as Mecca and Medina. The caliph's political motive was not difficult to fathom. Mecca was in the hands of the old Muslim aristocracy, which never ceased to look on the Umayyads as wealthy and worldly upstarts whose power stemmed from the luck of their military successes. While during the hundred years of the Umayyad caliphate (650–750) Mecca and Medina never lost their preeminence, the city of Jerusalem, because of al-Haram esh-Sharif, became something of a family shrine center for the Umayyad caliphs of Damascus.

As we have noted, the building of the Dome was a symbol of Islamic inheritance from and triumph over the religions of Jews and Christians, and equally an expression of the insecurity of Muslims in a city dominated by Christians from the initial Arab conquest in 638 until Saladin drove out the Crusaders in 1187. In making the Dome a taller, more imposing copy of the Holy Sepulchre, Caliph al-Malik was making visible to all Jerusalem's Christians the power and permanence of Islam in the Holy City. The caliph's artisans deliberately adopted Christian crosses and Persian crowns, symbols of imperial majesty and sanctity, to express the point that these empires had been defeated, and in the case of Persia its unbelievers converted to Islam.

The popular appeal of the Dome of the Rock and the Haram esh-Sharif to Muslims explains how the Koran's stories of Muhammad's Night Journey and Ascension to Heaven were connected with this sacred area. Years after its construction, it came to be believed that the Dome commemorated the fabled night in which, according to the Koran, Muhammad was transported from Mecca to a place called the "Farthest Mosque" and then to heaven to receive the final revelation of truth from God. In fact, there is no explicit reference to Jerusalem in the Koran, and only reference to the Holy Land (*al-Ard al-Muqaddosa*, Koran 5:21). But folk tradition is usually more powerful than historical accuracy. Muslim pilgrimage to Jerusalem undoubtedly influenced interpretation of the Koran stories. Once the connection between Jerusalem and Muhammad's Night Journey and Ascension had been made in popular belief, Jerusalem officially gained its place as a "holy city" in Islamic theology.

The handsome silver-domed al-Aksa Mosque, standing on the extreme south end of the Haram, would dominate the Temple Mount were it not for the more lustrous beauty of her sister, the Dome of the Rock. Taking its name from the Koranic account of Muhammad's Night Journey, al-Aksa, the "farthest mosque," was built in the period 709–715 over the site of Justinian's Church of Saint Mary and incorporated much of the church in its own construction. The mosque's builder, Caliph al-Walid, al-Malik's son, rivaled King Herod in commissioning numerous great monuments such as Medina's central mosque and the great mosques of Damascus and Cairo. Upon completion, al-Aksa became Jerusalem's central congregational mosque. According to English scholar John Gray, "Al Aksa is a classic example of how close the two faiths of Christianity and Islam may be on the level of popular tradition, for the prayer-niche giving the worshippers the orientation towards Mecca is associated in Muslim tradition with the Annunciation to Mary, and a stone basin is reputed to be the cradle of Jesus where he spoke to the people . . . . "

—Aryeh Kaplan, Made in Heaven

CHURCH OF THE HOLY SEPULCHRE

Pilgrims and tourists from the West are usually shocked to find that the Church of the Holy Sepulchre is not what they expected. They are surprised to discover that the Protestants have practically no presence in the church. And the Roman Catholics possess only a minor chapel, known as the Chapel of the Apparition. To be sure, the Roman Catholics are proud of their small chapel because it is located on the spot where Jesus is believed to have appeared to his mother after his resurrection. The chapel also houses several precious relics among which are part of the Column of Flagellation and the sword and spurs of Godfrey of Bouillon, the first Crusader, who ruled in Jerusalem. But the Greek Orthodox Church owns the main cathedral in the Church of the Holy Sepulchre. And on Calvary the Greeks possess the chapel which stands on the place of the Crucifixion, while the Latins—as the Roman Catholics are called—possess the lesser chapel which stands on the place where Jesus was nailed to the Cross. The Greek chapel is actually on the top of the hill and it stands on solid rock. The Latin chapel is only an upper room beneath which are chambers where the Greeks store some of the relics. And, most important, the Greeks are the custodians of the Holy Sepulchre itself.

What shocks the visitor even more is the absence of the aura of sanctity which Westerners anticipate in a place of worship, especially one that houses the Holy Sepulchre. The Western visitor expects to find in this holiest of Christian shrines perfect decorum, harmonious music, and earnest devotion. What the visitor often finds is pandemonium.

R. R. Madden, a devout Irish Catholic physician, expressed his shock at the Oriental Christian mode of worship. His experience was at the Sepulchre of the Virgin Mary. He writes in his two-volume work, *Travels in Turkey, Egypt, and Palestine:*

In the valley between the Mount of Olives and walls of Jerusalem, on the eastern side of the Brook Cedron, which is now without water, I visited "the Sepulchre of the Virgin." The Greeks were celebrating the festival of the Madonna, firing pistols before the altar, at which half a dozen priests were officiating, and squabbling in the most indecent manner on the very steps of the altar.

The grotto was crowded with Greek and Turkish (Arab) women; and the husbands of the latter were amusing themselves by firing pistols close to my ear, and pulling off the turbans of their neighbours. But what most astonished me, was to hear the Greeks, on coming out, boasting of what a good festival they had, of the great many shots that had been fired, as if they literally hoped to make sure of heaven by a "holy" violence.

Still another nineteenth-century traveler, Thomas Skinner, described a scene in the Church of the Holy Sepulchre, which shocked him as it would have scandalized any Western visitor in this Christian holiest of holy places. He reported that

The devout mothers had brought their infants with them; and, as it became necessary to satisfy their appetites, the women drew away from the crowd, and, ranged in a line to the east of the sepulchre, gave their children the breast. It was too hot to cover the heads of the babes; the more, therefore, the mothers exposed their bosoms. More than a hundred were engaged in this interesting duty.

The Greek Orthodox tradition predominates in the Christian shrines of Jerusalem, and the Oriental tradition does not regard indecorous worship as inappropriate. The Oriental worshiper is no less reverential or as pious than the Western Christian. He feels at home in his church and reacts as he does at home. Western standards are different, but not necessarily superior in piety and devotion. Armed with this awareness, the Western visitor will not be shocked at the disorder which may otherwise be disturbing in the Church of the Holy Sepulchre and in some of the other holy places in Jerusalem.

During the four hundred years of Turkish rule in the Holy City, the Moslems have employed several crude expedients to exalt Islam and to humiliate the infidels. Thus they entrusted the keys to the Church of the Holy Sepulchre to a certain Arab family who open and close the church in accordance with an established schedule—and at unscheduled times for an appropriate bakshish. This hereditary privilege has continued to this day.

Another expedient for humiliating the Christians consisted of placing Arab custodians within the church during the hours of Christian worship. The custodians sat on an elevated stand inside the church entrance and whiled away the hours sipping Turkish coffee or smoking nargillahs. Every time a Christian entered or left the church he was reminded that he worshiped in the Church of the Holy Sepulchre by the grace of the Moslem custodians. And up to the middle of the nineteenth century a small tribute in the form of an entrance fee was exacted from all Christians entering the church. This humiliating practice was abolished by Mohammed Ali when the Egyptians conquered the Holy City. When the city was returned to the Turks this fee was not reimposed.

Still another humiliating practice was the stationing of soldiers within the church to maintain order, especially during Holy Week. To be sure, there was always the danger of disorder due to the rivalries between the Christian sects. The pasha was responsible for the orderly conduct within the church and he could not afford to take chances. But the Turkish soldiers were coarse and often brutal in the performance of their duty. When the British mandatory government ruled in Palestine, they managed to keep the peace in the church without offending Christian sensibilities. Their soldiers were stationed at a discreet distance. The Israeli government, too, has been tactful in keeping the peace at the Holy Sepulchre.

Today the Christian visitor is no longer shocked by the presence of soldiers within their holiest shrine. The platform with the Arabs smoking their nargillahs or sipping their coffee is gone. More important, the violent historic rivalries between the Christian sects have subsided. There is even active cooperation among the sects in the current restoration of the church. The enlightened rule of the British between 1918 and 1948 and that of the Israeli government since 1967 have had their salutary effects on the age-old enmities between the Christian sects. An era of peace and cooperation is clearly in sight. But the keys to the Church of the Holy Sepulchre are still held by the Arab custodians. Neither the British nor the Israeli government has dared to alter the sacrosanct law of the *Status Quo.*

—Abraham Millgram, The Church of
the Holy Sepulchre

The Empty Tomb

"Now, in the place where he was crucified, there was a garden; and in the garden a new sepulchre wherein was never yet man laid. There they laid Jesus, therefore, because of the Jews' preparation day, for the sepulchre was nigh at hand." The Passion of Jesus is fully described in St. John's gospel: "Nigh to the City—Outside the Gate." The first followers of Jesus must have known exactly where the events took place.

If the sepulchre was in a garden, the tomb was that of a very well known member of the Sanhedrin, Joseph of Arimathea. He had hewn it out of the rock himself. This garden was presumably his own private property. Even when Herod Agrippa, in extending the city, enclosed it within the walls, the garden would not have been built on. Because it had been a burial place, it was unclean land. If it had remained in Christian hands, how easy it would have been to point out to future generations where these great events had happened! There is a natural instinct in all men to remember the sites of great historical happenings; surely this site would have been preserved by early Christians. They would point out to their children the sacred places so carefully described in the gospels.

In AD 66 began the revolt of the Jews against the power of Rome, which ended in the destruction of Jerusalem, under Titus, in the year AD 70.

The Christian community in the city, however small, continued to exist, for we have records of every single bishop of Jerusalem during this period. Although Titus is said to have destroyed the city, the sites of the crucifixion and resurrection, never having been built over, must have been comparatively unaffected by the rubble of destruction. There they remained for Christians to see. The bishops of Jerusalem must have pointed them out. And it may safely be said that the tradition of these Holy Places continued down through those unhappy years.

Once again, revolt broke out in the year 135, under Bar Kochbar. Once again, the city suffered defeat and demolition. Hadrian captured and entirely rebuilt it on the lines of a Roman colonial city. He renamed it Aelia Capitolina. Considering the Christian religion a Jewish sect, he tried to erase or desecrate the Christian sites. Hadrian built a great concrete terrace over the two sites of the crucifixion and resurrection. On this he erected a statue of Jupiter over Calvary and a temple of Venus over the tomb. (Part of the terrace is still to be seen in the Russian excavations.) Hadrian's action, however, had exactly the opposite results to what he had planned. For, under the providence of God, that mass of concrete served to mark indelibly the site of both the crucifixion and resurrection.

For the next two hundred years, Aelia Capitolina remained a Roman colony. Christians of Jewish race were exiled, but Christians of Greco-Roman origin were allowed to stay. The Church in Jerusalem grew and prospered as a Gentile Church, but kept in communion with the exiled Judaeo-Christians outside. We have again a record of all the Greco-Roman bishops of Aelia. Here begins at this time a record of pilgrimage and of interest in the Holy Places, although they were still hidden and covered by Hadrian's concrete.

Christendom, in so far as it had a headquarters, had it in Rome rather than in Jerusalem. Even in the life of the Palestinian Christian Church, the bishop of Jerusalem was to become only a suffragan to the bishop of Caesarea. It was not until 451 that the Council of Chalcedon made Jerusalem a patriarchate independent of Caesarea. Despite persecution, by the time of Constantine Christianity was well established in Syria and Palestine and there is good reason to believe that the exact location of the Holy Places was known from a tradition going back to apostolic times.

Perhaps Constantine, like us, was surprised to find these sites inside the then city walls. If he had just intended to found a place of pilgrimage in honor of Jesus, would not he have chosen a site outside the walls? Macarius was bishop of Jerusalem at that time and pointed out the sites to Constantine, within the city. Then began the destruction of one emperors temple of the imperial state religion by another emperor, and this for the sole purpose of erecting the central shrine of Christendom! In a letter to Bishop Macarius, Constantine wrote: "No words can express how good the Saviour has been to us. That the monument of his Holy Passion, hidden for so many years, has not at last been restored to the faithful is indeed a miracle. My great wish is, after freeing the site of impious idols, to adorn it with splendid buildings."

Constantine planned to make these holy places an object of Christian pilgrimage and devotion. So he set about the task in this order: (1) Demolition of pagan shrines. (2) Excavation of concrete podium. (3) Discovery of the Knoll of Calvary and of the Tomb below. (4) Leveling off to form a floor-level for his church. (5) Excavation into the hillside to build a rotunda for the Anastasis, a circular ambulatory round the Tomb of Jesus. (6) Leaving the shell of the tomb in a circular space, or rotunda. (7) He left a symbolic cuboid of the Rock of Calvary. (Of the shell of the tomb Eusebius wrote: "Is it not astonishing to see this rock standing isolated in the middle of a levelled space and with a cave inside it?")

Of the cuboid of rock Eusebius describes how the token "mound" stood with a single cross on top, in an open colonnaded court.

The cathedral or "martyrium" was beyond this open court. It was entered through an atrium or courtyard from the open street, which ran at right angles to the axis of the church (east to west). We can see in the Madeba Mosaic the magnificent setting of the basilica within the Byzantine city; to the north was the Damascus Gate, at which there was a single colossal column. Indeed the Arabic name for the Damascus Gate is still "Bag-el-Amoud," Gate of the Column. From this column ran a colonnaded street, all through the city, to the great facade of the basilica.

If the reproduction of the Madeba Mosaic is turned upside down, the following will be clearly seen, front to back, east to west: (1) A broad front-age ascending in five steps. (2) A triple doorway of a central large and smaller side doors. (3) A huge building, orientated east to west, with a pitched roof. (4) A section with no roof, indicating an open courtyard. (5) Finally, at the west end, a separate domed building.

The details of the facade cannot be clearly shown, but it included part of the city wall from the time of Christ, adapted and faced with white marble, against which there was an imposing line of black basalt columns. The three entrances into the basilica are still to be seen behind the Arab market or suq—one in a cafe, one in a Russian convent, one under the crypt of the Constantinian basilica, also still to be seen today, was the cistern in which were found three crosses. One of these was "identified" as the true cross.

Constantine built a sloping staircase leading down to the Chapel of St. Helena (now in the possession of the Armenians). The massive pillars which support its cupola are Byzantine work of the seventh century. From the Chapel of St. Helena is a flight of thirteen steps which leads down to the Chapel of the finding of the Cross. The walls of the stairway are covered with graffiti of medieval pilgrims. The chapel, which looks like an old disused cistern, is served now by the Latins and the Greeks. It was here, of course, the story says, that the true cross was found on the initiative of St. Helena. There is no evidence dating back any earlier than seventy years after her death of Helena's claim to have discovered the cross, nor has the Church ever made any pronouncement about the story. There are obvious and apparent improbabilities about the story, but when all is said, wood is not quickly destroyed except by fire. It can survive for may years in water and it is not difficult to think that the Romans carelessly threw away their crosses when they had served their purpose, and that there were plenty of used crosses lying about in neighboring cisterns. But such general arguments clearly cut both ways. If there were plenty of crosses lying about, what reason was there for believing that they were the three crosses in question? The Romans must have crucified hundreds of people during those years.

Within the church of St. Pudenziana in Rome, there is a contemporary fourth-century mosaic of Constantine's buildings in the apse and there, in the center of the mosaic, is the Rock of Calvary with its grille, above which stands a large decorative cross. Although the scene of the mosaic is very conventionalized, it does coincide rather remarkably with the remains in Jerusalem and with the ancient descriptions.

Here, Pere Couasnon, able to excavate not for the first time in eight hundred years, lately found that the Rock of Calvary was still four and a half meters wide by four and a half meters long—with a height of at least ten meters! It is not for nothing that the endless stream of pilgrims—some with bare feet—some with dripping swords—some who still see it all through the range-finders of their cameras—it is not for nothing that this stream has flowed past this traditional Rock of Calvary and the Tomb of Jesus.

—Christopher Hollis and Ronald
Brownrag essay

Deepening the Sources

The week prior to this class meeting ask for volunteers to lead tours of the three sites. The guides can utilize the source materials and are encouraged to add pictures, audiovisual aids, stories, songs, etc.

For the three sites, Western Wall, Church of the Holy Sepulchre, and Dome of the Rock, presenters should explore: A) The meaning of its name. B) How the structure looks today. Where it is located. C) Who constructed it. When it was built. How the site was chosen. Why it was built. D) Its role throughout history. How it has changed. E) Songs, stories, art, or poetry it has inspired. F) The purpose it serves today. Customs related to it. Ceremonies conducted at the site. What it means to people today.

Anyone who has visited the Western Wall, or seen pictures of people worshiping there, cannot but be struck by the diversity of Jews who come there. They dress differently, they speak different languages, they represent different nationalities, they even observe different customs. Yet, they are all Jews. Explore some of the communities of Jews that live in Jerusalem and make it the fascinating city it is.

IN SUMMATION

- Jerusalem's holiness grows out of the Torah and Prophets that teach that Jerusalem was chosen as our holy city by God and emanates from biblical experiences involving efforts to possess, rebuild, defend, and worship in Jerusalem.
- From the time that Jerusalem became part of the transition of the Jewish people from landless, independent tribes to nation, it never lost its holiness, its link with what extends beyond the earthly. Therefore, when it was destroyed and Jews were exiled, Jerusalem never lost its magnetism, its special relationship with the Jewish people.

  Pilgrims traveled to Jerusalem not only to see its sacred sites and to pray there but also to hear the word of God.

- Each of the three major religious groups has a major center of prayer in the city of Jerusalem.
- The Western Wall is a remnant of the Temple Mount's retaining wall left standing after Titus destroyed Jerusalem.
- The Church of the Holy Sepulchre is a monument to the life of Jesus.
- The Dome of the Rock is on the site from which Mohammed is said to have ascended to heaven.

PERTINENT SITES TO VISIT IN ISRAEL

- Western Wall
- Dome of the Rock
- Stations of the Cross
- Al-Aksa Mosque
- Church of the Holy Sepulchre
- Medaba Map (Cardo, or Jordan, or YMCA)

CHAPTER 11

THE SEARCH
FOR PEACE

BACKGROUND

King David, a man of war, conquered Jerusalem three thousand years ago. King David, a man of peace, composed a psalm that reads:

Pray for the peace of Jerusalem; They shall prosper
  that love thee Peace be within thy walls,
And prosperity within thy palaces.

Psalm 122: 6–7

The words remain relevant today, the prayer as fervent, the need as great. Why have the moments of peace for Jews in Jerusalem been so few and so fleeting? Why has peace been so elusive in this small corner of the world? Why have we persisted so stubbornly against tremendous odds in the struggle for peace?

At the very moment this is being written the efforts continue and we are perhaps closer to peace than we have been in almost fifty years. An examination of current efforts to attain peace must be coupled with an understanding of where the journey has taken us in this century in order to understand life in Jerusalem today.

Jerusalem was a divided city from 1948 until 1967 during which time Jordan occupied the walled, Old City. The New City became the capital of the State of Israel and thrived as a modern, growing metropolis. Government offices were moved there and the Knesset built. The Hebrew University and Hadassah Hospital both opened new facilities to replace those on Mount Scopus, which had become inaccessible to Jews. The population almost doubled in size as immigrants came from all corners of the world.

It was not a time of peace. Constant attacks by Arab terrorists threatened the civilian population and Israeli troops. In 1967 Israel launched a pre-emptive attack on the Egyptian army massing on the Israel-Egypt border. The successful campaign left the Sinai in the hands of Israel where it remained until the 1979 peace treaty signed by Begin and Sadat.

June 5, 1967, marks one of those life-time events whose witnesses can recall exactly where they were when they first heard of it. Israelis and Egyptians fought fiercely in the south. Israel urged King Hussein not to open an eastern front and bring the war into Jerusalem. But mortar shells began falling on Jewish Jerusalem that morning. By Wednesday, June 7, Israeli forces had captured most of the strategic points around Jerusalem and had taken the Old City.

At 10:15 in the morning, preceded by a paratroop unit, Haim Bar-Lev, deputy chief of staff, Uzi Narkiss, commander of the forces around Jerusalem and chaplain Rabbi Shlomo Goren arrived at the Temple Mount. Rabbi Goren carried a shofar and a Torah scroll. Standing at the Western Wall, he offered thanksgiving for the victory and recited the memorial prayer for those who had been killed in the liberation of the city. He then blew a long, powerful shofar blast that echoed throughout the world. Jerusalem was unified under Jewish rule once more.

Despite the victory, which included conquest of the Golan Heights to the north, great tensions continued to stand in the way of anything resembling peace. Attacks by the PLO and other terrorist groups continued. Events like the murder of Israelis at the Munich Olympics, the Yom Kippur War, the hijacking of an Air France plane to Entebbe, Operation Peace for the Galilee, and the Intifada (Palestinian uprisings in the administered territories) all were part of the continuing conflict between Arab extremists and Israel. Monumental changes in the Middle East took place in 1994. The historic handshake on the White House lawn sealed an agreement between two enemies, Yasser Arafat and Yitzhak Rabin, to work toward peace. The next year King Hussein of Jordan, signed a peace treaty. Negotiations with Syria continue as this is being written.

DIVIDED JERUSALEM
Arab-Jewish Relationship From Early Zionist Days Until Today

Time Line

ANTI-JEWISH VIOLENCE ERUPTS IN PALESTINE
1920: After Britain takes control of Palestine, violent Arab protest erupts against the 1917 Balfour Declaration's promise "to facilitate the establishment in Palestine of a national home for the Jewish people." In response, Britain places restrictions on Jewish immigration and settlement.

ARABS RENEW ATTACKS ON JEWS
1929: A dispute over Jewish access to the Western Wall sparks widespread violence against Jewish communities, including a massacre of Jews in Hebron. British inquiry urges restricting Jewish immigration.

ARAB UPRISING ENTERS THIRD YEAR
1939: Widespread anti-Jewish riots, beginning in 1936, further weaken British support for a Jewish homeland. On the eve of the Holocaust, a 1939 British White Paper limits Jewish immigration to a total of only 75,000 over the next five years, with further immigration prohibited. Land sales are also severely restricted.

ARABS SCUTTLE U.N. PEACE PLAN
1947: Unable to resolve the conflict, Britain submits the Palestine problem to the United Nations, which votes to partition the territory west of the Jordan into separate Jewish and Arab states, with Jerusalem an international city. Jews in Palestine accept the plan, although it allots them scant territory. Arabs violently reject the plan and prepare to prevent the establishment of the Jewish state through war.

ISRAEL DRIVES BACK ARAB INVADERS
1948: The State of Israel proclaims its independence on May 14, 1948, the date the British forces withdraw. Included in Israel's Declaration of Independence is a call for peace: "We extend our hand to all neighboring States and their peoples in an offer of peace and good neighborliness, and appeal to them to establish bonds of cooperation and mutual help with the sovereign Jewish people settled in its own land." The Arab response comes on the next day, May 15, when the armies of Egypt, Syria, Lebanon, Jordan, and Iraq joined by units from Saudi Arabia, invade Israel's borders. By July 1949, Israel has driven back the invaders and signed armistice agreements with provisions for later peace talks (Iraq and Saudi Arabia refuse). The talks, however, end in deadlock.

EGYPTIAN THREAT OVERCOME IN THE SINAI
1956: Faced with an immense Egyptian military buildup after years of Egyptian-backed terrorist raids,

and a blockade of its shipping in the South, Israel strikes at Egypt's bases in the Gaza Strip and Sinai, quickly reaching the Suez Canal. The territories are returned in 1957 when U.N. troops enter the Sinai to maintain peace along the border and Israel receives promises that freedom of shipping in the South will be secure.

ARAB STATES FORM PLO

1964: Based on the decision of the Arab League, Palestinian Arab terrorists, dedicated to the destruction of Israel, meet with representatives of the Arab states in Arab-controlled east Jerusalem and establish the Palestine Liberation Organization.

ISRAEL DEFEATS ARABS IN SIX-DAY WAR

1967: Increased terrorist attacks and Syrian shelling of Israeli settlements set the stage for renewed war. In May, Egypt orders U.N. troops from the Sinai and renews its naval blockade, coordinating war plans with Syria and Jordan. On June 5, Israel responds with air strikes, destroying Egypt's air force on the ground. In the following six days, fighting on three fronts, Israel gains control of territories that offer a buffer against future Arab attacks: the Sinai Peninsula and Gaza Strip, the Golan Heights and Judea and Samaria along the west bank of the Jordan. Israel's offer to negotiate for peace is rejected by the Arab summit at Khartoum.

EGYPT LAUNCHES "WAR OF ATTRITION"

1968: Egyptian shelling across the Suez Canal opens hostilities that last nearly two years. Israel responds with artillery, commando raids, and air strikes against Egypt's Soviet air support. Following the August 1970 cease-fire, Egypt stations Soviet missiles along the canal, in violation of agreement.

ARABS ATTACK ON JEWISH HOLY DAY

1973: Egypt and Syria launch simultaneous attacks against Israel on Yom Kippur, Judaism's holiest day. Despite heavy initial losses, Israel repels the attacking armies, pushing across the Suez Canal and to the outskirts of Damascus. U.N. sponsored cease-fire ends fighting after two weeks.

"SHUTTLE DIPLOMACY" RAISES HOPES FOR PEACE

1974: Shuttling between their capital cities, U.S. Secretary of State Henry Kissinger opens a channel for disengagement talks between Israel, Egypt, and Syria. Agreements signed in 1974 restore Arab territories lost in the Yom Kippur War. 1975 agreement with Egypt restores strategic sites in the Sinai.

SADAT TALKS PEACE IN JERUSALEM

1977: President Anwar Sadat of Egypt accepts Israel's long-standing offer to negotiate a peace. On November 19–21, Sadat travels to Jerusalem to begin the first direct talks between Israel and any of its Arab neighbors.

ISRAEL AND EGYPT SIGN PEACE TREATY

1979: Meeting with U.S. president Jimmy Carter at Camp David in 1978, Egyptian president Sadat and Israeli prime minister Menachem Begin workout a comprehensive framework for peace in the Middle East and a framework for peace between Israel and Egypt. In March 1979, they meet in Washington to sign a treaty based on these negotiations. Under terms of this treaty, Israel withdraws from the Sinai in 1982, giving up the fruits of fifteen years' intensive economic development in exchange for a secure border and peaceful relations, including full diplomatic ties.

ISRAEL STRIKES AT TERRORIST STRONGHOLDS

1982: Increased PLO terror abroad and intense PLO rocket attacks against Israel's northern communities force Israeli intervention against PLO positions in Lebanon. Israeli units pursue PLO fighters to Beirut, forcing the PLO to evacuate the city. With the arrival of an international peace-keeping force, Israel withdraws and eventually recalls its troops in 1985, maintaining only a security zone along the border.

ARAB VIOLENCE ERUPTS IN THE TERRITORIES

1987: When Arabs residing in Gaza, Judea, and Samaria stage violent disturbances, Israeli troops respond to restore calm and stability. Unrest continues into 1989, marked by boycotts and repeated violence, including PLO attacks on nonmilitant Palestinian Arabs, scores of whom are murdered.

ISRAEL OFFERS NEW PEACE INITIATIVE

1989: On the tenth anniversary of its Treaty with Egypt, Israel proposes a four point peace plan which calls for: (1) commitment by the Camp David partners to further progress toward peace; (2) negotiations between Israel and its hostile Arab neighbors; (3) international efforts to solve the problem of Arab refugees still living in Judea, Samaria, and the Gaza District; (4) free democratic elections among the Palestinian Arabs in these areas as a first step toward interim self-rule, followed by negotiations to arrive at a permanent solution that includes lasting peace with Jordan.

ISRAEL AND PLO SIGN ACCORD

1993: Israel and the PLO sign the Oslo Agreement, which promises (1) mutual recognition; (2) self rule for Palestinians living in the Gaza Strip and the West Bank.

ISRAEL AND JORDAN SIGN FIVE POINT PEACE TREATY

1994: The treaty promises (1) some return of some land taken in the Six Day War; (2) cooperation efforts regarding water supply and availability; (3) Jordan will neither join alliances against Israel nor permit attacks from within its borders; (4) Israel agrees to consult Jordan regarding the eventual fate of refugees; and (5) cooperative effort regarding tourism and diplomatic relations.

Deepening the Sources

Study the time line of events that characterize the relationship between Arabs and Jews during the twentieth century. What do you conclude from your analysis? How do the present circumstances compare with situations in earlier decades?

JERUSALEM OF GOLD
Jerusalem of Gold

The wine-clear mountain air

And the scent of pines
Are wafted on the winds of dusk
Together with the sound of bells.

And with slumbering tree and stone
The solitary city
With a wall through its heart
Is held captive in its dream.

Chorus: Jerusalem of gold, of light, of bronze . . .
  (x 2)
I am the violin for all your songs.

The wells are dry
And the marketplace empty.
No one visits the Temple Mount
In the Old City.

Through the caves in the rocks
The winds howl
And no one goes down to the Dead Sea
By way of Jericho.

Chorus: Jerusalem of gold . . .

Still, today as I come to sing to you
And fashion for you crowns
I feel smaller than your youngest sons,
Less than the least of your poets.
For your name will scorch my lips

Like a seraph's kiss
If I forget you Jerusalem,
City all of gold.

Chorus: Jerusalem of gold . . .

We have come back now to the water cisterns
Back to the marketplace.
The sound of the shofar is heard
From the Wailing Wall in the ancient city.

And from the rocky caves in the mountains,
A thousand suns are rising.
We shall go now to the Dead Sea,
Go by way of Jericho!

Chorus: Jerusalem of gold . . .

—Words and music by Naomi Shemer

The Song That Took a City

In Tel Aviv, Naomi Shemer sits and ponders her latest creation. For her, it was a miracle which began on May 15, 1967. Some 3,500 people had crowded into Nation Hall (Binyhanei Haooma) in modern Jerusalem to attend the annual song festival commemorating Israeli Independence Day.

For two months she wrote nothing at all. But as she went about her daily activities, she thought about the Jerusalem she had known as a girl. She remembered how her Polish parents spoke of their own birthplace of Vilna as "the Jerusalem of the Diaspora"—as if every other city could only be second-best. She remembers the colors, the sounds, the silent mood of Jerusalem, her childhood visits to biblical places, closed forever to her since 1948. She thought, too, of a story from the Talmud in which the wife of the great Rabbi Akiva lived in poverty for years so that her husband might pursue his studies. When Rabbi Akiva became a famous and learned man, he rewarded his wife with a "Jerusalem of gold," a gold brooch hammered out in the shape of the ancient city, to be worn as a symbol of her devotion.

Naomi Shemer took the Talmudic phrase, "Yerushalayim shel zahav," "Jerusalem made of gold," and used it as the title for her song. It was to be a song of nostalgia, an intimate regret for a city she had personally lost. "Jerusalem of gold, of copper and of light," went the refrain. Then, quoting from the medieval Hebrew writer, Yehuda Halevi, she continued, "Let me be a violin for all your songs." For the first time in modern song, she referred to the "ancient wall" which Jerusalem "carries around her heart," and talked of the sights of the Old City, sights Jews of today would never see:

The water cisterns are dry,
The marketplace is empty.
We cannot go to the Dead Sea
By way of Jericho.
Your name burns my lips like a seraphim's kiss.
Let me not forget thee, O Jerusalem of gold!

At Nation Hall in Jerusalem, it was already close to midnight when the song was sung. Fourteen other melodies had already been performed to full orchestral accompaniment and polite applause. Then a young girl, discovered by the composer herself only a few days before and unknown to the general audience, walked out on stage. Her only accompaniment was her guitar. As she sang "Yerushalayim Shel Zahav," the audience grew hushed. When the girl finished, there was a second of silence, then earsplitting applause for nearly seven minutes. Naomi Shemer's personal sense of loss, it turned out, was every Israeli's. "Jerusalem of Gold" had to be played once more, by popular demand. This time—the second time the song had ever been performed—the entire audience joined in the refrain.

On the same night that the Jewish audience was singing of a Jerusalem they would never see, Abdel Nasser was moving his troops into the Sinai Peninsula. In the days after Naomi Shemers song was premiered, the soldiers of Israel began to leave their homes and prepare for battle. They took with them almost no personal belongings, but somehow—as the song was played over and over on the radio during the early days of mobilization—they took the song.

Then the telephone calls and letters began. Soldiers wrote to tell Naomi Shemer how they sang her song in the fields during the evening. Performers called to ask if they might begin and end their programs for the military with her song, since the soldiers inevitably requested it. A high member of the armed forces called to invite Miss Shemer to sing her song for the troops stationed around Jerusalem. Although she does not often perform, she accepted.

On Sunday, June 4, Naomi Shemer was called to one of the army's central command posts, to be given a new troop-entertainment assignment. She was introduced to some of the top military leaders in Israel, including Brig. Gen. Ezer Weizman, deputy to Maj. Gen. Itzhak Rabin, and Brig. Gen. Ariel Sharon, division commander who was to lead one of the main thrusts of the Sinai campaign. Sharon turned to her, and in his usual blunt fashion said, "It's important you should come to sing for us." It was arranged for Naomi Shemer to go down to Sharon's base in the Negev in Ezer Weizman's plane.

Late that afternoon the songwriter from Tel Aviv and the deputy commander of Israel's armed forces flew together to the encampment of Sharon's troops in the south. Dinner that night consisted of tomatoes, cucumbers, and eggs. Nobody talked much. After dinner the young woman waited to be asked to sing, but she was not. Finally, Sharon's aide drew her aside. "The war will be tough," he began. "And we have reason to believe it will be soon—very soon. We have decided there will be no singing tonight." She said nothing. "Still," he added, "you do not know how important it is to us to have you here. It's difficult to explain," he continued, "but you are a poet, a musician—and somehow we wanted someone with a soul to share this time with us."

Late that night, very late, the men moved out and, on Monday morning, radios announced that war had broken out. Naomi Shemer set out to help in the only way she knew. On Tuesday, she joined the troops outside Rafa, singing for them in the evening. On Wednesday they moved to El Arish, where scattered infantry fighting was still going on. She and several other entertainers were huddled around a column built, ironically, by the Egyptians to commemorate their 1956 "victory" over the Israelis in Sinai.

Someone had a transistor radio. Suddenly an announcer broke into the music. "The city of Jerusalem has been taken!" The program switched to Jerusalem itself. Gunfire could be heard behind the announcer's voice as he described the para-

troopers block-by-block fight into the heart of the Old City. Now some of the troops were advancing toward the Wailing Wall, he said. Then, in the background, indistinctly at first, there was the sound of a song—or hymn, rather—sung by what sounded like hundreds of men, in hoarse voices, gasping for breath between lines: "Yerushalayim shel zahav, veshel nehoshet veshel or, Halo lechol shiraih ani kinor." ("Jerusalem of gold, of copper and of light, Let me be a violin for all your songs!") Tears ran down her cheeks.

Then in the middle of the sounds of battle in El Arish and in Jerusalem, a very small, personal, professional thought occurred to her: She would have to rewrite the second stanza of her song. There was no longer any need for nostalgia: Jerusalem was theirs!

Later that evening, when the Israeli soldiers had gathered in their camp in the desert, the young woman got up before them. "I shall sing for you a stanza I have just added to 'Jerusalem of Gold,' " she told them. "Because when I first wrote the song, Jerusalem was just a beautiful dream for all of us, and now it belongs to us!"

The soldiers clapped and clapped without stopping until she said to them, "I am the one who should applaud you, because it is easier to change a song than to change a city."

—Linda Gottlieb, "The Song That
Took a City" from CAJE's
Yerushalayim, pp. 32–34

Deepening the Sources

Listen to or sing "Jerusalem of Gold." Read the words in English. Talk about the associations participants have with the song and its meaning. Read the article by Linda Gottlieb that tells the story of the song. What do these reveal about Jewish attitudes toward Jerusalem?

Israel, Egypt Sign Truce Accord

Both Sides "Correct" at Brief Ceremony

The American-inspired, six-point cease-fire agreement was signed by Egyptian and Israeli officers yesterday in a drab army tent pitched in the desert at Kilometre 101 on the Cairo-Suez road.

The principals arrived promptly at 3 p.m. They

exchange salutes—not handshakes—with each other. The Israeli delegation of six sat on the east side of the tent opposite the four Egyptians. At the head table sat three UN officers.

The Israelis were led by Aluf Ahron Yariv and the Egyptians by General Mohammed Gamazy. The UNEF commander, General Ensio Sillasvuo, sat at the head table, and called the proceedings to order. He said: "Gentlemen, let's sign," according to the spokesman of the UNEF, who came from Cairo for the ceremony. He said it took place just a few minutes after the men took their seats. Each side signed three copies in English, handed them over to the others, and then signed their three. He described the mood in the tent as "correct."

In a statement made during the intermission, Aluf Yariv said that the agreement was the "first step on the long and difficult road that leads to settlement of the conflict and to peace."

(A United Nations spokesman in Cairo said last night that the second meeting between Egyptians and Israelis to discuss the implementation of the agreement would be held today at 10 a.m. again at Kilometre 101.)

(The spokesman, Rudolf Stadjuhar, said the two parties, after the signing, started discussion yesterday on modalities of the implementation of the agreement. He described the talks that followed the signing of the agreement as "useful and constructive." Today's meeting will be attended by Gen. Gamazy and Aluf Yariv.)

It was learned later that the talks went on for several hours as the two sides tried to hammer out an acceptable interpretation of the text they had signed.

—*Jerusalem Post*, November 12, 1973

PEACE AND ITS PRICE
Camp David Agreements, September 17, 1978

A Framework for Peace in the Middle East by Muhammed Anwar al-Sadat, President of the Arab Republic of Egypt, and Menachem Begin, Prime Minister of Israel met with Jimmy Carter, President of the United States of America, at Camp David from September 5 to September 17, 1978, and have agreed on the following framework for peace in the Middle East. They invite other parties to the Arab-Israeli conflict to adhere to it.

Preamble

The search for peace in the Middle East must be guided by the following:

The agreed basis for a peaceful settlement of the conflict between Israel and its neighbors is United Nations Security Council Resolution 242, in all its parts.

After four wars during thirty years, despite intensive human efforts, the Middle East, which is the cradle of civilization and the birthplace of three great religions, does not yet enjoy the blessings of peace. The people of the Middle East yearn for peace, so that the vast human and natural resources of the region can be turned to the pursuits of peace and so that this area can become a model for coexistence and cooperation among nations . . . .

The provisions of the Charter of the United Nations and the other accepted norms of international law and legitimacy now provide accepted standards for the conduct of relations among all states.

To achieve a relationship of peace, in the spirit of Article 2 of the United Nations Charter, future negotiations between Israel and any neighbor prepared to negotiate peace and security with it, are necessary for the purpose of carrying out all the provisions and principles of Resolutions 242 and 338.

Peace requires respect for the sovereignty, territorial integrity, and political independence of every state in the area and their right to live in peace within secure and recognized boundaries free from threats or acts of force. Progress toward that goal can accelerate movement toward a new era of reconciliation in the Middle East marked by cooperation in promoting economic development, in maintaining stability, and in assuring security.

Security is enhanced by a relationship of peace and by cooperation between nations which enjoy normal relations. In addition, under the terms of peace treaties, the parties can, on the basis of reciprocity, agree to special security arrangements such as demilitarized zones, limited armaments areas, early warning stations, the presence of international forces, liaison, agreed measures for monitoring, and other arrangements that they agree are useful.

Framework

Taking these factors into account, the parties are determined to reach a just, comprehensive, and durable settlement of the Middle East conflict through the conclusion of peace treaties based on Security Council Resolutions 242 and 338 in all their parts. Their purpose is to achieve peace and good neighborly relations. They recognize that, for peace to endure, it must involve all those who have been most deeply affected by the conflict. They therefore agree that this framework as appropriate is intended by them to constitute a basis for peace not only between Egypt and Israel, but also between Israel and each of its other neighbors which is prepared to negotiate peace with Israel on this basis. With that objective in mind, they have agreed to proceed as follows:

A. West Bank and Gaza

1. Egypt, Israel, Jordan and the representatives of the Palestinian people should participate in negotiations on the resolution of the Palestinian problem in all its aspects. To achieve that objective, negotiations relating to the West Bank and Gaza should proceed in three stages:

   (a) Egypt and Israel agree that, in order to ensure a peaceful and orderly transfer of authority, and taking into account the security concerns of all the parties, there should be transitional arrangements for the West Bank and Gaza for a period not exceeding five years. In order to provide full autonomy to the inhabitants, under these arrangements the Israeli military government and its civilian administration will be withdrawn as soon as a self-governing authority has been freely elected by the inhabitants of these areas to replace the existing military government. To negotiate the details of a transitional arrangement, the government of Jordan will be invited to join the negotiations on the basis of this framework. These new arrangements should give due consideration both to the principle of self-government by the inhabitants of these territories and to the legitimate security concerns of the parties involved.

   (b) Egypt, Israel, and Jordan will agree on the modalities for establishing the elected self-governing authority in the West Bank and Gaza. The delegations of Egypt and Jordan may include Palestinians from the West Bank and Gaza or other Palestinians as mutually agreed. The parties will negotiate an agreement which will define the powers and responsibilities of the self-governing authority to be exercised in the West Bank and Gaza. A withdrawal of Israeli armed forces will take place and there will be a redeployment of the remaining Israeli forces into specified security locations. The agreement will also include arrangements for assuring internal and external security and public order. A strong local police force will be established, which may include Jordanian citizens. In addition, Israeli and Jordanian forces will participate in joint patrols and in the manning of control posts to assure the security of the borders.

   (c) When the self-governing authority (administrative council) in the West Bank and Gaza is established and inaugurated, the transitional period of five years will begin. As soon as possible, but not later than the third year after the beginning of the transitional period, negotiations will take place to determine the final status of the West Bank and Gaza and its relationship with its neighbors, and to conclude a peace treaty between Israel and Jordan by the end of the transitional period. These negotiations will be conducted among Egypt, Israel, Jordan, and the elected representatives of the inhabitants of the West Bank and Gaza. Two separate but related committee will be convened, one committee, consisting of representatives of the four parties which will negotiate and agree on the final status of the West Bank and Gaza, and its relationship with its neighbors, and the second committee, consisting of representatives of Israel and representatives of Jordan to be joined by the elected representatives of the inhabitants of the West Bank and Gaza, to negotiate the peace treaty between Israel and Jordan, taking into account the agreement reached on the final status of the West Bank and Gaza. The negotiations shall be based on all the provisions and principles of U.N. Security Council Resolution 242. The negotiation will resolve, among other matters, the location of the boundaries and the nature of the security arrangements. The solution from the negotiations must also recognize the legitimate rights of the Palestinian people and their just requirements. In this way, the Palestinians will participate in the determination of their own future through: (i) the negotiations among Egypt, Israel, Jordan and the representatives of the inhabitants of the West Bank and Gaza to agree on the final status of the West Bank and Gaza and other outstanding issues by the end of the transitional period; (ii) submitting their agreement to a vote by the elected representatives of the inhabitants of the West Bank and Gaza; (iii) providing for the elected representatives of the inhabitants of the West Bank and Gaza to decide how they shall govern themselves consistent with the provisions of their agreement; (iv) participating as stated above in the work of the committee negotiating the peace treaty between Israel and Jordan.

2. All necessary measures will be taken and provisions made to assure the security of Israel and its neighbors during the transitional period and beyond. To assist in providing such security, a strong local police force will be constituted by the self-governing authority. It will be composed of inhabitants of the West Bank and Gaza. The police will maintain continuing liaison on internal security matters with the designated Israeli, Jordanian, and Egyptian officers.

3. During the transitional period, representatives of Egypt, Israel, Jordan, and the self-governing authority will constitute a continuing committee to decide by agreement on the modalities of admission of persons displaced from the West Bank and Gaza in 1967, together with necessary measures to prevent disruption and disorder. Other matters of common concern may also be dealt with by this committee.

4. Egypt and Israel will work with each other and with other interested parties to establish agreed procedures for a prompt, just, and permanent implementation of the resolution of the refugee problem.

B. Egypt-Israel

1. Egypt and Israel undertake not to resort to the threat or the use of force to settle disputes. Any disputes shall be settled by peaceful means in accordance with the provisions of Article 33 of the Charter of the United Nations.

2. In order to achieve peace between them, the parties agree to negotiate in good faith with a goal of concluding within three months from the signing of this Framework a peace treaty between them, while inviting the other parties to the conflict to proceed simultaneously to negotiate and conclude similar peace treaties with a view to achieving a comprehensive peace in the area. The Framework for the Conclusion of a Peace Treaty between Egypt and Israel will govern the peace negotiations between them. The parties will agree on the modalities and the timetable for the implementation of their obligations under the treaty.

C. Associated Principles

1. Egypt and Israel state that the principles and provisions described below should apply to peace treaties between Israel and each of its neighbors—Egypt, Jordan, Syria, and Lebanon.

2. Signatories shall establish among themselves relationships normal to states at peace with one another. To this end, they should undertake to abide by all the provisions of the Charter of the United Nations. Steps to be taken in this report include: (a) full recognition; (b) abolishing economic boycotts; (c) guaranteeing that under their jurisdiction the citizens of the other parties shall enjoy the protection of the due process of law.

3. Signatories should explore possibilities for economic development in the context of final peace treaties, with the objective of contributing to the atmosphere of peace, cooperation, and friendship which is their common goal.

4. Claims Commissions may be established for the mutual settlement of all financial claims.

5. The United States shall be invited to participate in the talks on matters related to the modalities of the implementation of the agreements and working out the timetable for the carrying out of the obligations of the parties.

6. The United Nations Security Council shall be requested to endorse the peace treaties and ensure that their provisions shall not be violated. The permanent members of the Security Council shall be requested to underwrite the peace treaties and ensure respect for their provisions. They shall also be requested to conform their policies' actions with the undertakings contained in this framework.

—Laqueur, 1984

Time For Peace Has Come

ISRAEL, PLO SIGN ACCORDS; RABIN AND ARAFAT SHAKE HANDS

Peres: Yesterday a dream, today a commitment

Prime Minister Yitzhak Rabin and PLO chairman Yasser Arafat sealed their peace accord with a handshake at a historic White House ceremony yesterday.

Rabin pledged to do his best to "embark upon a new era in the history of the Middle East," and to end the enmity that has brought wars, terrorism, and decades of ceaseless strife to Israelis and Palestinians.

The premier also cited Ecclesiastes, and concluded: "Ladies and gentlemen, the time for peace has come."

The 3,000 guests at the emotion-laden ceremony on the White House lawn, including former presidents George Bush and Jimmy Carter, heard President Bill Clinton say the occasion put "a peace of the brave within our reach."

Secretary of State Warren Christopher and Russian Foreign Minister Andrei Kozyrev served as official witnesses as Foreign Minister Shimon Peres and senior PLO official Mahmoud Abbas (Abu Mazen) signed the Declaration of Principles for Palestinian self-rule in the territories, beginning with Gaza and Jericho. They also counter-signed the letters of recognition Rabin and Arafat signed last week.

Before signing the declaration, Peres stated, "Yesterday a dream, today a commitment."

As applause rang out after the accord was signed, Arafat extended his hand to Rabin, Clinton threw his arm over Rabin's shoulder to draw him closer, and Rabin grabbed Arafat's hand and shook it.

In an uplifting speech, Rabin spoke directly to the Palestinians, saying, "We who have come from a land where parents bury their children, we who have fought against you, the Palestinians, we say to you today in a loud and clear voice: Enough of blood and tears, enough!"

"We wish to open a new chapter in the sad book of our lives together, a chapter of mutual recognition, of good neighborliness, of mutual respect, of understanding. We hope to embark on a new era in the history of the Middle East.

Arafat, wearing an olive green military-style uniform and his trademark black-and-white checkered keffiyeh and speaking in Arabic, said, "My people are hoping that this agreement which we are signing today marks the beginning of the end of a chapter of pain and suffering which has lasted throughout this century. My people are hoping that this agreement which we are signing today will usher in an age of peace, coexistence and equal rights.

"The battle for peace is the most difficult battle of our lives. It deserves our utmost efforts because the land of peace, the land of peace yearns for a just and comprehensive peace."

After Arafat finished his speech, he shook Rabins hand.

—*Jerusalem Post*, September 11, 1993

DECLARATION OF PRINCIPLES ON PALESTINIAN SELF-RULE

13 September 1993

The Government of the State of Israel and the Palestinian team (in the Jordanian-Palestinian delegation to the Middle East Peace Conference) (the "Palestinian Delegation") representing the Palestinian people, agree that it is time to put an end to decades of confrontation and conflict, recognize their mutual legitimate and political rights, and strive to live in peaceful coexistence and mutual dignity and security and achieve a just, lasting and comprehensive peace settlement and historic reconciliation through the agreed political process.

Accordingly, the two sides agreed to the following principles:

Article I
Aim of the negotiations

The aim of the Israeli-Palestinian negotiations within the current Middle East peace process is, among other things, to establish a Palestinian Interim Self-Government Authority, the elected Council, (the "Council") for the Palestinian people in the West Bank and the Gaza Strip, for a transitional period not exceeding five years, leading to a permanent settlement based on Security Council Resolutions 242 and 338.

It is understood that the interim arrangements are an integral part of the overall peace process and that final status negotiations will lead to the implementation of Security Council Resolution 242 and 338.

Article II
Framework for the interim period

The agreed framework for the interim period is set forth in the Declaration of Principles.

Article III
Elections

1. In order that the Palestinian people in the West Bank and Gaza Strip may govern themselves according to democratic principles, direct, free and general political elections will be held for the Council under agreed supervision and international observation, while the Palestinian police will ensure public order.
2. An agreement will be concluded on the exact mode and conditions of the elections in accordance with the protocol attached as Annex I, with the goal of holding the elections not later than nine months after the entry into force of this Declaration of Principles.
3. These elections will constitute a significant interim preparatory step toward the realization of the legitimate rights of the Palestinian people and their just requirements.

Article IV

Jurisdiction of the Council will cover West Bank and Gaza Strip territory, except for issues that will be negotiated in the permanent status negotiations. The two sides view the West Bank and the Baza Strip as a single territorial unit, whose integrity will be preserved during the interim period.

Article V
Transitional period and permanent
status negotiations

1. The five-year transitional period will begin upon the withdrawal from the Gaza Strip and Jericho area.
2. Permanent status negotiations will commence as soon as possible, but not later than the beginning of the third year of the interim period, between the Government of Israel and the Palestinian people representatives.
3. It is understood that these negotiations will cover remaining Jerusalem, refugees, settlements, borders, relations and cooperation with other neighbors, and other issues of common interest.
4. The two parties agree that the outcome of the permanent status negotiations should not be prejudiced or preempted by agreements reached for the interim period.

Article VI
Preparatory transfer of powers
and responsibilities

1. Upon the entry into force of the Declaration of Principles and the withdrawal from the Gaza Strip and Jericho area, a transfer of authority from the Israel military government and its Civil Administration to the authorized Palestinians for this task, as detailed herein, will commence. This transfer of authority will be of preparatory nature until the inauguration of the Council.
2. Immediately after the entry into force of this Declaration of Principles and the withdrawal from the Gaza Strip and Jericho area, with the view to promoting economic development in the West Bank and Gaza Strip, authority will be transferred to the Palestinians in the following spheres: education and culture, health, social welfare, direct taxation, and tourism.

The Palestinian side will commence in building the Palestinian police force, as agreed upon. Pending the inauguration of the Council, the two parties may negotiate the transfer of additional powers and responsibilities as agreed upon.

Article VII
Interim agreement

1. The Israeli and Palestinian delegations will negotiate an agreement on the interim period (the "Interim Agreement").
2. The Interim Agreement shall specify, among other things, the structure of the Council, the number of its members, and the transfer of powers and responsibilities from the Israeli military government and its Civil Administration to the Council. The Interim Agreement shall also specify the Councils executive authority, legislative authority in accordance with Article IX below, and the independent Palestinian judicial organs.
3. The Interim Agreement shall include arrangements, to be implemented upon the inauguration of the Council, for the assumption by the Council of all of the powers and responsibilities transferred previously in accordance with Article VI above.
4. In order to enable the Council to promote economic growth, upon its inauguration, the Council will establish, among other things, a Palestinian Electricity Authority, a Gaza Sea Port Authority, a Palestinian Development Bank, a Palestinian Export Promotion Board, a Palestinian Environmental Authority, a Palestinian Land Authority and a Palestinian Water Administration Authority, and any other authorities agreed upon, in accordance with the Interim Agreement that will specify their powers and responsibilities.
5. After the inauguration of the Council, the Civil Administration will be dissolved, and the Israeli military government will be withdrawn.

Article VIII
Public order and Security

In order to guarantee public order and internal security for the Palestinians of the West Bank and the Gaza Strip, the Council will establish a strong police force, while Israel will continue to carry the responsibility for defending against external threats, as well as the responsibility for overall security of the Israelis to protect their internal security and public order.

Article IX
Laws and military orders

1. The Council will be empowered to legislate, in accordance with the Interim Agreement, within all authorities transferred to it.
2. Both parties will review jointly laws and military orders presently in force in remaining spheres.

Article X
Joint Israel-Palestinian liaison committee

In order to provide for a smooth implementation of this Declaration of Principles and any subsequent agreements pertaining to the interim period, upon the entry into force of this Declaration of Principles, a Joint Israeli-Palestinian Liaison Committee will be established in order to deal with issues requiring coordination, other issues of common interest, and disputes.

Article XI
Israeli-Palestinian cooperation in economic fields

Recognizing the mutual benefit of cooperation in promoting the development of the West Bank, the Gaza Strip, and Israel, upon the entry into force of this Declaration of Principles, an Israeli-Palestinian Economic Cooperation Committee will be established in order to develop and implement in a cooperative manner the programs identified in the protocols attached as Annex III and Annex IV.

Article XII
Liaison and cooperation with Jordan and Egypt

The two parties will invite the Governments of Jordan and Egypt to participate in establishing further liaison and cooperation arrangements between the Government of Israel and the Palestinian representatives, on one hand, and the Governments of Jordan and Egypt, on the other hand, to promote cooperation between them. These arrangements will include the constitution of a Continuing Committee that will decide by agreement on the modalities of the admission of persons displaced from the West Bank and Gaza Strip in 1967, together with necessary measures to prevent disruption and disorder. Other matters of common concern will be dealt with by this Committee.

Article XIII
Redeployment of Israeli forces

1. After the entry into force of this Declaration of Principles, and not later than the eve of elections for the Council, a redeployment of Israeli military forces in the West Bank and the Gaza Strip will take place, in addition to withdrawal of Israeli forces carried out in accordance with Article XIV.
2. In redeploying its military forces, Israel will be guided by the principle that its military forces should be redeployed outside the populated areas.
3. Further redeployments to specified locations will be gradually implemented commensurate with the assumption of responsibility for public order and internal security by the Palestinian police force pursuant to Article VIII above.

Article XIV
Israeli withdrawal from the Gaza Strip and Jericho area

Israel will withdraw from the Gaza Strip and Jericho area, as detailed in the protocol attached as Annex II.

Article XV
Resolution of disputes

1. Disputes arising out of the application or interpretation of this Declaration of Principles, or any subsequent agreements pertaining to the interim period, shall be resolved by negotiations through the Joint Liaison Committee to be established pursuant to Article X above.
2. Disputes which cannot be settled by negotiations may be resolved by a mechanism of conciliation to be agreed upon by the parties.
3. The parties may agree to submit to arbitration disputes relating to the interim period, which cannot be settled through conciliation. To

this end, upon the agreement of both parties, the parties will establish an Arbitration Committee.

Article XVI
Israeli-Palestinian cooperation concerning regional programs

Both parties view the multilateral working groups as an appropriate instrument for promoting a "Marshall Plan," the regional programs and other programs, including special programs for the West Bank and Gaza Strip, as indicated in the protocol attached as Annex I.

Article XVII
Miscellaneous provisions

1. This Declaration of Principles will enter into force one month after its signing.
2. All protocols annexed to this Declaration of Principles and Agreed Minutes pertaining thereto shall be regarded as an integral part hereof.

Annex I—
Protocol on the Mode and Conditions of Elections

1. Palestinians of Jerusalem who live there will have the right to participate in the election process, according to an agreement between the two sides.
2. In addition, the election agreement should cover, among other things, the following issues:
   a. the system of elections,
   b. the mode of the agreed supervision and international observation and their personal composition, and
   c. rules and regulations regarding election campaigns, including agreed arrangements for the organizing of mass media, and the possibility of licensing a broadcasting and TV station.
3. The future status of displaced Palestinians who were registered on 4th June 1967 will not be prejudiced because they are unable to participate in the election process due to practical reasons.

Annex II—
Protocol on Withdrawal of Israeli Forces from
the Gaza Strip and Jericho Area

1. The two sides will conclude and sign within two months from the date of entry into force of this Declaration of Principles, an agreement on the withdrawal of Israeli military forces from the Gaza Strip and Jericho area. This agreement will include comprehensive arrangements to apply in the Gaza Strip and the Jericho area subsequent to the Israel withdrawal.

2. Israel will implement an accelerated and scheduled withdrawal of Israeli military forces from the Gaza Strip and Jericho area, beginning immediately with the signing of the agreement on the Gaza Strip and Jericho area and to be completed within a period not exceeding four months after the signing of this agreement.

3. The above agreement will include, among other things:
   a. Arrangements for a smooth and peaceful transfer of authority from the Israeli military government and Civil Administration to the Palestinian representatives.
   b. Structure, powers, and responsibilities of the Palestinian authority in these areas, except, external security, settlements, Israelis, foreign relations, and other subjects mutually agreed upon.
   c. Arrangements for assumption of internal security and public order by the Palestinian police force consisting of police officers recruited locally and from abroad (holding Jordanian passports and Palestinian documents issued by Egypt). Those who will participate in the Palestinian police force coming from abroad should be trained as police and police officers.
   d. A temporary international or foreign presence, as agreed upon.
   e. Establishment of a joint Palestinian-Israeli coordination and cooperation committee for mutual security purposes.
   f. An economic development and stabilization program, including the establishment of an Emergency Fund, to encourage foreign investment, and financial and economic

support. Both sides will coordinate and cooperate jointly and unilaterally with regional and international parties to support these aims.
   g. Arrangements for a safe passage for persons and transportation between the Gaza Strip and Jericho area.

4. The above agreement will include arrangements for coordination between both parties regarding passages:
   a. Gaza-Egypt; and
   b. Jericho-Jordan

5. The officers responsible for carrying out the powers and responsibilities of the Palestinian authority under this Annex II and Article VI of the Declaration of the Principles will be located in the Gaza Strip and in the Jericho area pending the inauguration of the Council.

6. Other than these agreed arrangements, the status of the Gaza Strip and Jericho area will continue to be an integral part of the West Bank and Gaza Strip, and will not be changed in the interim period.

PROTOCOL ON ISRAELI-PALESTINIAN COOPERATION IN ECONOMIC AND DEVELOPMENT PROGRAMS

The two sides agree to establish an Israeli-Palestinian Continuing Committee for Economic Cooperation, focusing, among other things, on the following:

1. Cooperation in the field of water, including a Water Development Program prepared by experts from both sides, which will also specify the mode of cooperation in the management of water resources in the West Bank and Gaza Strip, and will include proposals for studies and plans on water rights of each party, as well as on the equitable utilization of joint water resources for implementation in and beyond the interim period.

2. Cooperation in the field of electricity, including an Electricity Development Program, which will also specify the mode of cooperation for the production, maintenance, purchase, and sale of electricity resources.

3. Cooperation in the field of energy, including an Energy Development Program, which will provide for the exploitation of oil and gas for

industrial purposes, particularly in the Gaza Strip and in the Negev, and will encourage further joint exploitation of other energy resources. This Program may also provide for the construction of a petrochemical industrial complex in the Gaza Strip and the construction of oil and gas pipelines.

4. Cooperation in the field of finance, including a Financial Development and Action Program for the encouragement of international investment in the West Bank and the Gaza Strip, and in Israel, as well as the establishment of a Palestinian Development Bank.

5. Cooperation in the fields of transport and communications, including a Program which will define guidelines for the establishment of a Gaza Sea Port Area, and will provide for the establishing of a transport and communications lines to and from the West Bank and the Gaza Strip to Israel and other countries. In addition, this Program will provide for carrying out the necessary construction of roads, railways, communication lines, etc.

6. Cooperation in the field of trade, including studies, and Trade Promotion Programs, which will encourage local, regional, and inter-regional trade, as well as a feasibility study of creating free trade zones in the Gaza Strip and in Israel, mutual access to these zones, and cooperation in other areas related to trade and commerce.

7. Cooperation in the field of industry, including industrial Development Programs, which will provide for the establishment of joint Israeli-Palestinian Research and Development Centers, will promote Palestinian-Israeli joint ventures, and provide guidelines for cooperation in the textile, food, pharmaceutical, electronics, diamonds, computer and science-based industries.

8. A program for cooperation in, and regulation of, labor relations and cooperation in social welfare issues.

9. A Human Resources Development and Cooperation Plan, providing for joint Israeli-Palestinian workshops and seminars, and for the establishment of joint vocational training centres, research institutes, and data banks.

10. An Environmental Protection Plan, providing for joint and/or coordinated measures in this sphere.

11. A program for developing coordination and cooperation in the field of communication and media.

12. Any other program of mutual interest.

PROTOCOL ON ISRAELI-PALESTINIAN COOPERATION CONCERNING REGIONAL DEVELOPMENT PROGRAMS

1. The two sides will cooperate in the context of the multilateral peace efforts in promoting a Development Program for the region, including the West Bank and Gaza Strip, to be initiated by the G-7. The parties will request the G-7 to seek the participation in this program of other interested states, such as members of the Organization for Economic Cooperation and Development, regional Arab states and institutions, as well as members of the private sector.

2. The Development Program will consist of two elements:
   a) an Economic Development Program for the West Bank and the Gaza Strip;
   b) A Regional Economic Development Program.

   A. *The Economic Development Program for the West Bank and the Gaza Strip* will consist of the following elements:
   (1) A Social Rehabilitation Program including a Housing and Construction Program.
   (2) A Small and Medium Business Development Plan.
   (3) An Infrastructure Development Program (water, electricity, transportation and communications, etc.)
   (4) A Human Resources Plan.
   (5) Other programs.

   B. *The Regional Economic Development Program* may consist of the following elements:
   (1) The establishment of a Middle East Development Fund, as a first step, and a Middle East Development Bank, as a second step.
   (2) The development of a joint Israeli-Pales-

tinian-Jordanian Plan for coordinated exploitation of the Dead Sea Area.

(3) The Mediterranean Sea (Gaza)—Dead Sea Canal

(4) Regional Desalinization and other water development projects.

(5) A regional plan for agricultural development, including a coordinated regional effort for the prevention of desertification.

(6) Interconnection of electricity grids.

(7) Regional cooperation for the transfer, distribution and industrial exploitation of gas, oil and other energy resources.

(8) A regional Tourism, Transportation, and Telecommunications Development Plan.

(9) Regional co-operation in other spheres.

3. The two sides will encourage the multi-lateral working groups, and will coordinate toward its success. The two parties will encourage international activities, as well as prefeasibility and feasibility studies, within the various multilateral working groups.

—"Oslo Agreement on
Palestinian Self-Rule," 1993,
Source: Government of Israel

Rabin, Arafat Sign Gaza/Jericho Pact

PLO Chairman Yasser Arafat asked Israel to slow the pace of transition in Gaza-Jericho by "up to four weeks" to assure an orderly transfer to the new Palestinian authority, Prime Minister Yitzhak Rabin told reporters here yesterday. He said that although Israel originally hoped to leave in 10 days, he would comply.

Rabin's remarks came at the end of a landmark day, which saw the signing of the 200-page accord signaling the first time that Palestinians will be given control over their own lives.

The ceremony was marred by an embarrassingly visible confrontation over whether Arafat would sign the agreement's accompanying maps, which included a smaller Jericho area than he had wanted. An angry, red-faced Rabin threatened to halt the ceremony, as the center-stage pressures on Arafat from all sides were easily discerned by the 2,500 spectators in the hall and millions watching on television.

The ceremony was abruptly adjourned for a few

minutes amid concern that the entire agreement could unravel.

Arafat eventually signed the maps, but added a lengthy proviso that the validity of his signature was dependent on Rabin's agreement to an existing accompanying letter, which says that Israel will discuss increasing the 62 sq. km. allotted to autonomous Jericho, along with a promise to settle differences over whether a Palestinian policeman would be stationed on the Allenby Bridge and whether a Palestinian would run the Rafiah crossing terminal.

PLO spokesman Marwah Kanafani said it was unfair to blame Arafat, since it was known he did not like the proposed size of Jericho and "he did not know that maps would be signed." Israeli officials disagreed, noting that the Palestinians participated fully in preparations for the ceremony.

Israeli officials charged Arafat brought brinkmanship to a new level and a top Rabin aide called the spectacle a "disgrace."

In his remarks to reporters yesterday afternoon, Rabin played down what he called a "minor incident," preferring to focus on the future. "We could complete the handing over in two to three weeks, perhaps even in 10 days," he said. "The problem today, as the chairman of the PLO said last night, is that he might delay up to two, three, or four weeks. We would like to get out as quickly as possible."

While cautious not to attack Arafat openly, Rabin did issue veiled criticism, suggesting that the delay is due to the PLO's preoccupation with symbols to the detriment of the nuts and bolts of governance. Israeli officials complained that they pleaded with the PLO to dispatch 300 Palestinian police early to begin an overlapping period, only to meet with refusal.

Now, the PLO realizes there is a problem. It sent 22 policemen to Gaza yesterday, Rabin said, and is now willing to send officials to take the reins of the 38 spheres of civilian life in the territories. He openly questioned where the PLO will get the funds to pay the salaries of the approximately 24,000 Palestinian workers of the civil administration, and how it will manage to keep 18,000 Palestinians on public works projects.

He hoped that the international donors panel,

which committed $2.2 billion to the Palestinian authority over a five-year period, would help.

Chief Palestinian negotiator Nabil Sha'ath later confirmed the PLO had asked Israel to delay the withdrawal.

"Mr. Arafat did ask him to make sure that the overlap will take place [so] that they will not leave too soon before we are in," Sha'ath told reporters. "We are talking about a few weeks, not talking about years. I don't think that reflects . . . . any crisis," he added.

Rabin and his entourage returned last night to a festive welcome at Ben-Gurion airport. He later attended an outdoor rally in Tel Aviv in support of the Gaza/Jericho accord. "Don't pay attention to those who celebrate bloodshed," he told thousands outside the Tel Aviv museum. At the signing ceremony, Arafat signed the three copies of the accord, which included security, civilian, economic, and legal annexes, then quickly thumbed through the six accompanied maps without signing.

When it was Rabin's turn to sign, Foreign Ministry legal adviser Yoel Singer whispered, "He didn't sign the maps." Rabin replied, "Then neither will I."

Returning to his place alongside Mubarak, Rabin visibly complained about Arafat's refusal to sign. Using unmistakable body language, including shaking his head, he said he would not speak unless Arafat signed. However, using his own hand gestures of refusal, plus a stony-faced stance, Arafat refused.

Foreign Minister Shimon Peres and Egyptian Foreign Minister Amr Moussa became involved, and both, along with Egyptian President Hosni Mubarak, motioned that Arafat must sign. US Secretary of State Warren Christopher stood alongside Arafat, awkward and motionless, only to become involved in talking with Mubarak and Arafat after calling his aide, Dennis Ross, to the podium.

Other Palestinians and Israelis were also called to the podium, and the discussions continued during the speeches. With the public ignoring the speeches and riveted on the political theater, the ceremony was abruptly halted.

Talking to reporters afterward, Rabin recalled his 6 1/2 hour conversation with Arafat the night before, during which he agreed to extend the area of Jericho from 55 sq. km. to 62 sq. km. Arafat, however, wanted more.

"I agreed that we would sign on the basis of my position, and could continue to discuss the issues. But when we signed, it would be on the basis of my answers." He added, "There is no agreement without maps."

—*Jerusalem Post*, May 5, 1994

Five Key Points Made Agreement Possible

Five key understandings made the peace treaty possible, a very senior official said in a briefing for reporters last night, as he disclosed the main provisions of the accord.

The five understandings reached are: The two countries will trade small parcels of territory, and Israel would lease other areas from Jordan; Israel agreed to yield 50 million cu. m. of water and participate in projects that would yield 100 million cu. m. more; and Jordan agreed that its territory would not be a launching pad for third-party attacks against Israel.

Also, Israel will consult Jordan before it begins talks on the future of Palestinian refugees there in final-status talks with the PLO, and the two countries will exchange embassies within a month after the treaty is ratified by the respective parliaments.

Meanwhile, Prime Minister Yitzhak Rabin phoned both Egyptian president Hosni Mubarak and PLO chairman Yasser Arafat to brief them on the accord. Mubarak informed Rabin that Syrian president Hafez Assad is flying to Cairo today, presumably to discuss the implications of the treaty.

Rabin also briefed leaders of the political opposition last night on the main points of the accord.

Likud leader Binyamin Netanyahu said that "the general direction is positive. This shows peace can be made without unilateral concessions. Territory can be exchanged. I still want to withhold comment on all the specifics, however, until I study the wording."

The official 15-page text of the treaty has not been released.

According to the senior official, the main provisions are:

- Border demarcation: Israel will return over 300 sq. km. to Jordan. The two countries agreed to respect the 1922 British Mandate map, while Israeli farmers would not be forced off lands currently being cultivated. Jordan accepted some 30 sq. km. of the Arava in exchange for these lands.

"We gave them inch for inch. Jordan did not lose an inch of territory," the official said. He admitted Israel wrongfully seized Jordanian land in the Arava, saying it was fair for Israel to trade for such territory if it sought to keep some of these fields.

Other areas will come under Jordan sovereignty, but be immediately leased back for 25 years, with an option to renew. They are: 2,000 dunams farmed by Kibbutz Tsofar in the Arava and 800 dunams near the Yarmuk River called Naharayim. Israeli policemen will be allowed to enter the territory with weapons for self-defense.

"One could have gone to arbitration," he said, "but it could have taken years," alluding to Taba, when Israel lost its case after years of wrangling.

The official did not deny suggestions that this model of territorial exchange and leasing could be used as a precedent in negotiations with Syria.

- Water: Israel agreed to yield 40 million cu. m. of Yarmuk River water annually, and 10 million cu. m. more will be provided through desalination of brackish water sources near the Kinneret. No water will be taken from the Kinneret itself, as Israel fears this would be a bad precedent in future talks with Syria.

Beyond this 50 million cu. m., the two countries will construct two dams on the Yarmuk and Jordan rivers. Israel is not responsible for financing these projects, but will approach other countries to ask for financing. Another 50 million cu. m. may be found should the regional development "visions of [Foreign Minister Shimon] Peres" succeed, the official said, but "we did not commit ourselves."

- Security threats: Jordan will neither join alliances against Israel nor will it let its territory serve as a launching pad for attacks. Jordan also agreed that it will not allow third parties to deploy inside its territory in ways that threaten Israel, and vice versa.

Israel originally wanted to forbid foreign forces from ever entering Jordan, but settled on more general wording to satisfy concerns that such broad language would rule out joint maneuvers with the US.

The official hinted that the same wording used in the Israel-Egyptian peace treaty to offset the 1954 Arab League collective security agreement would be repeated in this treaty.

- Refugees: Israel agreed to consult with Jordan before it negotiates the fate of refugees from 1948 in final-status talks with the Palestinians. Those talks are scheduled to begin less than two years from now. At least half the Jordanian population is Palestinian.

This marks the second time that Rabin is officially making Jordan a player in the final-status talks with the PLO. In July's Washington Declaration, Israel said it would take into consideration Jordan's special status in safeguarding of Moslem holy places in Jerusalem.

It also reaffirms the commitments made in the Camp David and Oslo accords on Palestinians displaced by the Six Day War—that Israel, Jordan, the Palestinians, and Egypt will discuss their future.

- Normalization: The official suggested there are no disagreements over the two basic elements of normalization—diplomatic relations and tourism.

According to the treaty, embassies will be established a month after ratification. Jordan and Israel are both eager to create tourism packages, especially for tourists from third countries.

The senior official said he believed the peace treaty would improve the prospects for peace between Israel and its other Arab neighbors, including Syria.

—*Jerusalem Post*, October 18, 1994

Israeli-Jordanian Peace Treaty, 1994

Below is the full text of the peace treaty signed October 26 on the Jordanian-Israeli border by Jordanian prime minister Abdessalam Majali and Israeli prime minister Yitzhak Rabin, with President Bill Clinton signing as witness.

Preamble

The Government of the State of Israel and the Government of the Hashemite Kingdom of Jordan:

Bearing in mind the Washington Declaration, signed by them of 25th July, 1994, and which they are both committed to honor;

Aiming at the achievement of a just, lasting, and comprehensive peace in the Middle East based on Security Council resolutions 242 and 338 in all their aspects;

Bearing in mind the importance of maintaining and strengthening peace based on freedom, equality, justice, and respect for fundamental human rights, thereby overcoming psychological barriers and promoting human dignity;

Reaffirming their faith in the purposes and principles of the Charter of the United Nations and recognizing their right and obligation to live in peace with each other as well as with all states, within secure and recognized boundaries;

Desiring to develop friendly relations and cooperation between them in accordance with the principles of international law governing international relations in time of peace;

Desiring as well to ensure lasting security for both their States and in particular to avoid threats and the use of force between them;

Bearing in mind that in their Washington Declaration of 25th July, 1994, they declared the termination of the state of belligerency between them;

Deciding to establish peace between them in accordance with this Treaty of Peace;

Have agreed as follows:

Article I—Establishment of Peace

Peace hereby established between the State of Israel and the Hashemite Kingdom of Jordan (the "Parties") effective from the exchange of the instruments of ratification of this Treaty.

Article II—General Principles

The Parties will apply between them the provisions of the Charter of the United Nations and the principles of international law governing relations among states in times of peace. In particular:

1. They recognize and will respect each others sovereignty, territorial integrity, and political independence;
2. They recognize and will respect each others right to live in peace within secure and recognized boundaries;
3. They will develop good neighborly relations of cooperation between them to ensure lasting security, will refrain from the threat or use of force against each other, and will settle all disputes between them by peaceful means;
4. They respect and recognize the sovereignty, territorial integrity, and political independence of every state in the region;
5. They respect and recognize the pivotal role of human development and dignity in regional and bilateral relationships;
6. They further believe that within their control, involuntary movements of persons in such a way as to adversely prejudice the security of either Party should not be permitted.

MAIN POINTS: TREATY OF PEACE BETWEEN ISRAEL, JORDAN

In addition to banning all hostile activities, the peace treaty with Jordan recognizes the importance of cooperation in all spheres, developing good neighborly relations, and respecting the role of human development and dignity in the region.

The treaty with Jordan comprises thirty articles and five annexes which address boundary demarcations, water issues, police cooperation, environmental issues, and mutual border crossings.

In particular, the Agreement establishes the following arrangements:

1. International Boundary:

The Agreement delimits the agreed international boundary between Israel and Jordan, including territorial waters and airspace. This boundary is delimited with reference to the Mandate boundary, and is shown on the maps attached to the Agreement.

The Agreement provides for some minor mutual border modifications, which will enable Israeli farmers in the Arava to continue to cultivate their land.

The Naharayim/Baqura Area and Zofar Area will fall under Jordanian sovereignty, with Israeli private land use rights. These rights include unimpeded freedom of entry to, exit from, and movement within the area. These areas are not subject to the customs of immigration legislation. These rights will remain in force for twenty-five years, and will be renewed automatically for the same period unless either country wishes to terminate the arrangement, in which case consultations will be taken.

2. Security:

The two parties will refrain from any act of belligerency or hostility, will ensure that no threats of violence against the other party originate from within their territory, and will take necessary and effective measures to prevent acts of terrorism. They will also refrain from joining a coalition whose objectives include military aggression against the other party.

The two countries will establish a Conference on Security and Cooperation in the Middle East (CSCME), which will be modeled after the Conference on Security and Cooperation in Europe (CSCE). This is an ambitious attempt to replace the more traditional view of security by substituting the old notions of deterrence and military preparedness with confidence-building measures. In due time, confidence building will lead to the establishment of mutual trust and institutions aimed at preventing war and enhancing cooperation.

3. Relations Between Jordan and Israel:

Not only does the peace treaty deal with an end to war, but it also calls for normalization. The two countries will establish full diplomatic relations, including the appointment of ambassadors and the establishment of embassies. Various articles of the treaty deal with practical issues of normalization in such matters as culture and science, the war against crime and drugs, transportation and roads,

postal services and telecommunications, tourism, the environment, energy, health, agriculture, and the development of the Jordan Rift Valley and the Aqaba/Eilat area.

Israel and Jordan will abstain from hostile propaganda and will repeal all discriminatory references and expressions of hostility in their respective legislation.

Economic cooperation is seen as one of the pillars of peace, vital to the promotion of secure and harmonious relations between the two peoples. To this end, negotiations are underway in order to conclude agreements on economic cooperation, including, of course, the termination of boycotts, the establishment of a free-trade area, investment, banking, industrial cooperation, and labor.

Direct telephone and fax lines have already been set up between the two countries. Postal links will be set up shortly, together with wireless, cable, and television relays. An agreement to facilitate and encourage tourism is close to ratification.

4. Water:

Israel and Jordan have agreed on allocations of water from the Jordan and Yarmouk Rivers and from the Araba/Arava groundwaters. Israel has agreed to transfer to Jordan 50 million cubic meters (1.8 billion cubic feet) of water annually from the northern part of the country. In addition, the two countries have agreed to cooperate to alleviate the water shortage by developing existing and new water resources, by preventing contamination of water resources, and by minimizing water wastage.

5. Refugees and Displaced Persons:

The parties recognize the human problems caused by the conflict in the Middle East, and agree to alleviate them on a bilateral level, and to try to resolve them through three channels:

1. The quadripartite committee with Egypt and the Palestinians with regard to displaced persons.
2. The Multilateral Working Group on Refugees.
3. Negotiations in a framework to be agreed upon—bilateral, or otherwise—in conjunction with permanent-status negotiations detailed in the Declaration of Principles.

6. Places of Historical, Religious Significance:

There will be freedom of access to the places of religious and historical significance. In accordance with the Washington Declaration, Israel respects the present special role of the Hashemite Kingdom of Jordan in Muslim holy shrines in Jerusalem. When negotiations on the permanent status will take place, as detailed in the Declaration of Principles, Israel will give high priority to the Jordanian historic role in these shrines.

7. Freedom of Passage:

Nationals from both countries and their vehicles will be permitted freedom of movement through open roads and border crossings. Vessels from either country will have the right to passage through territorial waters, and will be granted access to ports. Negotiations are underway toward a Civil Aviation Agreement. The Strain of Tiran and the Gulf of Aqaba are considered international waterways, open to all nations for freedom of navigation and overflight.

8. Interim Period:

Even before the establishment of diplomatic relations and the completion of a comprehensive tourism agreement, interim measures regarding tourism will begin immediately after the ratification of the treaty. For example, a total of 550 visas a day will be granted to Israelis wishing to tour in Jordan during the interim period.

9. Joint Projects:

Jordan and Israel will maintain good neighborly relations by cooperating in many spheres on joint projects. Among the projects are: development of energy and water resources, protecting the natural environment, and joint tourism development of the Jordan Rift Valley.

> —Israel-Jordan Peace Treaty, 1994,
> *Source:* Government of Israel from
> Near East Report

Deepening the Sources

Summarize and read aloud selections from the three documents: (1) Israel and Egypt—Camp David Agreement; (2) Israel and the PLO—Oslo Accords; (3) Israel and Jordan. What are the major issues at stake in each treaty? Have these treaties been maintained?

Terrorism has created painful obstacles to peace. Some Israelis want to abandon the peace negotiations and others feel that they must be maintained at any price. What are the arguments on each side? What is your opinion?

As this is being written in February 1995, Syria remains the one neighbor with whom Israel has not entered into a formal treaty. Syria is asking Israel to give up the Golan Heights as part of the agreement. Israel is considering this in light of the possible availability of electronic satellite surveillance equipment that, along with a demilitarized zone, could provide secure borders. The problem this does not address is the status of the cities and settlements Israel built in the Golan. Refer to current newspapers and other contemporary sources and consider how you would resolve the situation.

NOTE: These activities (and all the activities in this chapter) should be revised as circumstances change in these very fluid situations.

Read the articles from the Jerusalem Post on the Israel-Egypt truce ending the Yom Kippur War (1973) and the Camp David Agreements (1979); the articles on the pullback from Lebanon (1985), the peace agreement with the PLO (1994), and the treaty with Jordan (1994).

Arabs raise the question of the future of Jerusalem. There are three major proposals: to maintain its status quo as a unified city under Israel's control; to divide Jerusalem as it was prior to 1967; and to make it an international city.

The idea of internationalization of Jerusalem grows out of the 1947 Partition Plan of the United Nations General Assembly. The plan called for Jerusalem to be administered by an international regime that would devise "suitable guarantees for the protection of the Holy Places both within and outside Jerusalem." Discuss your reactions to these proposals.

The phrase "status quo" refers to an understanding in existence since Ottoman days based on a distinction between religious rights and secular authority. The agreement is not contingent on the city being administered by the followers of any particular religion. It does not depend upon Christians or Moslems sharing in the secular au-

thority as an expression and assertion of their due rights in the places holy to them. It requires that all religions be free to control the religious nature of the holy places. This is and has been respected by Israel.

An excellent discussion of this is found in the pamphlet "Jerusalem, Issues and Perspectives," from the Israel Information Centre, Jerusalem, 1977.

IN SUMMATION

- Israel wants peace.
- The Arabs formerly wanted to destroy Israel. With the disappearance of the power and support of the Soviet Union, most Arab nations are now willing to negotiate a peace.
- The peace process is not just about the absence of war; it is about territorial concessions, boundaries, security, and relations between self-governing entities.
- Israel is attempting to make peace not with one country only but with numerous nations.
- Great progress in the last few years is documented by treaties with the PLO and Jordan in addition to the 1979 treaty with Egypt.
- The question of the future of Jerusalem continues to be a potentially volatile issue.

ADDITIONAL LEARNING POSSIBILITIES

1. Invite an Israeli to speak to the group about his/her experiences during the Six-Day War.

2. The music and art of Israel represent dreaming and striving for peace; other works capture the deep sorrow and bitterness. Analyze the music and poetry of the last several decades for the attitudes toward peace reflected in them.

3. View the film *Late Summer Blues*, which depicts the brutally harsh story of high school graduates facing army duty in a country in a constant state of war.

4. Lead a congregational observance for Yom Yerushalayim. The sources can be used as reference materials. Additional materials can be obtained from the ARZA office.

PERTINENT SITES TO VISIT IN ISRAEL

- Walk along the safe areas of the pre-'48 border between Jordan and Israel
- Follow the footsteps of those who united Jerusalem: Police Station, Ammunition Hill, Lion's Gate, Western Wall
- Visit with settlers in the Golan to discuss issues of territorial concessions
- Dialogue with Knesset speakers on peace efforts
- Rockefeller Museum
- Damascus Gate
- Notre Dame
- Music of Israel with David Israel

CHAPTER 12

JERUSALEM IN JEWISH PRAYER AND LAW

BACKGROUND

Every article or book on the centrality of Jerusalem includes observances, quotations, and prayers that have been a part of Judaism for centuries. Even when there was no Jewish nation in its land, Jerusalem remained central to our life and thought. Each day when we thank God for our food, we pray also for Jerusalem.

Three times daily, in the recitation of the *Amidah*, Jerusalem as the dwelling place of God is the theme of the fourteenth blessing. Each time we recite it, weekday or Shabbat, we ask that our prayers be acceptable and look forward to the time when God's presence "returns to Zion."

The Torah service as well contains references to Zion, to Jerusalem.

Under the bridal canopy a glass is broken in solemn remembrance of the destruction of the Temple in Jerusalem. Ashkenazi Jews shout "Mazel Tov" while Sephardic Jews recite the verse, "If I forget you, O Jerusalem, let my right hand forget its cunning."

The great majority of synagogues throughout the world are built facing Jerusalem. Jews praying alone or in a minyan face the Holy City.

Holidays are celebrated according to a calendar reflecting and adjusting itself to the seasons in Jerusalem's land.

We conclude the Passover Seder with "Next Year in Jerusalem." In a Seder ritual in the Sephardic tradition participants ask each other, "Where are you going?" The response: "I am going to Jerusalem." We end the most solemn of Yom Kippur services, the Ne'ila, the closing service, with those same words, "Next Year in Jerusalem." Jews throughout the world celebrate Yom Yerushalayim commemorating the reunification of Jerusalem during the Six-Day War. When we paint and plaster our homes, we leave an empty space to recall Jerusalem. When a Jew dies, earth from Jerusalem is placed inside the coffin.

Jerusalem has been, is, and will always be a vital part of our system of belief, a word that is constantly on our lips and a concept that is represented in many of our religious acts.

JERUSALEM AS CENTER
From the *Amidah*

Sound the great Shofar for our freedom; lift up the banner to bring our exiles together, and assemble us from the four corners of the earth. Blessed art thou, Adonai, who gatherest the dispersed of thy people Israel.

Return in mercy to thy city Jerusalem and dwell in it as thou hast promised; rebuild it soon, in our days, as an everlasting structure, and speedily establish in it the throne of David. Blessed art thou, Adonai, Builder of Jerusalem.

May our eyes behold thy return in mercy

to Zion. Blessed art thou, O Lord, who restorest thy divine presence to Zion.

Deepening the Sources

The Amidah *selections focus on one aspect of our prayers for Israel. What is that? The prayers deal with both political and spiritual visions. Which apply to which?*

Excerpt from the Torah Service

Ki mitzion tetze Torah ud'var Adonai miyerushalayim.
For out of Zion shall go forth Torah, and the word of Adonai from Jerusalem.

Baruch sh'natan Torah l'amo Yisrael bik'dushato.
Praised be the One who in holiness has given the Torah to the people Israel.

Sh'ma Yisrael Adonai Eloheynu Adonai Echad.
Hear, O Israel: Adonai is our God, Adonai is One!

Echad Eloheynu, Gadol Adoneynu, kadosh sh'mo.
Our God is One; our God is great; holy is God's name.

Gad'lu Adonai iti un'rom'mah sh'mo yachdav.
O magnify Adonai with me, and together let us exalt God's name.

Deepening the Sources

When the Torah is taken from the ark we chant these passages from Isaiah. What is the impact of linking the Torah service to Jerusalem? What does it make you think about?

Excerpts from the Grace after Meals

For this good earth that you have entrusted to our mothers and fathers, and to us; for our deliverance from bondage; for the convenant You have sealed into our hearts; for Your life-giving love and grace; for Torah, our way of life, and for the food that sustains us day by day, we give You thanks.

For all this we thank You. Let Your praise ever be on the lips of all who live, as it is written: 'When you have eaten and are satisfied, give praise to your God who has given you this good earth.'

We praise You, O God, for the earth, and for its sustenance. Amen

Eternal God, source of our being, show compassion for Israel Your people, Jerusalem Your city, and Zion, the ancient dwelling-place of Your glory. Guide and sustain us in all our habitations, and be a help to us in all our troubles. May we ever be able to help ourselves and one another, even as we rely on Your open and generous bounty.

Let Jerusalem, the holy city, be renewed in our time. We praise You, O God; in compassion You rebuild Jerusalem. Amen.

from *On the Doorposts of Your House*, CCAR, 1994, pp. 10–14

Deepening the Sources

Review the biblical history contained in the Grace after Meals. Did we ever give up our spiritual claim to Eretz Yisrael? What is "the covenant which thou has sealed in our flesh?" What does linking the land with our daily food do for us, both in terms of our perception of God's relationship to us and our relationship to the land? The reciting of Grace is supposed to take something very mundane and raise it to a level of holiness. How is this accomplished?

Selections from Psalms

Jerusalem which is built as a city
that fosters togetherness . . .
Inquire after the peace of Jerusalem;
May those who love you enjoy serenity.

—Psalm 122

Those who trust in God are as Mount Zion
which cannot be moved, but abides forever.
Jerusalem, mountains surround it as God
is round about the people, from now and forever.

—Psalm 125

When God restored the exiles to Zion, it seemed like a dream. Our mouths were filled with laughter, our tongues with joyful song. Then they said among the nations: God has done great things for them. Yes, God is doing great things for us, and we are joyful. Restore our fortunes, O God, as streams revive the desert. Then those who have sown in tears shall reap in joy. Those who go forth weeping, carrying bags of seeds, shall come home with shouts of joy, bearing their sheaves.

—Psalm 126, *Note: This is also the introductory psalm to* Birkat Ha-Mazon, *Grace after Meals, when recited on Sabbaths and Festivals. From* On the Doorposts of Your House, *p. 9.*

May God bless you out of Zion!
And may you see the goodness of
Jerusalem all the days of your life.

—Psalms 128 and 134

Deepening the Sources

Many psalms sing the praises of Jerusalem. What are the qualities ascribed to Jerusalem? In what kinds of ways can Jerusalem affect us? What is the relationship between God and Jerusalem? What does it mean to "see the goodness of Jerusalem?"

Eretz Yisrael in the Talmud

When the Temple was destroyed, many Jews became ascetics, binding themselves neither to eat meat nor to drink wine. R. Joshua got into conversation with them and said: "My sons, why do you not eat meat?" They replied: "Shall we eat flesh, which used to be brought daily as an offering on the altar now that this altar is in abeyance? Shall we drink wine which used to be poured as a libation on the altar, but now no longer?" He said to them: "If that is so, we should not eat figs or grapes either, because there is no longer an offering of first fruits. We should not drink water, because there is no longer a ceremony of the pouring of the water." To this they could find no answer; so he said to them: "Not to mourn at all is impossible because the blow has fallen. To mourn overmuch is also impossible." The sages, therefore, have ordained thus: A man may stucco his house, but he should leave a little bare in memory of Jerusalem. A man may prepare a full-course banquet, but he should leave out an item or two in memory of Jerusalem. For so it is said: "If I forget thee, Oh Jerusalem, let my right hand forget its cunning, let my tongue cleave to the roof of my mouth if I remember thee not, if I prefer Jerusalem above my chief joy." (Psalm 137:5–6)

—Baba Batra 60b

Deepening the Sources

The rabbis shaped our response to the destruction of the Temple and the Exile. What did they feel was the right response? The examples provide ways, in the ordinary things we do, to remember the destruction. What other ways do you know?

If the husband wishes to go to Palestine, but his wife refuses, she may be compelled to go; if she refuses to comply, she may be divorced and forfeits her marriage contract. If she wishes to go, while he refuses, he may be compelled to go; if he refuses, he is compelled to divorce her and pay her marriage contract in full.

—Ketubot 110b

Deepening the Sources

Considering the value of marriage and the home, what does the statement about husbands and wives say about the importance of Jerusalem?

If one buys a house from a heathen in Eretz Yisrael the title deed may be written for him even on the Sabbath. On the Sabbath! Is that possible? But as Rava explained, he may order a non-Jew to write it, even though instructing a non-Jew to do a work prohibited to Jews on the Sabbath is forbidden by rabbinic ordination, the rabbis waived their decree on account of the settlement of Eretz Yisrael.

—Baba Kama 80b

Deepening the Sources

Shabbat is another very high value in Judaism. This too can be set aside to enable someone to settle in Jerusalem!

Shimon bar Ba came to ask R. Hanina for a letter of recommendation to help him earn a livelihood outside the Land. R. Hanina refused, saying: "When I die they will say to me—one glorious plant we had in Eretz Yisrael and yet you allowed it to leave the country."

—Yerushalmi Moed Katan 83,1

Deepening the Sources

Here again Israel becomes a higher value than the student-teacher, or friend, relationship and Israel is so important that it is linked to the world to come (see passage below).

"One that gives a soul unto the people that are upon it and a spirit to them that walk therein" (Isaiah 42:5); They said in the name of R. Yochanan: Whoever walks four cubits in Eretz Yisrael may be assured of life in the world to come.

—Ketubot 111a

Even those who live in the East, even India, in the isles of the sea who need rain in the summer do not pray for it except when it is needed in Eretz Yisrael. For if you say they should pray for rain at the season when they need it, even if that means in summer, it will cause them to regard themselves as living in their own homeland. Let them, however, regard themselves as guests (when in the Diaspora), their hearts directed toward Eretz Yisrael. Their prayer for rain will be in accordance with the seasons in Eretz Yisrael.

Deepening the Sources

Even though Jews were living outside of their land, they remained attached to it psychologically in that they prayed and celebrated holidays according to the seasons in Israel.

Taken together, the sources from the Talmud illustrate how attached we remained to Israel when we were in exile and how the attachment has been integrated into Jewish life throughout the centuries.

From the *Neilah* Service

May there be acceptance
of the prayers and supplications
of the entire House of Israel
before their Father in heaven.
And say, Amen.

May there be abundant peace from heaven
and life
for us and for all Israel,
—and say Amen.

God Who makes peace in the high Heavens
may God make peace
for us and for all Israel,
—and say Amen.

Next year in Jerusalem!

Deepening the Sources

Both in the Neilah Service and at the end of the Passover Seder, Jews recite the words "Next Year in Jerusalem." What is the significance of placing this phrase at the end of observances? The phrase had a very specific meaning during the years when we were without a land. It can still have a similar meaning to those who may be traveling or who are anticipating travel to Israel. Today it has taken on a variety of metaphorical meanings, some of them incorporating a Messianic vision. What can this phrase mean to contemporary Jews? What does it mean to you?

From the Wedding Ceremony

May the barren [land] rejoice and be glad, when its children are gathered back to it in joy. Blessed are You, O God, who makes Zion rejoice in her children.

May You grant great joy to these dearly beloved, just as You granted joy to the work of Your hands long ago in the Garden of Eden. Blessed are You, O God, who grants joy to the bridegroom and bride. Blessed are You, Adonai our God, Ruler of the Universe, who created happiness and joy, bridegroom and bride, rejoicing and song, delight and cheer, love and harmony, peace and fellowship.

Soon, Adonai our God, may there be heard in the cities of Judah and in the streets of Jerusalem, the sound of gladness, the sound of joy, the sound of the bridegroom, the sound of the bride, the sound of bridegrooms rejoicing at their weddings, and young people at their feasts of song. Blessed are You, O God, who grants joy to the bridegoom with the bride.

Deepening the Sources

What is the significance of the reference to Jerusalem in this part of the wedding ceremony? What is meant by the prayer for hearing the sounds of gladness and joy in Jerusalem? The breaking of the glass is also part of the wedding ceremony that links us to Jerusalem. What is its significance?

ADDITIONAL POSSIBILITIES

1. JERUSALEM AS CENTER: Even when Jews did not possess the land, Jerusalem remained a central part of Jewish life. What have we learned in this course, or what do you know from your own Jewish life, that emphasizes the centrality of Jerusalem in our actions and prayers as Jews? Brainstorm and see how long a list you can create.

2. TIMELESS TEXTS: TIMELESS CITY: Introduce the traditional Jewish practice of studying in Hevrusa, with a partner, a friend. Refer to the statement in Pirke Avot, *k'na l'cha haver*, "get yourself a study partner." Utilizing the metaphor that sparks are created when two sticks are rubbed together, talk about the advantages of two individuals exchanging ideas, challenging and supporting the ideas of one another. This has been a traditional Jewish mode of studying. The tradition discourages studying alone like a monk in a monastery. Hevrusa is associated with the Talmudic academy, the cheder, and the Yeshiva. We are going to use it to study texts that are part of our Jewish life that connect us in diverse ways to Jerusalem. Students will divide into Hevrusot for approximately forty-five minutes to examine the texts (those from the Talmud are especially appropriate) and answer the questions related to each one. The group will reconvene the last half hour to discuss answers to the questions and raise additional questions.

3. A SUMMARY DISCUSSION: Can we categorize the content of these prayers? What are the ways that Jews express their attachment to their land?

IN SUMMATION

- Even though Jews were exiled from Jerusalem and for many centuries were not permitted to live there, Jerusalem remained central in our prayers, our observances, and our teachings.
- The meanings of references to Jerusalem in our prayers and observances have changed in this century. Now that Jerusalem is in our possession, the Jerusalem of our prayers is seen in a new light.

CHAPTER 13

JERUSALEM IN JEWISH THOUGHT

BACKGROUND

Jerusalem is a holy city to the Jewish people. It is said that every Jew has two homes, the one in which you live and Jerusalem. Its holiness rises out of its historical memory, its mystical experience, its synagogues and schools, and its stunning beauty. Much of this resides in an allusive, ineffable, emotional mist of existence expressed in the fact that many feel better able to relate to God when they are in Jerusalem. Jerusalem is deeply embedded in Jewish thought, in Jewish text. It is one of the most thought-about, written-about subjects in Jewish life.

Jerusalem is not only a part of our past and present; it is a key element in the vision of our future. When we are in Jerusalem the past, present, and future come together. Because of its eternal nature, we have never abandoned the idea of Jerusalem and the idea of its being rebuilt when it lay in ruins under the rule of hostile conquerors. Part of our faith in God and God's plan for us and our world is faith in Jerusalem. Part of our personal faith, of knowing who we are as Jews, is knowing Jerusalem.

THE BEGINNING: EYE OF THE UNIVERSE

Jerusalem as Eye of the World

The construction of the earth was begun at the center with the foundation stone of the Temple, the *Even Shetiyah.* For the Holy Land is at the central point of the surface of the earth, Jerusalem is at the central point of Palestine, and the Temple is situated at the center of the Holy City.

The body of man is a microcosm, the whole world in miniature, and the world in turn is a reflex of man. The hair upon his head corresponds to the woods of the earth, his tears to a river, his mouth to the ocean. The world resembles the ball of his eye; the ocean that encircles the earth is like the white of the eye, the dry land is the iris, Jerusalem the pupil, and the Temple the image mirrored in the pupil of the eye.

—Midrash

The Historical Geography of the Holy Land

[Jerusalem has] no harbors; no river, no trunk-road, no convenient market for the nations on either side. In their commerce with each other these pass by Judea, finding their emporiums in the cities of Philistia, or, as of old, at Petra and Bosra on the east of the Jordan. Gaza has outdone Hebron as the port of the desert. Jerusalem is no match for Shechem [Nablus] in fertility or convenience or site. The whole plateau stands aloof, waterless, on the road to nowhere. There are none of the natural conditions of a great city.

And yet it was here that She arose who, more than Athens and more than Rome, taught the nations civic justice, and gave her name to the ideal city men are ever striving to build on earth, to the City of God that shall one day descend from heaven—the New Jerusalem. For her builder was not Nature nor the wisdom of men, but on that secluded and barren site the Work of God, by her prophets, laid her eternal foundations in righteousness, and reared her walls in her peoples faith in God.

—George Adam Smith,
"The Historical Geography of the
Holy Land" in Millgrim

Deepening the Sources

Jewish law kept Israel a part of daily Jewish life. Legend, however, made it part of our imagination. Read the texts from the Midrash and George Adam Smith. These very diverse readings only begin to represent the ways Jerusalem's centrality has been perceived through the centuries.

THE MIDDLE: EARTHLY AND HEAVENLY JERUSALEM

Fifteen things were said of Jerusalem:

Jerusalem's houses do not become unclean through leprosy;

It is not to be declared a condemned city;

Neither beams nor balconies nor sockets may project there over the public thoroughfare lest, by overshadowing, they give passage to the corpse uncleanness;

The dead may not be lodged there overnight;

The bones of a dead man may not be carried through it;

No place is made available there for a resident alien;

No graves may be kept there excepting the graves of the house of David, and, of Huldah the prophetess which were there since the days of the early prophet . . .

No plants may be planted there, neither gardens nor orchards may be cultivated there, excepting rose gardens which were there since the days of the early prophets;

Neither geese nor chickens may be raised there, nor, needless to say, pigs;

No dunghills may be kept there because of uncleanness;

No trial of a stubborn and rebellious son may be held there, such is the view of Rabbi Nathan (see Deuteronomy 21:18 ff.);

No houses may be sold there save from the ground up [only the structure, not the ground, could be sold];

The sale of houses is not round up for longer than twelve months;

No payment for a bed is accepted there [from the pilgrims who come for the Festivals]—Rabbi Judah says: Not even payment for beds and coverings;

The hides of the sacrificial beasts are not for sale there.

<Halakhah made Jerusalem part of the daily life of the Jew, but it was Aggadah that fired the imagination. Through rabbinic tales, interpretations, and lore touching on every phase of the city's origins and history, Jerusalem remained a living presence for Jews in all the lands of the dispersion.>

He who has not seen Jerusalem in her splendor has not seen a desirable city in his life.

There is no wisdom like the wisdom of the Land of Israel. There is no beauty like the beauty of Jerusalem.

Jerusalem is the light of the world . . . and who is the light of Jerusalem? God.

There are six things that were chosen: the priestly family, the levitical family, Israel, the royal house of David, Jerusalem, the Sanctuary.

Jerusalem is destined to expand until it reaches the Throne of Glory.

Not only on the face of this earth is there a Jerusalem, called in Hebrew *Yerushalayim Shel Matta* (the Lower), but also in heaven is there such a city: *Yerushalayim Shel Ma-alah*—Jerusalem the Upper.

Rabbi Yohanan said: "The Holy One, blessed be He, said: I will not enter Jerusalem the Upper, until I can enter Jerusalem the Lower."

In the upper Jerusalem there is also a Temple, and when the high priest of Israel entered the Temple on Mount Moriah and offered sacrifices and incense, the archangel Michael entered the heavenly Temple and offered sacrifices and incense.

Everyone who wishes can go to Jerusalem on earth, but not to Jerusalem in heaven. Here only those who are invited can enter. When Moses was taken by the angel, God opened before him the seven heavens and showed him Jerusalem with its Temple.

Jeremiah prophesied: "Behold, I will turn the captivity of Jacob's tents,/ And have compassion on his dwelling-places; / And the city shall be builded upon her own mound, / And the palace shall be inhabited upon its wonted place."

The legend interprets the words of the prophet: "And the city shall be builded upon her own heap" refers to Jerusalem the Lower. "And the palace shall remain after the manner thereof" refers to Jerusalem the Upper.

In the second century the church father Tertullian writes about the divinely built city of Jerusalem which is in heaven: "It is evident from the testimony of even heathen witnesses that in Judea there was a city suspended in the sky early every morning . . . As the day advanced, the entire figure of the walls would wane gradually, and sometimes it would vanish instantly."

—ZevVilnay, Summary of the Talmud
on Heavenly Jerusalem

Deepening the Sources

Read the quotations from the Talmud on the earthly Jerusalem. When were these written? The rabbis were building on the yearning to return and rebuild Jerusalem as a Jewish city. After the fall of Jerusalem the rabbis accepted one of their principal tasks to be to keep the presence of Jerusalem alive.

Yet they maintained a connection with the prophetic vision of Isaiah 6, which describes a heavenly Temple and leads to the idea of a heavenly Jerusalem. The rabbis taught that while the Temple was prepared before the world was created, the heavenly Jerusalem was fashioned out of great love for the earthly Jerusalem. The Aggadah rejected the Christian view that gave priority to the heavenly Jerusalem. It states that the earthly Jerusalem will extend and rise upward until it *reaches the throne of Divine majesty. The earthly Jerusalem influences heaven, not the other way around.*

THE END: JERUSALEM AND THE MESSIAH

The word that Isaiah the son of Amoz saw concerning Judah and Jerusalem. And it shall come to pass in the last days, that the mountain of God's house shall be established on the top of the mountains, and shall be exalted above the hills; and all nations shall flow to it. And many people shall go and say, Come, and let us go up to the mountain of the Adonai, to the house of the God of Jacob; and God will teach us the way, and we will walk in God's paths; for from Zion shall go forth Torah, and the word of the the Adonai from Jerusalem. And God shall judge among the nations, and shall decide for many people; and they shall beat their swords into plowshares, and their spears into pruning hooks; nation shall not lift up sword against nation, nor shall they learn war any more. O house of Jacob, come, and let us walk in the light of Adonai. For you have abandoned your people, the house of Jacob, because they are replenished from the east, and are soothsayers like the Philistines, and they please themselves in the children of strangers. And their land is full of silver and gold, and there is no end to their treasures; and their land is full of horses, and there is no end to their chariots; And their land is full of idols; they worship the work of their own hands, that which their own fingers have made; And humanity is humbled, and humanity is brought low; forgive them not. Enter into the rock, and hide in the dust, for fear of Adonai, and for the glory of God's majesty. The lofty looks of humanity shall be brought low, and the arrogance of humanity shall be brought low, and Adonai alone shall be exalted in that day. For the day of Adonai shall be upon every one who is arrogant and lofty, and upon every one who is lifted up and shall be brought low; And upon all the cedars of Lebanon, that are high and lifted up, and upon all the oaks of Bashan, And upon all the high mountains, and upon all the lofty hills, And upon every high tower, and upon every fortified wall, And upon all the ships of Tarshish, and upon all delightful craftsmanship. And the haughtiness of humanity shall be bowed down, and the arrogance of humanity shall be brought down, and Adonai alone shall be exalted in that day. And the idols God shall completely abolish. And they shall go into the holes of the rocks, and into the caves of the earth, for fear of Adonai, and for the glory of God's majesty, when Adonai arises to shake terribly the earth. In that day humanity shall cast idols of silver, and idols of gold, which they made to worship, to the moles and to the bats; To go into the clefts of the rocks, and into the crevices of the rocks, for fear of Adonai, and for the glory of God's majesty, when he arises to shake terribly the earth. Cease you from humanity, in whose nostrils is a breath; for in what is humanity to be accounted for?

—Isaiah 2

The wolf and the lamb shall feed together, and the lion shall eat straw like the ox; and dust shall be the serpent's food. They shall not hurt nor destroy in all my holy mountain, says the Adonai.

—Isaiah 2, 65:25

For, behold, in those days, and in that time, when I shall bring back the captivity of Judah and Jerusalem, I will also gather all nations, and will bring them down into the valley of Jehoshaphat, and will enter into judgment with them there for my people and for my heritage Israel, whom they have scattered among the nations, and have divided my land. And they have cast lots for my people; and have given a boy for a harlot, and sold a girl for wine, that they might drink. And also, What are you to me, O Tyre, and Sidon, and all the regions of Philistia? Are you paying me back for something? If you are paying me back, swiftly and speedily I will return your deed upon your own head; Because you have taken my silver and my gold, and have carried into your temples my goodly treasures; And the people of Judah and the people of Jerusalem have you sold to the Yavanim, removing them far from their own border. Behold, I will raise them from the place where you have sold them, and will return your deed upon your own head; And I will sell your sons and your daughters to the hand of the people of Judah, and they shall sell them to the Sabeans, to a people far off; for Adonai has spoken it. Proclaim this among the nations; Prepare war, stir up the mighty, let all the warriors draw near; let them come up; Beat your plowshares into swords, and your pruning hooks into spears; let the weak say, I am strong. Hasten and come, all you nations, and gather yourselves together around; cause your mighty ones to come down, O Adonai. Let the nations be stirred up, and come to the valley of Jehoshaphat; for there I will sit to judge all the nations around. Put in the sickle, for the harvest is ripe; come, tread down; for the press is full, the vats overflow; for their wickedness is great. Multitudes, multitudes in the valley of decision; for the day of Adonai is near in the valley of decision. The sun and the moon are darkened, and the stars withdraw their shining. And Adonai roars out of Zion, and utters from Jerusalem; and the heavens and the earth shake; but Adonai will be a refuge and a fortress for the people of Israel. And you shall know that I am Adonai your God dwelling in Zion, my holy mountain; then shall Jerusalem be holy, and no strangers shall pass through her any more. And it shall come to pass on that day, that the mountains shall drop sweet wine, and the hills shall flow with milk, and all the streams of Judah shall flow with waters, and a fountain shall issue from the house of Adonai, and shall water the valley of Shittim. Egypt shall be a desolation, and Edom shall be a desolate wilderness, for the violence done against the people of Judah, because they have shed innocent blood in their land. But Judah shall remain for ever, and Jerusalem from generation to generation. For though I have acquitted them, I have not acquitted those who shed their blood. And Adonai dwells in Zion.

—Joel 4

Jerusalem in the End of Time

1. When Will Jerusalem Be Restored?

The rabbis relate: "Jerusalem will not be rebuilt in its entirety till all the children of Israel will be gathered from exile . . . As it is written [in Psalms]: 'The Lord doth built up Jerusalem, He gathereth together the dispersed of Israel.' "

In the end of time, Jerusalem, the tent of God, will spread forth in all directions. All the children of Israel will return from exile and find rest and peace within her border, so it is prophesied by Isaiah: "Enlarge the place of thy tent, / And let them stretch forth the curtain of thy habitations, spare not; / Lengthen thy cords, and strengthen thy stakes. / For thou shalt spread abroad on the right hand and on the left."

"God will gather the outcast of Israel in peace!"

"In the end of time, Jerusalem will become the metropolis for all lands."

"In the end of time, Jerusalem will be a shining light to all the nations of the earth, who will walk in its brightness."

2. Jerusalem in the Future

The prophet Isaiah describes Jerusalem's restoration: "Behold, I will set thy stones in fair colors, / And lay thy foundations with sapphires. / And I will make thy pinnacles of rubies, / And thy gates of carbuncles, / And all thy borders of precious stones."

"The Holy One, blessed be He, will in time to come add to Jerusalem a thousand gardens, a thousand towers, a thousand palaces, and a thousand mansions."

The Almighty will surround Jerusalem with seven walls: a wall of silver and a wall of gold; a wall of precious stones and a wall of lazulite; a wall of sapphire, a wall of emeralds, and a wall of fire; and its brilliant splendor will radiate to the four corners of the globe.

The borders of Jerusalem in the future will be full of precious stones and pearls, and all Israel will come and take what they please.

3. The Pilgrimage in the Future

"In the end of time, Jerusalem will spread over the whole of the land of Israel. And the land of Israel will spread over the whole world."

How shall the people come from all corners of the earth and pray in Jerusalem? The clouds of the heavens will carry them to Jerusalem the first day of every month and every Sabbath, and bring them back to the place from which they came.

The prophet Isaiah praises them and says: "Who are these that fly as a cloud?"

The prophet Nahum describes the redemption in the future: "Behold upon the mountains the feet of him / That bringeth good tidings, that announceth peace! / . . . the chariots rush madly in the streets . . . / The appearance of them is like torches, / They run to and fro like the lightnings."

The words of the prophet refer to the children of Israel in the end of time: "The lightning spread from one end of the world to another in a very short time. So the children of Israel run to Jerusalem, from the ends of the world, and sacrifice and return to their places swiftly."

—ZevVilnay,
"Jerusalem in the End of Time"

Deepening the Sources

The real mystery of Jerusalem is not in its past or present but in the future! Read the passage from Isaiah. Summarize the first two stanzas. What is the relationship of law, judgment, and peace in the world, and the relationship of Jerusalem to each of these?

IN SUMMATION

- The Beginning: Jerusalem as Eye/Center of the Universe
- The Middle: Jewish thought encompasses both upper and lower Jerusalem, a heavenly Jerusalem and one of this world.
- The End: Jerusalem in the end of days is linked with the ingathering of all Jews and the coming of the Messiah or the Messianic Age.

BIBLIOGRAPHY

Alpert, Fran. *Getting Jerusalem Together*, Jerusalem: Archeological Seminar, 1984.

Amichai, Yehuda. *Poems of Jerusalem and Love Poems*, New York: Sheep Meadow, 1981.

Avi-Yona, Michael. *A History of the Holy Land*, New York: Macmillan, 1969.

Avi-Yona, Michael. *Jerusalem*, New York: Arco, 1960.

Babylonian Talmud, Shabbat, London, Jerusalem: Soncino, 1972.

Bahat, Dan. *Carta's Historical Atlas of Jerusalem*, Jerusalem: Carta, 1973.

Bahat, Dan. *The Illustrated Atlas of Jerusalem*, New York: Simon & Schuster, 1989.

Begin, Menachem. *The Revolt*, Jerusalem: Steimatzky's Agency Ltd, 1974.

Ben-Arieh, Yehoshua. *Jerusalem in the 19th Century: Emergence of the New City*, New York: St. Martin's Press, 1986.

Ben-Dor, Gabriel. *The Druzes in Israel a Political Study*, Jerusalem: Magnes Press, 1979.

Ben Dov, Meir, Mordechai Naor, and Zeev Aner. *The Western Wall*, Tel Aviv: Ministry of Defense, 1983.

The Books of the Maccabees Comm: John L. Bartlett, Cambridge, England: Cambridge University Press, 1973.

Breakstone, David. *Israel Connection*, Jerusalem: Melton Centre for Jewish Education in the Diaspora, 1986.

Coalition for the Advancement of Jewish Education. *Yerushalayim*, New York, 1992.

Collins, Larry and Dominick Lapierre. *O Jerusalem*. New York: Simon & Schuster, 1972.

Eisenberg, Azriel. *Jerusalem Eternal*, New York, NYBJE, 1971.

Eisenberg, Azriel. *Modern Jewish Life in Literature*, New York: United Synagogue Commission on Jewish Education, 1952.

Elazar, Daniel J. *Israel:Building a New Society*, Bloomington, IN: Indiana University Press, 1986.

Facts About Israel, Jerusalem: "The State" Ministry of Education, 1985.

Gilbert, Martin. *The Atlas of Jewish History*, New York: William & Morrow, 1992.

Gilbert, Martin. *Jerusalem: Illustrated History Atlas*, New York: Macmillan, 1977.

Gorenberg, Gershom. "Myth of the Secular Majority," *Jerusalem Report*, February 24, 1994.

Hacohen, Menachem. *Avanim M'saprot*, Jerusalem: Department of Security, 1967.

Halevi, Yossi Klein. "A Tale of Two Cities," *Jerusalem Report*, June 17, 1993.

Halevi, Yossi Klein. "We Shall Not Be Moved," *Jerusalem Report*, November 18, 1993.

Haliv, Ben Avraham. *A Modern Guide to the Jewish Holy Places*, Jerusalem: Posner & Sons, 1981.

Harlow, Julius. *Lessons from Our Living Past*, New York: Behrman House, 1972.

Hertzberg, Arthur. *The Zionist Idea*, New York: Athenium, 1976.

Hirschberg, Peter. "A High Price to Pay for Peace," *Jerusalem Report*, February 10, 1994.

Hollis, Christopher and Ronald Brownrag. *Holy Places*, New York: Praeger, 1969.

Holtz, Avraham. *The Holy City*, New York: Norton & Co, 1971.

Idiopulos, Thomas A. *Jerusalem Blessed, Jerusalem Cursed*, Chicago: Ivan R. Dee, 1991.

Jaffe, Eliezer. *Yemin Moshe*, New York: Praeger, 1988.

Jagodnik, Franklin, ed., *Jerusalem Most Fair of Cities*, New York: Vilo, 1981.

The Jerusalem Post, Nov. 12, 1973; Mar. 27, 1979; Feb. 17, 1985; Sept. 14, 1993; May 4, 1994; Oct. 18, 1994; Mar. 19, 1992; Aug. 29, 1973; April 13, 1990.

Jewish Publication Society Bible, Philadelphia, New York, 1913.

Josephus. *The Complete Works of Josephus*, Grand Rapids, MI: Baker Book House, 1993.

Kaplan, Rabbi Ariyeh. *Made in Heaven*, New York: Mozarim, 1983.

Klausner, Joseph. *The Messianic Idea in Israel*, New York: Macmillan, 1955.

Kollek, Teddy and Moshe Pearlman. *Jerusalem Sacred City of Mankind: A History of Forty Centuries*, Jerusalem: Steimatzky's Agency Ltd., 1978.

Labovitz, Annette and Eugene Labovitz. *A Sacred Trust*, Vol. II, Los Angeles: Isaac Nathan, 1995. ("I Have a Dream")

Laqueur, Walter and Barry Rubin, eds. *The Israeli-Arab Reader*, New York: Penguin, 1984.

Les Dossiers D'Archeologie. *Jerusalem, 5000 Years of History*, Jerusalem, 1992.

Liptz, Paul. "Israeli Politics 1992–1995," unpublished manuscript, May 1995.

Lowenthal, Marvin. *The Diaries of Theodore Herzl*, New York: Dial, 1956.

Manor, Moshe. *Roads to Statehood*, Jerusalem: Dept. of Education and Culture, 1984.

Maranz, Felice. "Israel 2010," *Jerusalem Report*, September 10, 1992.

Matthews, Charles D. *Palestine: Mohammedan Holy Land*, New Haven, CT: Yale University, 1949.

Mazar, Benjamin. *The Mountain of the Lord*, New York: Doubleday, 1975.

The Middle East and North Africa, 41st ed., Rochester, England: Europa Publications Ltd., 1995.

Midrash Rabbah, Stephan Austin, Hartford, CT: 1939.

Millgrim, Abraham E. *Jerusalem Curiosities*, Philadelphia, New York: Jewish Publication Society, 1990.

Narkiss, Bezalel, ed., *Picture History of Jewish Civilization*, New York: Abrams, 1970.

Nathan, Joan and Judith Goldman. *The Flavor of Jerusalem*, Boston: Little Brown, 1974.

Near East Report, Vol. XXXVIII, No. 44, Oct. 31, 1994.

Nir-Lichtenberg, Rachel. *Jerusalem & I*, New York: JAJZE, 1995.

Oesterreicher, John M. and Anne Sinai, eds., *Jerusalem*, New York: John Day, 1974.

Oxford Annotated Bible, New York: Oxford Press, 1973.

Palestine Royal Commission Report, London: His Majesty's Stationery Office, 1937.

Parkes, James. *Whose Land?*, New York: Taplinger, 1970.

Peters, F.E. *Jerusalem*, Princeton, NJ: Princeton University, 1985.

Rabinovich, Abraham. *Jerusalem on Earth*, New York: Macmillan, 1988.

Rabinovich, Itamar and Jehuda Reinharz. *Israel in the Middle East: 1948–Present*, New York: Oxford Univ. Press, 1984.

Reimer, Jack and Nathanial Stampfer. *Jewish Ethical Wills*, New York: Schocken Books, 1994.

Roskies, David G., ed., *The Dybbuk and Other Stories*, New York: Schocken, 1992.

Sawicki, Tom. "The Ultra-Orthodox Takeover of Jerusalem," *Jerusalem Report*, December 20, 1994.

Sheniak, Mazal. *Why Hebrew?* Jerusalem: Melton Centre for Jewish Education in the Diaspora, 1984.

Shepherd, Naomi. *The Mayor and the Citadel*, London: Weidenfeld and Nicolson, 1987.

Siegel, Danny. "Poems from Jerusalem," *Keeping Posted*, February 1972.

Simhovich, Shira. *Here and There in the City of Jerusalem*, Jerusalem: Melton Centre for Jewish Education in the Diaspora, no date.

Stern, Chaim, ed., with Berman, Donna, Edward Graham, and H. Leonard Poller. *On the Doorposts of Your House*, New York: Central Conference of Rabbis, 1994.

Twain, Mark/Samuel Clemens. *Innocents Abroad*, New York, Hippocrene Books, 1989.

Vilnay, Zev. *Legends of Jerusalem*, Philadelphia: JPS, 1980.

The Washington Post, "Archeology Fight Tests Israeli Coalition," Sept. 24, 1981.

Werblowsky, R.J. Zev. *The Meaning of Jerusalem to Jews, Christians, and Muslims*, Jerusalem: Old City Press, 1983.

Wiesel, Elie. *Beggar in Jerusalem*, New York: Random House, 1970.

Wilkin, Robert. *The Land Called Holy*, New Haven, CT: Yale Univ. Press, 1992.

Wolman, Baron. *Above the Holy Land*, San Francisco: Chronicle Books, 1987.

ACKNOWLEDGMENTS

For permission to reprint the copyrighted selections in this volume, thanks are due to the following authors and publishers:

American Academic Association for Peace in the Middle East, New York, NY: *Jerusalem*, by John M. Oesterreicher and Anne Sinai.

Archeological Seminars, Jerusalem: *Getting Jerusalem Together*, by Fran Alpert.

Armon Publishing: Jerusalem and Vilo Publishers, New York, NY: *Jerusalem Most Fair of Cities*.

Baker Book House, Grand Rapids, MI: *The Complete Works of Josephus*, by Josephus.

Behrman House, West Orange, NJ: *Lessons From Our Living Past*, by Julius Harlow.

Carta, Jerusalem: *Carta's Historical Atlas of Jerusalem*, by Dan Bahat.

Coalition for the Advancement of Jewish Education, New York, NY: *Yerushalayim*.

Division of Christian Education of the National Council of the Churches of Christ in the USA, New York, NY: *Revised Standard Version of the Bible*.

Europa Publications Limited, London, England: The *Middle East and North Africa*, 41st Edition.

Harper and Row, New York, NY: *Songs of Jerusalem and Myself*.

JAJZE, Department of Education and Culture in the Diaspora, New York, NY: *Jerusalem and I*, edited by Rachel Nir Lichtenberg.

Jerusalem Blessed, Jerusalem Cursed by Thomas A. Idinopulos, copyright © 1991 by Thomas A. Idinopulos, published by Ivan R. Dee.

The Jerusalem Post, Jerusalem: "Against All Odds: Knesset Votes for Direct Election of PM," by Dan Izenberg.

The Jerusalem Post, Jerusalem: "Israel and Egypt Sign Peace Treaty Declaring End to 30-Year State of War," by Ari Rath, Wolf Blitzer, David Landau, and Malka Rabinowitz.

The Jerusalem Post, Jerusalem: "Israel, Jordan Initial Peace Treaty," by David Makovsky.

The Jerusalem Post, Jerusalem: "Old City Dig Poised on Brink of David's Time," by Abraham Rabinovich.

The Jerusalem Post, Jerusalem: "Rabin, Arafat Sign Gaza/Jericho Pact" by David Makovsky.

The Jerusalem Post, Jerusalem: "Riot Erupts in Old City," by Haim Shapiro and Ron Kampeas.

The Jerusalem Post, Jerusalem: "Troops Redeploy Along Interim S. Lebanese Line, IDF Completes Pullback I," by Hirsch Goodman and Joshua Brilliant.

The Jerusalem Report, Jerusalem: "A Huge Price to Pay for Peace," by Peter Hirschberg.

Jewish Publication Society, Philadelphia, PA: *Jerusalem Curiosities*, by Abraham E. Millgrim.

Jewish Publication Society, Philadelphia, PA: *Legends of Jerusalem*, by Zev Vilnay.

Keeping Posted: Poems From Yerushalayim, by Danny Siegel.

Little Brown & Co. Inc, Boston, MA: *The Flavor of Jerusalem*, by Joan Nathan and Judith Goldman.

Macmillan Publishing Co, New York, NY: Jerusalem, *Illustrated History Atlas*, by Martin Gilbert.

The Melton Centre for Jewish Education in the Diaspora, Jerusalem: *Israel Connection*, by David Breakstone.

The Near East Report, Washington, DC: Vol. XXXVIII, No. 44, October 31, 1994.

New York Board of Jewish Education, New York, NY: *Jerusalem Eternal*, by Azriel Eisenberg.

Posner & Sons Ltd, Jerusalem: *A Modern Guide to Jewish Holy Places*, by Ben Avraham Halevi.

Princeton University Press, Princeton, NJ: *Jerusalem*, by F.E. Peters.

St. Martin's Press, New York, NY: *Jerusalem in the 19th Century: Emergence of the New City*, by Yehoshua Ben-Arieh.

Schocken Books, New York, NY: *Jewish Ethical Wills*, by Jack Reimer & Nathaniel Stampfer.

Simon & Schuster, New York, NY: *0 Jerusalem*, by Larry Collins and Dominick Lapierre.

Steimatzky Ltd, Jerusalem: *The Revolt*, by Menachem Begin.

Steimatzky Ltd, Jerusalem: *Jerusalem Sacred City of Mankind: A History of Forty Centuries*, by Teddy Kollek and Moshe Pearlman.

Stern College, New York, NY: *Yerushalayim*.

United Synagogue Commission on Jewish Education, New York, NY: *Modern Jewish Life in Literature*, Book I, by Azriel Eisenberg.

Vilo, New York, NY: *Jerusalem Most Fair of Cities*, by Franklin Jagodnik.

The Washington Post, Washington, DC: "Archeology Fight Tests Israeli Coalition."

William Morrow & Company Inc, New York, NY: *The Atlas of Jewish History*, by Martin Gilbert.